DISASTER IN BANGLADESH

DISASTER IN BANGLADESH

EDITED BY LINCOLN C. CHEN, M.D.

NEW YORK   OXFORD UNIVERSITY PRESS   LONDON   TORONTO   1973

Dedication:

BETTER HEALTH FOR THE PEOPLE OF BANGLADESH

There they stand, heads bowed,
Mute; on their pale faces chronicled the sufferings
Of many centuries; on their shoulders they bear burdens
Which grow; carrying on, slowly, while life holds,
And then they pass them on to the children, for generations.
Fate they do not curse, nor complain, remembering the gods;
Men they do not blame, nor cherish any pity of love
For themselves; only a few grains of food they glean,
And their tormented lives, somehow, keep alive.
When even that meagre food someone robs,
Or hurts their life in blind might's cruel oppression,
They know not to whose door they will turn for justice;
Calling on the God of the Poor, for once, in their heaving sighs,
Silently they die.

Rabindranath Tagore

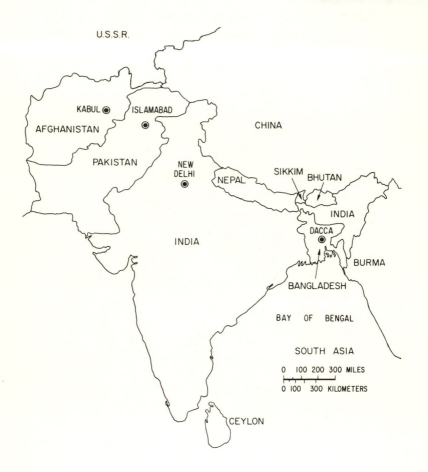

U.S.S.R.

KABUL ◉   ISLAMABAD

AFGHANISTAN   ◉

CHINA

PAKISTAN   NEW
DELHI   SIKKIM   BHUTAN
◉   NEPAL

INDIA

DACCA   INDIA
◉

BURMA

INDIA

BANGLADESH

BAY   OF   BENGAL

SOUTH   ASIA

0   100 200 300 MILES

0 100   300 KILOMETERS

CEYLON

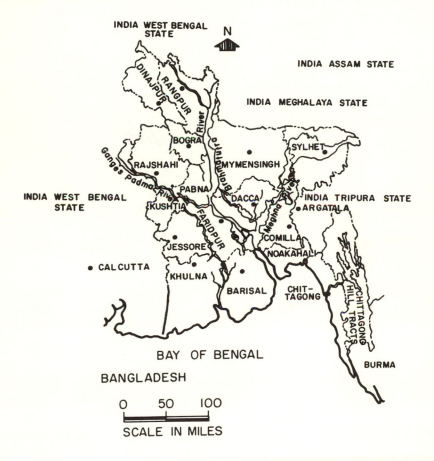

INDIA WEST BENGAL
STATE

N

INDIA ASSAM STATE

INDIA MEGHALAYA STATE

DINAJPUR

RANGPUR

Brahmaputra River

BOGRA

SYLHET

Ganges

RAJSHAHI

Padma River

MYMENSINGH

Brahmaputra

PABNA

INDIA WEST BENGAL
STATE

KUSHTIA

DACCA

Meghna

INDIA TRIPURA STATE

ARGATALA

FARIDPUR

JESSORE

COMILLA

NOAKAHALI

CALCUTTA

KHULNA

BARISAL

CHIT-
TAGONG

CHITTAGONG
HILL TRACTS

BAY OF BENGAL

BURMA

BANGLADESH

0   50   100

SCALE IN MILES

Contributors

LINCOLN C. CHEN	Technical Assistance Division, The Population Council
NORBERT HIRSCHHORN	Assistant Professor of Medicine, Johns Hopkins University School of Medicine
W. HENRY MOSLEY	Professor and Chairman, Department of Population Dynamics, Johns Hopkins University School of Hygiene and Public Health
MONOWAR HOSSAIN	Population and Human Resources Division, The World Bank
JOHN STOECKEL	Demographic Division, The Population Council
IRWIN H. ROSENBERG	Associate Professor of Medicine, Pritzker School of Medicine, University of Chicago
JOHN LINDENBAUM	Associate Professor of Medicine, College of Physicians and Surgeons, Columbia University
WILLIAM M. MCCORMACK	Assistant Professor of Medicine, Harvard Medical School
GEORGE T. CURLIN	Epidemiology Program, Center for Disease Control
RICHARD L. GUERRANT	Chief Resident in Medicine, University of Virginia School of Medicine

RICHARD A. CASH — Infectious Disease Fellow, University of Maryland School of Medicine

ROBERT S. NORTHRUP — Chief, Bacterial Vaccine Section, Bureau of Biologics Standards, Food and Drug Administration

ALFRED SOMMER — Epidemiology Program, Center for Disease Control

MATTHEW S. LOEWENSTEIN — Chief, Enteric Disease Section, Center for Disease Control

JON E. ROHDE — Senior Resident in Pediatrics, Children's Hospital Medical Center and Harvard Medical School

PIERCE GARDNER — Assistant Professor of Medicine, Harvard Medical School

DESAIX MYERS III — Ceylon-Nepal Desk Officer, United States Agency for International Development

NILTON ARNT — Medical Officer, The World Health Organization

STANLEY O. FOSTER — Chief of Research and Development, Smallpox Eradication Program, Center for Disease Control

WILLIAM B. GREENOUGH III — Associate Professor of Medicine, Johns Hopkins University School of Medicine

Foreword

The birth of Bangladesh has been a saga of human tragedy and courage rarely witnessed in modern times. Within the short span of little more than one year, the people of Bengal faced natural disaster, bloody repression, and civil war. Millions of Bengalis perished. Hundreds of thousands died in the violence unleashed by the Pakistan army, countless thousands more in the squalor of refugee camps, and uncounted more in the famine and disease of a ravaged countryside. But the spirit of Bengal survived, and Bangladesh won its freedom and independence.

Never has there been so massive a shift in population as when nearly 10 million refugees fled to India in less than eight months in 1971. It was, and will likely remain, one of the great human migrations of the twentieth century. Not unexpectedly, the refugees brought with them some of the most difficult humanitarian problems ever to confront any nation or the international community. Certainly, no one who traveled then into the refugee camps of India—as I had the opportunity to do—or to work in them as several of the authors of this book did, will ever forget the suffering and misery everywhere present.

Those who suffered most from the hunger, the congestion, the lack of medical supplies, and the frightful conditions of sanitation, were the young and the very old. Many of the infants and aged died before programs to help them could ever be established. One could see children with legs and feet swollen with edema and malnutrition, limp in the arms of their mothers. There were babies going blind for lack of vitamins, or covered with sores that would not heal. And in the eyes of their parents was the despair of ever seeing their children well again.

Humanitarians throughout the world cried out in frustration as diplomats in their capitals stood idle while weeks of tragedy passed. Only the tireless efforts of the Government of India and certain international relief agencies averted even greater tragedy.

The tragedy of Bangladesh was epochal. But just as its birth was a triumph for democratic principle and the struggle for self-determination, its battle for survival is symbolic of that facing many millions in the developing nations of the world. The human disaster which Bangladesh conquered is not, and will not, be dissimilar to the crises many developing nations will likely face in the coming decades, and the world must learn from it.

Clearly, one important lesson is that we still do not have the capacity to deal effectively with massive "people problems"—humanitarian problems of all kinds—which should and must call forth a response from the international community. The United Nations, particularly, has a unique humanitarian role and responsibility to each member of the family of man. Yet, it is still not equipped to fulfill this obligation. Former Secretary-General U Thant understood this when he called for the United Nations General Assembly to form a U.N. Disaster Relief Office. As he stated then:

I sometimes think that the drafters of the Charter were overly obsessed with political and military conflict. No doubt that obsession was justified in the situation prevailing at the time. In the world of today, it might be useful to add an article which would authorize the Secretary-General to bring to the attention of the membership, global threats to human well-being other than those to peace and security.

Although the U.N. Disaster Relief Office was established in 1971, and is a step in the right direction, it has never received the funds or the staff—or the support of the United States Government—sufficient to function as a permanent U.N. emergency relief service which is "on call" and ready to go.

The experience of Bangladesh is lesson enough that until such a service is permanently established there will be no readily available channel through which the international community can act to blunt the effects of some of the violent norms of international conduct or overcome bureaucratic inertia and diplomatic lethargy toward humanitarian crisis. The ad hoc creation in 1972 of the United Nations Relief Operation in Dacca (UNROD), and its excellent record, is also a positive step. But the disasters which overtake man—whether natural or, more particularly, man-made—require more than ad hoc responses. The United Nations, as well as the United States Government, needs a permanent organizational unit with the power, resources, and sense of priority, to respond efficiently to international humanitarian problems. As long as we fail to build mechanisms that might anticipate and prevent political disasters which erupt into civil or international conflict, the international community must have an organized capability to meet humanitarian crises when they do occur.

Within the United Nations, the patterns of procedures and activities developed by the United Nations High Commissioner for Refugees, offer some guidelines for the operation of such a U.N. emergency service. The service should be headed by an impartial diplomatic leadership for negotiating mercy agreements and consent for the deployment of the Relief Corps. Along with funds and personnel resources from other governments and agencies of the United Nations, regional organizations, and voluntary agencies—relief corps units could be deployed with maximum speed to stricken areas. Eventually the activities of the United Nations in disaster relief should be supported by a Declaration on Humanitarian Assistance to civilian populations in armed conflicts and other disasters.

Within the United States Government we need to establish a Bureau of Social and Humanitarian Services to be headed by an Assistant Secretary within the Department of State. The President, with Congressional consultation, can create such a bureau by Executive order. The time is long overdue to raise the level of responsibility and encourage stronger national leadership by our Government in international humanitarian affairs. Nothing illustrates more the need for such coordination and priority within our government than the record of shortcomings in our response to the Bangladesh disaster.

Finally, the experience of Bangladesh underscores the need for our nation to restructure our foreign assistance policies—to make clear whether our priorities are world development and humanitarian aid, or world destruction and armament sales. These competing impulses were seen all too graphically in the Bangladesh crisis. One part of our government busily shipped arms to the army of Pakistan, while another did too little to help the hungry Bengalis injured while facing those same guns.

The terrible fact is that U.S. military assistance programs continue to receive more support than American programs of economic, social, humanitarian, and political development. This discredited approach is deplored by those who see the problems of poor countries in terms of their international development instead of the sterile rhetoric of security. For most Third World countries this emphasis on military power is virtually irrelevant to their true needs and desires. The surplus sale or subsidy of arms will not help them in meeting the threats of poverty, misery, illiteracy and disease. Even the Generals of Pakistan have learned this.

It is time for the Congress and the American people to insist that our overseas aid should go where it is needed most: into the mouths of hungry infants, into the education of illiterate children, into bettering the hopeless lives of their parents, and into the general development of Third World countries. If America really means what it says about a concern for people, we will finally introduce a greater dimension of compassion into our national attitudes and policies toward the special needs of refugees, the homeless, and others who are struggling to build better lives for their children.

It is to these and other points that this thoroughly researched and reasoned book addresses itself. On the basis of personal experience tempered in the field, the contributors to this volume document the full dimension of the health and food crisis which Bangladesh faced—both during the cyclone disaster of 1970, the period of civil strife in 1971, and the postwar relief and rehabilitation effort in 1972. Throughout, the authors suggest some of the basic lessons which the international community must and can learn from the Bangladesh disaster. I am confident that this volume of essays will contribute to a better understanding of some of the fundamental "people problems" which will demand the attention of the international community the coming decades.

EDWARD M. KENNEDY

Chairman, Subcommittee for Refugees
Committee on the Judiciary U.S. Senate

Preface

This book is about health in Bangladesh. The first part presents a background description of the health problems which have chronically afflicted this nation. The second part focuses on the health crises precipitated by two recent disasters: the cyclone of 1970 and the civil war of 1971. The concluding part offers recommendations for more effective conduct of relief operations during future disasters. The aims of this volume are (1) to present the critical health issues confronting Bangladesh, (2) to examine scientifically the effect of disasters on health, and (3) to analyze the lessons learned from the disaster relief experiences as they may apply to the future.

All of the contributors to this volume have lived and worked in Bangladesh. Most were also directly involved with relief operations during the disasters. After the cyclone, ten contributors participated in voluntary relief activities and field assessment in the devastated region. Eight participants witnessed firsthand the outbreak of civil war. More than a dozen contributors have either worked in the refugee camps or have returned to Bangladesh after independence to assist with rehabilitation and reconstruction.

During 1971, the attention and concern of much of the world focused on the tragedy in Bengal. Despite this widespread interest, few understood the root of the crisis or the nature of the health problems associated with the disaster. For this reason, the Bangladesh Information Center was formed by concerned scholars, physicians, and students. Its primary goal was to disseminate information on the Bangladesh crisis. As part of this information program, many participants wrote articles for journals and magazines, testified before congressional committees, and lectured to a wide-range of audiences, including medical communities, relief organizations, charitable groups, schools, churches, and clubs. It was from these activities that this book evolved.

Although the book spans three health disciplines (population, nutrition, and infectious disease), every effort has been made to present the material in an easily digestible form. Rather than aim for comprehensiveness, the authors attempt to highlight the critical issues. A glossary of Bengali and technical terms is provided to assist the reader.

The contributors are grateful to the people of Bangladesh who have shown us courtesy and kindness while we lived among them as guests. The royalties from the sale of this book will be donated toward the reconstruction of Bangladesh.

The editor is grateful to the contributors who have devoted exceptional time and energy to write chapters expressly for this publication. Special thanks are due to Dr. William B. Greenough III, who has encouraged and supported this work since its inception. I am grateful to Dr. W. Henry Mosley who reviewed the manuscript and offered valuable suggestions. I also thank Mrs. Deborah Wimmer for her assistance in the preparation of the final manuscript. Finally, I acknowledge with affection the participation of my wife, who helped with the editing process and who sympathetically tolerated my prolonged preoccupations with this book.

The views expressed are those of the contributors and do not represent the position of the organizations listed.

LINCOLN C. CHEN, M.D.

Contents

INTRODUCTION

Carl E. Taylor, M.D., Dr. P.H.

Seldom have so many suffered so much as in Bengal during 1970 and 1971. The sequence of disasters led to epidemics, starvation, and many injuries. This volume attempts a scientific analysis of some of the medical problems resulting from the disasters and the health measures that were tried. Lessons learned apply not only to Bangladesh, but also to disasters generally.

The health crisis in Bangladesh is not yet over. In fact, the disasters provide the challenge of moving beyond rehabilitation to habilitation in finding better ways to improve the life of the people of Bangladesh. One of the greatest lessons we have learned is the importance of an intensive planning period as habilitation starts.

Disasters are becoming more severe in their impact on more people. The increase is not merely an apparent increase due to more rapid and complete news coverage. Their is a real increase in the impact of both manmade and natural disasters (Table 1).

In relating the crises in Bangladesh to a broad perspective of the worldwide pattern of disaster, an attempt has been made to conceptualize a medical approach (1). In familiar terminology this introduction reviews diagnosis, treatment, prevention, and habilitation to summarize the points of view in the chapters that follow.

DIAGNOSIS

The etymology of the word disaster carries the meaning "from the stars." In ancient times a sudden catastrophe was automatically attributed to supernatural causes and spiritual forces. Even though we seem somewhat more able to understand disasters today, we

TABLE 1

World-Wide Distribution of Major [a] Disasters as Reported by US/AID Foreign Disaster Relief Coordinator's Office, Washington, D.C.

Year	Africa	NE/S Asia	East Asia	Europe [b]	Latin America	Total	No. Killed	No. Victims
1965	15	12	7	2	14	50	47,089	5,504,173
1966	15	5	12	0	16	48	7,086	4,139,646
1967	11	15	15	2	19	62	17,547	14,223,092
1968	11	13	13	3	15	55	4,103	5,455,602
1969	12	5	8	1	10	36	1,018,534 [c]	32,482,216
1970	16	6	5	2	22	51	72,915	11,743,040 [d]
1971	16	12	4	1	17	50	522,212	68,069,760 [e]
Total	96	68	64	11	113	352	1,689,486	141,617,529 [d]

a. Major disasters reported here number those disasters in which victim country requested aid from U.S.
b. Countries of Europe less apt to request aid from U.S. than developing countries elsewhere in world.
c. Includes civil strife in Nigeria
d. Includes earthquake victims of Peru
e. Includes victims of cyclone in East Pakistan

Note: One world-wide disaster registered in Disaster Relief Office not included in these figures is the cholera epidemic covering many regions over a number of years.

Source: These figures were obtained through a personal communication with the Office of the Coordinator, US/AID Foreign Disaster Relief Operations Section, Washington, D.C., on May 24, 1972.

still do not manage very well in coping with or preventing them.

In defining causal factors, we usually start by trying to distinguish between natural and manmade disasters. It is apparent that man is increasingly contributing to his disasters. This is not only because of the increasing lethality and destructiveness of war, but also because human population growth creates conditions which make natural disasters more likely.

Disasters have always occurred with varying levels of frequency determined by local conditions. Natural catastrophes can be roughly divided into those that are medical problems and those that arise from environmental causes. The major medical crises are epidemics and famine, both of which are well illustrated in this volume (Chapters 13, 15). The major environmental catastrophes are floods, earthquakes, and storms (such as hurricanes, tornadoes, and cyclones) (Chapters 9, 10). Manmade disasters are usually related to war with its phenomenal social disruption and human suffering. The increasing flood of refugees around the world is caused mainly by wars and political disturbances (Chapter 11). They represent a much more serious long-range problem than the refugees produced by natural disasters because it is so much more difficult to get resettlement and rehabilitation after a war. Refugees often become a floating population rejected by both sides in a political conflict, while being used for bargaining and political leverage. A final group of manmade disasters will undoubtedly become an increasing threat as population density and industrialization increase; it includes explosions, chain automobile accidents on expressways, and periodic surges of environmental pollution.

A major feature of the worldwide pattern of disasters is the accelerating number of individuals involved. Like so much else in the world, this phenomenon is clearly related to population growth (Chapter 9). The closer we get to the world's limit of growth, the more prepared we should be for more and bigger catastrophes (2). It has long been predicted that the natural history of population pressure would lead to conditions conducive to catastrophes. There are three reasons for this prediction.

First, as populations expand people are pushed into marginal areas with insufficient time or resources to make an adaptive adjustment. Many of the recognized disaster zones are populated only because people cannot find anywhere else to live. One such example is the Ganges/Brahmaputra Delta in Bangladesh. The islands in the Bay of Bengal are scarcely above water level in normal weather and with the increasing frequency of floods they are regularly inundated. Even more hazardous is the regular occurrence of typhoons and cyclones that sweep in from the Indian Ocean. Bengalis used to live on the mainland raising crops on the islands only through periodic visiting. With population growth, settling progressed rapidly to the present high density, villagers having adjusted psychologically to living under the threat of recurrent disasters.

Second, population pressure also produces environmental changes which increase the likelihood of natural disasters. On the Indian subcontinent there is the growing problem of floods from North Indian rivers as a result of deforestation and erosion in the Himalayas. The Nepalese and other residents of the Himalayas used to live only in the valleys. As population pressure increased, terracing became a fine art and fields crept up the mountain slopes to more than 12,000 feet. Massive cutting of forests caused accelerating erosion. In addition, the grow-more-food campaign in India led to deliberate substitution of fields for *terai* forests. Following malaria eradication in both India and Nepal, there was a massive flow of population from the hills into the *terai*. The United Nations estimate is that Nepal's world-famous *terai* jungles will be all farmland in ten years. The monsoon rains sweep across India to dump most of their water on the southern slopes of the Himalayas. The forested mountains, and especially the *terai* jungle, used to function like a big sponge which gradually released water through the year in the many rivers flowing across North Indian plains. Water now pours down the deforested slopes and the frequency and severity of floods has increased sharply. This sort of deforestation cycle is not new in history; much archeological evidence indicates that high density river civilizations, as in Mesopotamia, declined sharply after forests were destroyed (3).

Third, population pressure also increases tensions between nations, ethnic groups, and religions (4). The complex historical development of the antagonism between India and Pakistan has been clearly aggravated by population pressure. A realistic appraisal of world trends leads to the unhappy conclusion that such crises and civil disturbances are going to increase, and that we should prepare to respond constructively.

TREATMENT

Disaster planning requires appropriate response machinery both locally and internationally. Evidence presented in this volume provides a basis for planning a flexible response (Chapter 17). It is particularly evident that international agencies and the United States Government should develop a systematic and planned approach. Within the United Nations agencies a central focus for coordination is needed. Political issues often dominate the acute stages of a disaster, and humanitarian efforts and interest unfortunately tend to be relegated to a secondary position.

The technical functions in relief work require a well-organized working group. A politically powerful coordinating group should be set up by the local government with full participation of international agencies. Previous experience in coping with disasters needs to be incorporated into a system which can be quickly mobilized as in India's "Famine Code." A recent symposium on famine provides a particularly useful summary of field procedures (5).

A lesson from Bangladesh experience is the importance of basing relief activities on competent scientific surveys. After the cyclone a rapid but technically sound survey was done that revealed many dead but few wounded (Chapter 9). The sick were generally the least able to escape the tidal wave. Rather than sending three emergency hospitals, therefore, U.S. relief concentrated on feeding and housing the survivors.

In the first outpouring of sympathy that follows news of a disaster, there is a tendency to respond quickly by sending whatever supplies happen to be on hand. This has repeatedly proved to be a mistake because nothing is more precious immediately after a disaster than transportation facilities. Careful priority setting of relief supplies would make the best use of limited transportation and distribution arrangements.

There is probably no situation in which waste is so easy or so great a problem as during a disaster. Even more serious than frequent logistic problems such as spoilage and deterioration of supplies are the difficulties of distributing them and giving assistance to the right people. Nutrition programs for Bengali refugees experienced the familiar problem that the children going to the feeding centers were those healthy enough to wait in line. The really malnourished children were unable to leave the shelters. An associated problem is getting access to the right supplies; the classical example of this is the shipping of American wheat to rice-eating people at prices far in excess of the cost of rice in neighboring countries. Finally, there is the even more delicate problem of providing the right kind of care. This often means keeping well-intentioned individuals with the wrong type of training out of refugee camps. The most complex part of arranging for optimum care is to ensure cooperation rather than competition among relief agencies and individuals.

PREVENTION

Prevention depends on accurate diagnosis and an understanding of causation. Treatment can be based on symptoms but prevention requires a better understanding of causes. A continuing need is to study the distribution of disasters and to define disaster-prone areas on the basis of both geographic and political considerations. Impending civil disorders cast their shadows far enough before them that preparation should be possible so as to minimize damage and suffering. We may even be able to predict such manmade disasters as smog and pollution.

Real prevention depends on altering the basic causes. Population pressure, however, makes major social changes increasingly difficult. For instance, resettlement would solve some problems but there are very few areas where refugees are welcomed. A promising possibility is to change building materials and methods in disaster-prone areas. One area where this could be done is in the villages of Iran and Turkey which have been subjected to so much damage from earthquakes. The traditional flat roofs are built of logs, flat stones, and mud. Their collapse causes much injury to anyone inside. Another example is to improve agriculture and to provide better nutrition and thus forestall famine.

HABILITATION

A fundamental principle is that relief should do more than just get a refugee group back to its previous status. The disaster should be considered an opportunity to start long-term development. The fundamental Marxist concept that revolution must occur before a new society can be started is relevant to this discussion. Although not promoting revolution, we should at least take advantage of whatever opportunity a spontaneously occurring catastrophe offers. Planning should be foresighted enough to have specific programs available because in an emergency it is difficult to think beyond immediate needs. This approach has long been recommended by epidemiologists such as Chapin, who said that the smart public health official learned how to use a good epidemic to institute programs that would otherwise not be implemented (6). Some disasters in themselves are a demonstration that something is wrong, and preliminary planning should include evidence that a better way is possible. For instance, it may be possible to introduce simple changes such as building well-planned facilities after a flood. Even more important perhaps would be to introduce changes in administrative structure or personnel relationships. In a disaster situation, it may be possible to use auxiliaries so effectively that they could then be brought into a regular health program. Especially important is the psychological principle that a disaster can create awareness of the need for change among both leaders and people so as to make it possible to get both financial support and community participation toward a new way of life.

As Bangladesh now proceeds with active rehabilitation there is still particular need for intensive planning. The great tendency in the presence of urgent need is to do just anything and it is always easier to try to go back to what was there before. For Bangladesh this would be a mistake. There were many things there which needed improving. People will accept news ways more readily now than after previous patterns have been re-established. What is really crucial is to put together quickly rational plans for innovative programs based on practical field experience. Social rehabilitation, for instance, is virtually impossible without intensive population control; yet an overt campaign would be politically sensitive. A massive program integrating family planning and maternal and child health could, however, reach the villages quickly. It would have the advantage of being labor intensive and it could live employment in village service to thousands of the educated youth.

References

1. Saylor, L. F., and Gordon, J. E. The Medical Component of Natural Disasters. *Am. J. Med. Scs.* 234:342–362, 1957.
2. Meadows, D. H., Meadows, D. L., Randers, J., and Behrens, W. W., III. *The Limits to Growth, A Report for the Club of Rome's Project on the Predicament of Mankind.* New York, Universe Books, 1972.
3. Jacobsen, T., and Adams, R. M. Salt and Silt in Ancient Mesopotanian Agriculture. *Science* 128:1251–1258, 1958.
4. Galle, O. R., Gove, W. R., and McPherson, J. M. Population Density and Pathology: What are the Relations for Man? *Science* 176:23–30, 1972.
5. Blix, G., Hofvander, Y., and Vahlquist, B., eds. *Famine: A Symposium Dealing with Nutrition and Relief Operations in Times of Disaster.* Uppsala, Sweden, Almquist & Wiksells, 1971.
6. Chapin, C. V. *The Sources and Modes of Infection.* New York, John Wiley & Sons, 1910.

Part One
HEALTH IN BANGLADESH

(1) PROSPECTS FOR
HEALTH IN BANGLADESH

Norbert Hirschhorn and Lincoln C. Chen

The World Health Organization defines health as a state of physical, mental, and social well-being. In the developing regions of the world, of which Bangladesh is an important example, the prevalence of illness is extremely high due to a multiplicity of virulent pathogens, difficult living conditions, and impaired host resistance. The annual mortality rate in Bangladesh is between 15 and 20 per thousand population, and the annual infant mortality rate is 125 per thousand livebirths. But these conventional measures of health cannot adequately depict the heavy burden imposed upon the society by disease, for the survivors of serious illness far outnumber those killed and the total economic and social costs are considerable.

The three principal health problems of Bangladesh are overpopulation, malnutrition, and communicable disease. Seventy-five million inhabitants are squeezed into an area the size of Greece, producing a population density of 1,500 per square mile, and the population continues to grow at an alarming 3 per cent each year. Arable land is limited and food production has not kept pace with the increase in population. Partly because of the food shortage, malnutrition of varying degrees afflicts a significant portion of the population, especially preschool-age children. Inadequate sanitation, contaminated water sources, and overcrowding predispose the weakened population to many serious infectious diseases (cholera, smallpox, dysentery, tuberculosis, tetanus, parasitic infestation, and so on).

The deaths and illnesses due to disease, considered in terms of both absolute numbers and rates, have not been appreciably diminished by modern medical technology. For some diseases, technology is still insufficient. Further, many recent medical advances are quite inapplicable to the needs of a developing nation. In any case, modern medical techniques and facilities are simply inaccessible or unavailable to the average Bengali villager. We estimate, in fact, that no more than 5 per cent of Bangladesh's population has access to modern medical facilities or even to clean water and sanitation.

Reasons for poor health are complex but no doubt include limited economic resources, lack of knowledge about personal hygiene, and certain cultural traditions. Another reason is the low priority which health programs have received. During the five-year period of 1965 to 1970, only 2 per cent of Pakistan's annual national budget (or 40 cents per person) was invested in health. This contrasts with approximately $300 per capita spent in the United States each year.

Scarce resources were devoted to agricultural and industrial development, and much was wasted on military expenditures. Economic planners were reluctant to invest in health programs because it was believed that these programs, by reducing the mortality rate, would further exacerbate the population explosion which we are now witnessing. From the seventeenth to the nineteenth century, the population of Bangladesh remained relatively stable; a very high birth rate was balanced by a high mortality rate. In this century, however, population growth has accelerated; the birth rate remained high while the mortality rate fell. Yet modern medical advances can claim little credit for the decline in mortality. In Bangladesh the only truly modern public health projects have been the malaria- and smallpox-eradication programs conducted in the past two decades. But malaria and smallpox caused fewer than 10 per cent of the total deaths in Bangladesh, and in addition their control has actually been incomplete.

In fact, it can be shown that this century's population explosion preceded the introduction of modern health measures. The acceleration of population growth takes much of its impetus from the sheer mathematical effect of geometric progression. Moreover, the process of modernization, by bringing improved shelter, more food (especially imported foodgrain), and better education, transportation, and sanitation, has probably contributed more to the falling mortality rate than specific health measures have. In Bangladesh the acceleration of population growth preceded the introduction of public health programs by decades.

From a historical perspective, the falling mortality observed in many regions of the world is more closely correlated with socioeconomic development than with health measures. From 1900 to 1930, for example, the infant mortality rate in New York City declined from 140 to 60 per thousand, principally because of reduction in the incidence of respiratory and diarrheal illnesses. Yet this dramatic transition occurred before the introduction of antibiotics, vaccines, disease eradication programs, and intravenous fluid therapy. The three decades were marked by intense economic and social progress.

Rather than apologizing for contributing to the population crisis, many international health experts point to the beneficial effects of disease eradication on economic development. A frequently cited example is the malaria eradication campaign in Ceylon. Elimination of malaria from sparsely settled regions permitted people from the overcrowded parts of the island to inhabit and cultivate previously fallow land. Disease control actually reduced overcrowding, enhanced agricultural production, and stimulated economic progress.

It has been argued that a successful attack on disease improves the human resources of a developing nation. Productivity increases, absenteeism decreases, and the quality of labor-output improves. Support for this contention is found within Bangladesh itself in the tea gardens of the District of Sylhet. On some tea estates the private companies devised and implemented an effective and efficient scheme for rural health care. Their intention was to overcome the shortage of labor, especially during the critical harvesting months. The improved health of the workers eased the shortage of labor, and productivity increased. These operations required yearly budgetary justification, and pragmatic businessmen learned quickly that a small investment in health can pay off handsomely in profits.

These arguments have focused primarily on the effect of improved health in adult men, who constitute the economically productive portion of the population. Yet most illnesses and deaths occur in the pediatric and female portion of the population. In

Bangladesh 13 out of every hundred liveborn infants do not reach their first birthday, and another 10 per cent do not reach their fifth birthday. More than half of all deaths occur in children under the age of 5 years. Comprehensive health programs must therefore deal largely with infants and children. A cruel dilemma poses itself. Will health programs that save children's lives simply exacerbate the population crisis without improving economic productivity?

Two contentions have been advanced to support the proposition that improved health for children will have a positive demographic and economic impact on the society. The first is that a reduction of the birth rate, and thus a relaxation of the population explosion, will not occur unless it is preceded by a further reduction in infant and childhood death rates. The second is that the complex of malnutrition and infection during early childhood produces irreversible organic brain damage, resulting in fewer creative, productive adults.

Support for the second contention is tenuous at best. It is possible to demonstrate that severe food deprivation during the fetal and neonatal periods leads to loss of brain substance in animals. It is another matter to extrapolate these data to the conclusion that mild and moderate malnutrition, by far the commonest forms, retard intelligence, inhibit creativity, and dull initiative in humans.

Support for the first argument is still largely inferential. From a historical perspective, the "demographic transition" experienced by Western society from a high to a low population growth rate occurred over many years. This transition began with a decline in infant and childhood mortality, followed generations later by a decline in births. Hence, a reduction in childhood deaths has historically anteceded a drop in births. Moreover, available data suggest that parents tend to have a sufficient number of children to ensure the survival of at least one or two sons. In Bengal this is evident. Children not only provide a form of social security for their elders, but also are a source of joy and pride, ensuring the continuance of cultural tradition. It is believed that a voluntary birth control program cannot succeed unless coupled to a health program which promotes the survival of children already born. The success of voluntary family-planning programs depends on a change of motivation, and better health and increased survival of children may lie at the root of this change. Well-designed studies are needed to test these hypotheses.

It is possible that no effort toward disease control and family planning, however wisely conceived or aggressively implemented, will succeed in preventing a doubling of Bangladesh's population over the next 20 years. This tragedy is compounded by the fact that these new members of the world community are likely to suffer the same diseases which afflict their parents today.

What, then, prompts us to recommend vigorous health efforts in Bangladesh?

In a world where global balances of power dictate national expenditures and where planners choose politically pragmatic paths, it may seem naïve to talk of humanitarianism. Yet we firmly believe that the human race has a moral obligation to care for those already born. Currently, in the affluent West we spend billions of dollars annually on ourselves to prevent and cure all manner of diseases, with insufficient questioning of cost-benefit ratios, or effects on our population growth, or our contribution to environmental pollution. Why should so little be done for the disadvantaged peoples of the world!

(2) POPULATION:

BACKGROUND AND PROSPECTS

W. Henry Mosley and Monowar Hossain

INTRODUCTION

Bangladesh, formerly East Pakistan, is the eighth most populous nation in the world. With more than 70 million people crowded into 55,126 square miles, it is also the most densely settled developing country of the world today. The number and the density of the population, however, do not depict the full complexion of Bangladesh's population problem. In this chapter additional demographic features, such as age structure, marriage pattern, family size, urban-rural distribution, and educational level, will be discussed. In addition, projections of future population growth and its impact on health in Bangladesh will be presented to provide an insight into the nature of the population problem facing this new nation.

HISTORICAL PATTERN

To understand the current demographic picture, a review of the historical pattern of population growth is necessary. Figure 2.1 illustrates the growth of the population for the region that is now Bangladesh from 1700 to 1970 (1). During the eighteenth century, the population was stable at about 17 million. The population began to grow slowly in the nineteenth century, reaching 29 million by 1901. Since then, the growth rate has steadily accelerated. By 1961, the time of the last official census, the population had

w. HENRY MOSLEY was formerly head of the Epidemiology Division of the Cholera Research Laboratory, Dacca, Bangladesh. MONOWAR HOSSAIN was formerly Director of the Institute of Statistical Research and Training, Dacca University, Bangladesh.

reached approximately 55 million.[1] In the decade of the sixties, the growth rate approximated 2.7 to 3.0 per cent per year. Thus a conservative estimate of the size of the population in 1970 is 71.6 million people. The enormous acceleration of the growth rate is reflected in the fact that the number of new additions in only ten years, 1961–71, nearly equals the number present in the entire country 150 years ago.

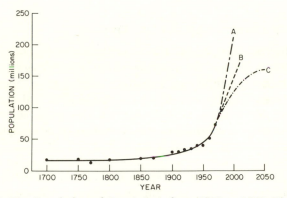

FIGURE 2.1. The Population of Bangladesh from 1700 to 2050. Lines A, B, and C represent three different projected growth rates from 1970. Line A represents a constant growth rate of 3 per cent. Line B represents our projected growth rate and Line C represents the anticipated growth rate if all couples were to reduce the number of children to two by 1980.

This acceleration reflects a recent decline in the mortality rate without a parallel fall in the birth rate. One hundred years ago the birth rate ranged from 45 to 50 livebirths per 1,000 population. But this high fertility was counterbalanced by a correspondingly high death rate of 40 to 45 per 1,000 persons. Moreover, episodic famine and epidemic diseases acted as intermittent brakes on population growth. Thus, population growth, which is the net difference between births and deaths in the absence of migration, was

1. The 1961 census actually counted a population of 51 million for the region that is now Bangladesh. Most observers, however, agree that there was an under-enumeration of the population, especially in the younger age groups, and the true population was felt to be closer to 55 million.

relatively slow and sporadic in the nineteenth century. Since the turn of this century, however, there has been a steady decline in the mortality rate, and since World War II this decline has accelerated. By 1960 the crude death rate had fallen to around 20 per 1,000, yet birth rates have remained high at 45 to 50 per 1,000. The growth rate during the decade of the sixties has been close to 3 per cent and, if this rate is sustained, the population will double in approximately 23 years.

DEMOGRAPHIC CHARACTERISTICS

A number of demographic characteristics are responsible for the continuing high fertility rates observed in Bangladesh. Among these are the youthful age structure, early age of marriage for women, large family size, desire for children for old-age security purposes, and low levels of literacy in this rural and tradition-bound society. The age and sex structure of the population in 1960 and 1970 is presented in Figure 2.2 (2). As illustrated, nearly 50 per cent of the population is under the age of 15 years. This high proportion of children (who do not contribute to economic productivity) not only imposes a heavy dependency burden on the nation, but also results in a built-in momentum for further population growth. The group that will be reproducing in the next generation has already been born. Since this group is larger than those currently in the reproductive ages, population will continue to grow in the near future, even if all families limited births to replacement levels immediately. This built-in momentum is illustrated in Figure 2.2, which shows an increase in the proportion of the younger age groups in the decade of the sixties.

Other factors conducive to high fertility are that nearly all women marry and that they marry at an early age (3,4). Fifty per cent of all females are married by age 13 years and over 99 per cent are married by the age of 19. On the average males are ten years older than their wives. Early and universal marriage obviously increases fertility by placing more women for longer periods of time in the potential reproductive pool. Moreover, the age differential between husband and wife at marriage inherently favors a high percentage of widows in the elderly age groups (Figure

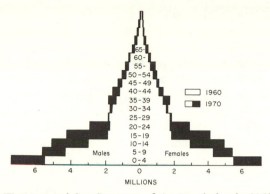

FIGURE 2.2. The Age and Sex Structure of the Population in 1960 and 1970. Nearly 50 per cent of the population is under age 15 years. Note that the younger age groups increased in greater proportion than the general population from 1960 to 1970.

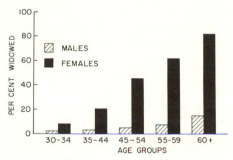

FIGURE 2.3. Percentage of Male and Female Widows According to Age.

2.3). One-fifth of the women are widows between the ages of 35 and 44; half of the women age 50 and under are widows; and eight out of ten of those 60 and under are. The corresponding percentage for men is lower since wives are considerably younger at marriage and thus are not likely to die before their husbands, and also because men commonly remarry after their wives die. The prospect of widowhood, no doubt, provides a strong incentive to young mothers to have many children since surviving sons provide the only means of support during old age.

The strong social, economic, and cultural incentives for surviving children are reflected in the average family size in Bangladesh of 5.6 members, enumerated in the 1961 census (1). Since this figure includes new families as well as those completing childbearing, another picture of the fertility pattern is revealed by the survey of Obaidullah which indicated that rural women who had completed childbearing averaged 6.5 livebirths (3). From a survey of pregnant women who were at the end of their childbearing years (40 to 49) in rural Matlab, it was found that each woman had an average of 8.5 prior pregnancies (5). Furthermore, they had experienced an average of 2.5 deaths of liveborn children per family, and at least 50 per cent of all women have witnessed the death in childhood of at least one of their offspring.

The population is relatively immobile and predominantly rural in distribution (1). In 1961, only 4 per cent of the population were living in a different district from their birthplace. Only 6 per cent of the population lived in urban centers (Table 1). The remaining 94 per cent were scattered in over 65,000 villages throughout the countryside. It is difficult to get educational facilities, health services, and family planning programs to such a dispersed rural population.

Bangladesh's population has an extremely low level of literacy. In the 1961 census, only 2.5 million persons (8 per cent) were registered as functional literates (five or more years of schooling). There were only 28,000 college graduates and 7,000 postgraduates, who represented less than 0.1 per cent of the population. Although a larger absolute number of literates and graduates is present today, it is unlikely that the percentage has increased, primarily because population growth has consistently outpaced the capacity of educational facilities to increase school enrollment ratios.

These demographic features, both individually and in concert, have been conducive to a sustained high fertility level in Bangladesh. Obviously, unless dramatic social changes occur, these factors will continue to influence the size of the population of Bangladesh.

POPULATION PROJECTIONS

Although a number of population projections for Bangladesh are available (6–9), a fresh assessment is necessary because of the recent disasters, the cyclone of 1970 and the civil war in 1971. To estimate the future population size of Bangladesh is extremely difficult, however, because necessary data are either unavailable or not fully reliable. Moreover, the full demographic impact of the recent disasters is unclear, and the population policies and programs of the new government are not yet fully developed. Nevertheless, projections of future trends of fertility, mortality, and population size are necessary to appreciate the complexity of the population problem facing this new nation.

Our projected trends of fertility and mortality from 1971 to

TABLE 1

Urban Population of
Bangladesh (1901–1971)

Year	Urban Population (thousands)	Per Cent of Total Population
1901	702	2.4
1911	807	2.5
1921	878	2.6
1931	1076	3.0
1941	1537	3.4
1951	1820	4.3
1961	2641	5.2
1971[a]	4200	6.0

a. estimated.
Source: Census of Pakistan, 1961.

2000 are presented in Figure 2.4. A comprehensive analysis of the data and assumptions supporting these trends are presented elsewhere (10). There is good evidence that both fertility and mortality declined slightly but consistently in the decade of the sixties.[2] These trends, however, were interrupted by the disasters which had significant demographic consequences. We have assumed a net loss of 2.5 million persons with these disasters: 0.5 million deaths

2. It is useful to note that a decline in fertility is not always associated with a corresponding decline in birth rates. Fertility is age and sex specific while the birth rate depends not only on the fertility but also on other demographic characteristics such as age structure and marital patterns.

from the cyclone, 1.5 million deaths associated with war, and 0.5 million refugees who have not returned to Bangladesh after the war. Due to the disruptions of war, we have also assumed that the mortality level returns only gradually to predisaster levels. It has been suggested that the large number of deaths, especially among children, may set off a pronatalist trend, hence increasing fertility. While this seems possible, we feel that fertility will increase only transiently until 1973 and will again decline after 1974.

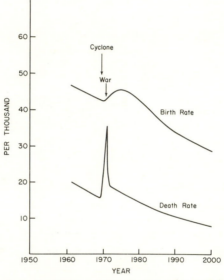

FIGURE 2.4. Trends in the Birth and Death Rates from 1961 to 2000. Note that the impact of the disasters has only transient effect on these trends.

The population projection to the year 2050 based on these assumptions and trends is illustrated in Figure 2.1, Line B. In spite of declining fertility from 1974 to 2000 and unusual deaths and migrations associated with recent disasters, the population of Bangladesh seems headed for at least a twofold increase between 1970 and the year 2000. Lines A and C delineate the most pessimistic and most optimistic projections, respectively. If the present growth rate of almost 3 per cent is sustained, the population will exceed 200 million by the next century (Figure 2.1, Line A). Even under the most optimistic assumption that fertility will decline dramatically so that in 1980 the average family will have two children, by the turn of the century the population will be 118 million (Figure 2.1, Line C) (11). Furthermore, the growth will not stabilize until 2050, at which time the population will be over 150 million. Continued growth will be due to the large number of children in the younger age groups, which provide built-in momentum for future growth. Whichever trend actually materializes, the fact remains that Bangladesh will experience an increasing pressure of population on land and other economic resources in the decades to come.

IMPACT OF RAPID POPULATION GROWTH

This rapid population growth will have profound economic, social, educational, health, and environmental effects on Bangladesh. Table 2 presents our projected changes of the age structure of Bangladesh's population from 1961 to 2000. Since the total population will grow from 55.3 million in 1961 to an estimated 145.9 million by the turn of the century, food, clothing, and shelter must be expanded nearly threefold during this period just to preserve the current standard of living.

The labor force (men, ages 15 to 64) will probably increase over twofold from 1971 to 2000. Many more jobs will need to be

TABLE 2

Age Structure Projection of
Bangladesh's Population (1961–2000)

Year	Age Groups				Total
	0–4	5–14	15–64	65+	
		(thousands)			
1961	10809	15153	27177	2167	55306
1971	12574	20686	36865	2221	72346
1981	16442	24329	51886	2543	95200
1991	17967	32661	66328	3512	120468
2000	18893	34926	87430	4712	145961

generated within the economy to accommodate the growing size of the labor force. Unless this expansion keeps pace with the growth rate, underemployment and unemployment will increase, exacerbating social tensions. As rural employment opportunities decline, urbanization will accelerate and there will be overcrowded housing. increased health hazards, and social disruption.

Social services will require enormous expansion. It will be extremely difficult, for example, to raise the school enrollment ratios among children. Children from ages 5 to 14 will increase from 20 million in 1971 to almost 35 million in 2000, and educational facilities will require enormous expansion to keep up. It will be even more difficult to make improvements in the quality of education. Preventive and curative health services will face similar difficulties. With more people, especially children and women, superimposed upon overcrowding, urbanization, malnutrition, and poor sanitation, health services will need to expand rapidly in order to prevent, contain, and treat a spectrum of endemic and epidemic diseases.

CONCLUSION

All in all, the prospect for better health in the economic, social, and physical sense will be greatly diminished by the growing population of Bangladesh. These problems were recognized ten years ago when a National Family Planning Program was initiated in Pakistan. By 1965, this program had been partially successful in promoting an awareness of the need for family planning at the village level. Actual practice was, however, more difficult to induce. Recent surveys have shown that fewer than 5 per cent of village couples have been practicing birth control. A critique of the family planning program and suggestions for programs of the future are beyond the scope of this chapter.

Meeting the challenge of population growth in Bangladesh will require unprecedented social change. The revolutionary events leading to the establishment of a new nation indicate that change is possible. Time will tell whether Bangladesh, and the world, will rise to meet the challenge.

References

1. Census of Pakistan. Volume II, *East Pakistan.* p. II–4, 1961.
2. Bean, L. L., Khan, M. R., and Rukanuddin, A. R. *Population Projections for Pakistan: 1960 to 2000.* Pakistan Institute of Development Economics, Karachi, Pakistan. Monograph No. 17, January 1968.
3. Obaidullah, M. *Demographic Survey in East Pakistan.* Part II. *On Marriage, Fertility, and Mortality.* Institute of Statistical Research and Training, Dacca University. 1961–1962.
4. Yusef, F. "Some Recent Estimates of Fertility of Pakistani Women Based on PGE Data" (unpublished memeo).
5. Chowdhury, A. K. M. A., Aziz, A. K. M., and Mosley, W. H. *Demographic Studies in Rural East Pakistan, Second Year, May 1967–April 1968,* Pakistan-SEATO Cholera Research Laboratory, Dacca, East Pakistan, 1969.
6. Benford, F. Basic Assumptions of Revelle, Thomas / East Pakistan. Center for Population Studies, Harvard University. Memo dated January 6, 1972.
7. Brackett, J. W., and Akers, D. S. *Projections of the Population of Pakistan by Age and Sex: 1965–1986.* Bureau of the Census, U.S. Dept. of Commerce. June 1965.
8. Bussink, W. C. F. "Ultimate Stationary Population Size for East Pakistan. June 1971" (unpublished).
9. Revelle, R., and Thomas, H. "Population and Food in East Pakistan." *J. of Ind. and Trop. Hyg.* October 1970.
10. Hossain, M. *Bangladesh: Population Projections, 1961–2000.* Population and Human Resources Division, International Bank for Reconstruction and Development. May 8, 1972.
11. U.S. Bureau of Census. *The Two Child Family and Population Growth: An International View.* U.S. Dept. of Commerce.

(3) POPULATION:
DEMOGRAPHIC TRENDS

John Stoeckel

INTRODUCTION

A comprehensive analysis of demographic trends in Bangladesh is rather difficult since reliable data have not been collected consistently for long periods of time. Censuses taken in 1951 and 1961 contained substantial errors of underreporting of infants and women, and the 1971 census was canceled after the outbreak of civil war. Hence, to provide an assessment of demographic trends, data sources other than the censuses have to be utilized. Fortunately, two such sources exist for the 1960's: the Population Growth Estimation (PGE) reports and the registration system of the Cholera Research Laboratory (CRL). Most of the following analysis will be based on data from these two sources. The design and collection procedures of the PGE and CRL will be discussed later in the chapter.

The objectives of the present analysis are (a) to assess the trends in fertility and mortality, (b) to study the major components of population growth, and (c) to identify any shifts in the age-sex structure and their implications for population growth. Two additional aspects of growth are also considered: the potential impact that declines in infant mortality could have upon growth, and the role that rural to urban migration may play in urban population growth.

JOHN STOECKEL was formerly Research Demographer. Cholera Research Laboratory, Dacca, Bangladesh.

DATA SOURCES

Population Growth Estimation (PGE)

The PGE experiment began in Pakistan in late 1961 with the objective of obtaining, through sample survey and registration, information on demographic factors relevant to the future development of the economy, i.e., births, deaths, and rates of natural increase. The experiment covered the urban and rural populations and utilized a complex sample design based upon "a multi-stage sample of clusters of households . . . employing a broad geographic stratification." Two types of collection procedures were established in selected sample areas. One was Longitudinal Registration (LR), wherein births and deaths were recorded as they occurred by special PGE registrars who lived in each sample area. The other approach, called Cross-Sectional Survey (CS), was designed to obtain data on population size, age, sex, marital status, family composition, occupation, pregnancy, and births and deaths which occurred in households in the PGE areas during the previous year. The CS household survey was conducted once every three months. Simultaneous use of LR and CS was made in eight of twelve areas. In each of these eight areas, a full-time resident registrar recorded births and deaths as they occurred, and quarterly enumeration was also undertaken. Two of these areas were urban and six rural. Of the remaining four areas, two were subjected to LR only and two to CS only. Events were registered and enumerated on a *de facto* basis. The births and deaths recorded by the two systems were matched one by one, and nonmatched events were investigated as far as possible (2). This process continued through 1965.

Cholera Research Laboratory (CRL)

The CRL began data collection in connection with cholera vaccine trials through a registration system of all births, deaths, and migrations in 132 villages (population = 111,748) of Matlab *Thana* in May 1966 (3). In this system a local female resident (field worker) of each village visited each household daily to check for any births, or deaths, and on persons who have migrated into or out of the village. Her work and record-keeping were supervised by male field assistants. Each field assistant had from three to five field workers under supervision. On the average these assistants visited each family weekly, recording the vital events on standard forms which were checked against the information collected by the female resident. Supervision of the work of the field assistant was conducted by Sanitary Inspectors who visited each household twice a month to check on the completeness of the registration. These workers in turn were supervised by the Field Surveillance Supervisor and his deputy, who were responsible for the coordination of the field work. This data collection system operated up to March 1971. The data currently available from the system extend through 1969.

RESULTS

Births and Deaths

Birth and death rates in Bangladesh were high and relatively stable in the 1960's (Table 1). On the average the early estimates of the crude birth rate by PGE show little or no difference from the later estimates of CRL, and CRL estimates of the crude death rate are slightly lower than the PGE, suggesting a small decline in mortality in the mid-1960's. (This decline was probably a result of the intensive treatment of all diarrheal illnesses in the area.) In general, however, the rate of natural increase or population growth for the period remained near an average of 3 per cent per year; only two other major Asian countries, the Philippines and Thailand, have growth rates which exceed this level (Table 2).

The population of Bangladesh increased from about 52 million in 1962 (4) to over 70 million in 1971 and can be expected to double in less than 25 years at the current rate of growth.[1] This estimate does not take into account losses from the cyclone disaster of 1970 or the military conflict of 1971. Even if losses from

1. The 1971 population (P) was calculated by the simple formula, $P_{1971} = P_{1962}(1 + r)$, where r equals the annual rate of increase (3 per cent) and n equals the time in years.

TABLE 1
Summary of Demographic Rates for Bangladesh, 1962–1965 (PGE)
and 1966–1967 through 1968–1969 (CRL)

	PGE (1)		CRL (3)	
Rates	1962–65	1966–67	1967–68	1968–69
Crude Birth Rate[a]	44–53	47	45	47
Crude Death Rate[b]	16–20	15	17	15
Natural Increase[c]	2.8–3.3	3.2	2.8	3.2
Total Fertility Rate[d]	6.3–7.4	6.6	6.3	6.3

a. $CBR = \dfrac{\text{No. of Live Births in the Year}}{\text{Total Population at Midyear}} \times 1{,}000.$

b. $CDR = \dfrac{\text{No. of Deaths in the Year}}{\text{Total Population at Midyear}} \times 1{,}000.$

c. NI = CBR per 100 − CDR per 100.

d. TFR = The sum of the age-specific birth rates for women 15–49 years.

TABLE 2
Summary Demographic Rates for
Selected Asian Countries

Country	Year	Crude Birth Rate[a]	Crude Death Rate[b]	Natural Increase	Total Fertility Rate[c]
Ceylon	1969	31.7	7.9	2.4	5.5
Hong Kong	1970	18.9	5.1	1.4	5.2
India	1968	42.8	16.7	2.6	5.4
Indonesia	1968	48.3	19.4	2.9	6.1
Japan	1970	18.9	6.9	1.2	2.0
Korea	1968	36.6	11.0	2.6	6.0
Philippines	1968	44.7	12.0	3.3	6.6
Singapore	1970	23.3	5.3	1.8	5.5
Taiwan	1970	28.1	5.1	2.3	5.8
Thailand	1968	42.8	10.4	3.2	6.0

a. United Nations, *1970 Demographic Yearbook*, U.N., New York, 1971, p. 657.

b. Ibid., p. 675.

c. Lee Jay Cho, Estimated Refined Measures of Fertility for All Major Countries of the World. *Demography* 1: 359–374 (1964).

these events reached the high estimate of 3 million persons, however, Bangladesh (at a 3 per cent rate of growth) would replace this number within a year and a half.

One final observation should be made from Table 1. The total fertility rate, which is not subject to the fluctuations in the age structure that affect the crude birth rate,[2] has remained above six for the entire period, and this rate is second only to that of the Philippines (Table 2). If women continue childbearing at this rate, their completed family sizes will exceed six children. The persistence of this high total fertility rate seems all the more ominous when one considers that it is most sensitive to shifts in marriage patterns and family limitation practices; it suggests that past family-planning programs and economic development have exerted little impact upon fertility.

Age Structure

No attempt will be made to assess trends in specific age groups since errors of age misstatement and underreporting may alter the individual cohorts. Instead, a general overview of the age structure is presented in the form of age-sex population pyramids based on data from the 1962 and 1965 PGE and 1968–69 CRL registration systems (Figure 3.1).

The pyramids fit the classical shape of a population characterized by consistently high rates of growth, and this shape generally does not appear to have altered greatly through the period. The bases are extremely broad—the high proportion of persons in the younger age groups is characteristic of high levels of fertility. The portions of the pyramids representing old age groups show the constrictions which are characteristic of high levels of mortality.

2. It should be noted that a population could have a high crude birth rate with a falling or low total fertility rate. That is, if the population has an age structure which favors a high proportion of women in the childbearing ages, then the ratio of births produced by these women to the total population would be high. A smaller number of women producing a larger number of births could result in a crude birth rate at a level equal to the population with a large number of childbearers but lower actual fertility, i.e., ratio of births to women in the specific age groups.

Probably the most important aspect of the age structure for future growth and its impact upon the society is the high proportion of the younger age groups. Almost half of the population of Bangladesh is under 15 years of age, which is the highest such proportion of the major Asian countries (Table 3). This is particularly striking when one considers the dependency burden this age group places on the economically active portion of the population and the present and future educational and occupational needs that must be met. Even if Bangladesh were able to reduce her fertility level substantially, she would still be faced with the problems re-

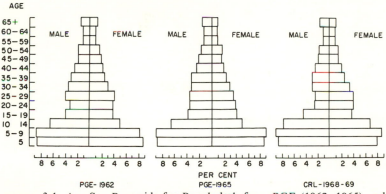

FIGURE 3.1. Age-Sex Pyramids for Bangladesh from PGE (1962, 1965) and CRL (1968–69)

sulting from an age structure heavily weighted in the direction of youth and the growth this group engenders when it enters the marriage and child-bearing period. That is, even if the members of this group lowered their absolute fertility, their sheer numbers would contribute to a substantial rate of growth. For example, Frejka has shown that even if fertility dropped drastically to the replacement level (i.e., mothers would replace themselves with one living daughter, a net reproduction rate of 1) by 1975, Bangladesh would still add another 30 million persons to its population by the year 2000 (4).

TABLE 3
Proportion of the Population of Bangladesh
Under 15 Years of Age (PGE 1962 and 1965,
CRL 1968–1969) and Other Asian Countries

Country	Year	Proportion Under 15 Years
Bangladesh	1962 (PGE)	46.4
	1965 (PGE)	47.3
	1968–69 (CRL)	49.3
Ceylon	1963	41.5[a]
Hong Kong	1969	38.1
India	1970	41.6
Indonesia	1964	43.9
Japan	1969	24.0
Korea	1970	40.4
Philippines	1968	46.8
Singapore	1970	38.8
Taiwan	1968	42.9
Thailand	1960	43.1

a. United Nations, *1970 Demographic Yearbook,* U.N., New York, 1971, pp. 268–298.

Infant Mortality

Infant mortality, which is comprised of neonatal and postneonatal deaths,[3] reaches a level of 125 per 1000 live births in Matlab and accounts for over 35 per cent of the total deaths in the population (Table 4). Given this high proportion of total deaths, a reduction in infant mortality, through maternal and child health care programs, could exert considerable impact upon the crude death rate (and consequently upon the growth rate). This potential impact through selected proportional reductions in both neonatal and postneonatal deaths is shown in Table 5 (5).[4]

3. Neonatal deaths are defined as deaths occurring in the first month of life, and postneonatal deaths are those occurring between the first and twelfth months of life.

4. The reduction (R) in the crude death rate was calculated by the simple formula:

$$R = CDR - \frac{D - X \, (P_{10 \ldots 50})}{T}$$

where CDR is the current crude death rate, D is the total number of deaths in the population, X is the number of neonatal or postneonatal deaths, P is the percentage reduction, and T is the total population.

TABLE 4

Neonatal and Postneonatal Deaths per 1,000 Live Births
and as Proportions of Total Deaths in the Population
of 132 Villages of Matlab Thana, May 1967,
through April 1969

Deaths	Number	Per Cent	Rate per 1000 Births[a]	Per Cent of Total Deaths[b]
Neonatal	805	60.6	75.5	22.0
Postneonatal	525	39.4	49.1	14.3
Total Infant	1,330	100.0	124.6	36.3

a. Total Births = 10,658, Crude Birth Rate = 46.
b. Total Deaths = 3,661, Crude Death Rate = 15.8.

TABLE 5

Change in the Crude Death Rate of 15.8 (Deaths per 1,000
Population) Produced by Selected Percentage Reductions
in Neonatal and Postneonatal Deaths in 132 Villages
of Matlab Thana, May 1967 through April 1969

Deaths	Reduction of Neonatal and Postneonatal				
	10 Per Cent	20 Per Cent	30 Per Cent	40 Per Cent	50 Per Cent
	Change in Crude Death Rate				
Neonatal	− 0.3	− 0.7	− 1.0	− 1.4	− 1.7
Postneonatal	− 0.2	− 0.5	− 0.7	− 0.9	− 1.1
Total Infant	− 0.5	− 1.2	− 1.7	− 2.3	− 2.8

Source: From Stoeckel and Chowdhury, 1972.

At the extreme, if neonatal deaths were reduced by half,[5] the
crude birth rate of 46 would have to fall by about 2 points just to
restrict the growth rate to its present high level of 3 per cent. A
comparable reduction in the postneonatal rate would require a

5. It would seem entirely possible that the neonatal death rate could be reduced by such a large proportion with the implementation of an effective
tetanus vaccine program. According to an unpublished analysis of infant
death reports in the area, deaths due to neonatal tetanus account for over
40 per cent of all neonatal deaths.

drop of one point in the crude birth rate to limit growth to the current rate.

Although a total reduction of about three points in the crude
death rate resulting from a 50 per cent reduction in infant mortality
appears rather small, its impact on a stable high crude birth rate
would require a drastic decline of eight points in the crude birth
rate just to reach a growth rate of 2.5 per cent, which would still
result in a doubling of the population in less than thirty years. It is
obvious that continued efforts in death control without extensive efforts in birth control will perpetuate this high rate of growth.

Out-migration

Rapid rural to urban shifts in population can have severe consequences for the social structure of a population, particularly in an
area already characterized by high unemployment, overcrowded
schools, and sprawling slums. Although very little is known about
such shifts in Bangladesh, data from the Matlab registration area
provide a basis for drawing inferences about this process at the
national level.

In a previous study it was found that in the year 1968–69, 64.2
per cent of all rural out-migrants from Matlab moved to an urban
area which results in an urban migration rate of 2.4 per 100 rural
population (6). Further, of 2,907 in-migrants, 1,449 came from
urban areas, and of 4,040 out-migrants, 2,592 moved to an urban
area. Thus, the increase in the urban population from rural out-
migrants is reduced by about 56 per cent and the net gain to the
urban population is 1.1 persons per 100 rural population. We will
assume that this rate can be applied to the total rural population
to obtain an estimate of the proportional increase in the urban
population which could result from rural to urban migration. Ad-
mittedly, the data arising from this assumption must be treated
with caution. In the absence of other information on migration
rates, however, the present data provide a crude estimate of the
urban growth due to inter-area migration streams.

To be conservative a second rate of migration at a lower level
will also be applied. The rationale for including a lower rate is

that the Matlab villages have slightly higher than average population density, which may act as a push factor to increase the out-migration rate to levels above that of populations with lower densities. Also, Matlab's relatively close proximity to two of the four largest urban areas, Dacca and Narayanganj, may act as a stronger pull factor than exists in those rural areas located at greater distances from urban areas. Although it is not possible to assess these factors quantitatively, we will assume that they may exert such an influence that the net gain in the urban area from migration is about 30 per cent lower than the rate found in Matlab. This assumption reduces the rate from 1.1 to 0.7 per 100 rural population.

Table 6 presents the impact of this internal migration on urban population growth. Given an urban population that was 6.0 per cent of the total population in 1969, an annual growth of 16 per cent would result from rural in-migration if the migration rate for all rural areas of Bangladesh was the same as in Matlab.[6] Under our conservative estimate of rural in-migration, the urban population would still increase by almost 11 per cent per year. Further, even if the urban population was approximately 9.4 per cent of the total population in 1969, the proportional annual growth added by net rural migration under the two rates would still equal 10 and 7 per cent, respectively.

It should again be noted that the intent of this analysis is simply to provide a crude range of estimates of urban growth which could result from net rural to urban migration. Without concurrent eco-

6. These rates are calculated from the following formula which estimates the proportional increase in the urban population in 1969 due to net out-migration from the rural to urban areas:

$$UI = \frac{P - (P)\ (EU_1 \ldots 5_1)}{(P)\ (EU_1 \ldots 5_1)} \cdot Rn$$

where UI is the proportional increase in urban population in 1969; P is the total population of Bangladesh in 1969 projected from the 1961 census population at a 3 per cent rate of natural increase per year; $EU_1 \ldots 5_1$ is the expected per cent of urban population in 1969 obtained by projecting the per cent of urban population in 1961 by the annual intercensal (1951–1961) rate of increase, "i," of the proportion urban; and Rn is the net rate of out-migration from the rural to urban area.

nomic expansion the consequences of net rural to urban migration, at even the more conservative estimate, for an area already under severe population pressure are obvious. Since most of the migrants to urban areas are males seeking better occupational opportunities (7), new positions in the existing occupational structure will have to be created to accommodate the surplus labor force. Housing facilities and educational institutions will also have to be expanded. Failure of the urban social structure to accommodate these increased needs will further contribute to the already familiar problems of unemployment, slums, and overcrowded schools.

TABLE 6

Estimated Proportional Increase in Urban Population of Bangladesh in 1969 Resulting from Net In-Migration from Rural Areas

Net In-Migration from Rural Areas per 100 Persons	*Per Cent Urban in 1969*				
	6.0	6.9	7.7	8.5	9.4
	Per Cent Increase in Urban				
1.1	16.4	14.3	12.4	11.3	10.2
0.7	10.9	9.5	8.3	7.5	6.8

Source: From Stoeckel, Chowdhury, and Aziz, 1972.

It has been shown that even under the more conservative assumption the urban population of Bangladesh may be estimated to have grown by at least 10 per cent annually in 1969 from rural out-migration alone. It would thus appear that population redistribution to urban areas is a problem of more immediate concern than the high rate of natural increase. Growth from net migration to urban areas will be over three times as great as growth from natural increase and will obviously exert a much greater impact in the short run. Although population control programs within the context of other developmental efforts are a necessity, the present data indicate the importance of implementing programs to meet the urban needs created by such rapid increases in population.[7]

7. The civil war in Bangladesh precludes making any generalizations from the findings beyond 1970. Certainly the selectivity of migrants and pattern

SUMMARY AND CONCLUSIONS

This analysis of demographic trends and their implications for Bangladesh has found that:

1. Population growth characterized by high birth and death rates averaged about 3 per cent in the 1960's. If the current rate of growth continues, Bangladesh will double in population in less than 25 years. The persistence of a high total fertility rate would appear to indicate that development and family-planning programs have had little impact in the past.

2. The age structure showed little variation through the 1960's. Almost half of the population is under 15 years of age, which places a sizable burden of dependency on the economically active population. Substantial population growth due to the presence of large numbers of future childbearers can be expected to continue even with reductions in absolute fertility.

3. The infant death rate accounts for over 35 per cent of total deaths in the population. If the infant rate were reduced by half, the current crude death rate would decrease from 16 to 13 per cent. Although this reduction would appear to be small, in the context of a current high growth rate of 3 per cent it would have a sizable impact. For example, it would take a reduction of 8 points in the crude birth rate of 46 just to achieve a growth rate of 2.5 per cent under these circumstances. Obviously birth control programs must parallel efforts to prevent infant deaths.

4. Conservative estimates of rural to urban migration indicate that urban areas of Bangladesh may be expected to increase by about 10 per cent per year. The immediate impact that this rapid rate of growth may have on the urban social structure cannot be overemphasized. Development programs will have to be implemented so that the existing educational and health institutions can accommodate the rapid influx. Occupational op-

of redistribution will have been altered by this event. However, the present data provide the only reliable basis of a future comparison which can evaluate the impact of the war on the population and generate information which can be used to direct new development programs.

portunities and housing facilities must also undergo rapid expansion. In the short run, urban growth from migration seems
a more pressing problem than growth due to natural increase.

It would be a gross understatement to say that Bangladesh indeed has a population problem. This analysis has barely scratched
the surface, and when one considers the additional complications
of extremely low ages at marriage, existing high population densities, and limited agricultural production, nothing but a pessimistic conclusion can be reached. At this point it would be rather
foolhardy to speculate on the possibilities of solving a problem of
such magnitude. Massive development efforts will be necessary for
even the slightest impact.

References

1. *Report of the Population Growth Estimation Experiment: Description and Some Results for 1962 and 1963.* Pakistan Institute of Development Economics, Karachi, p. 24 (1968).
2. Ibid., p. 24.
3. Mosley, W. H., Chowdhury, A. K. M. A., and Aziz, K. M. A. *Demographic Characteristics of a Population Laboratory in Rural
   East Pakistan.* Center for Population Research, National Institute
   of Health. September 1970.
4. Frejka, T. *Alternatives of World Population Growth: Demographic
   Paths to the Future.* New York, John Wiley & Sons. In press.
5. Stoeckel, J., and Chowdhury, A. K. M. A. Neonatal and Postneonatal Mortality in a Rural Area of Bangladesh. *Population Studies,*
   March 1972.
6. Stoeckel, J., Chowdhury, A. K. M. A., and Aziz, K. M. A. Out-
   Migration from a Rural Area of Bangladesh. *Rural Sociology.* June
   1972.
7. Ibid., p. 5.

(4) NUTRITION: FOOD PRODUCTION, DIETARY PATTERNS, AND NUTRITIONAL DEFICIENCIES

Irwin H. Rosenberg

INTRODUCTION

Nutrition has been a primary concern of Bangladesh throughout its modern history. In the best of times the food supply has been barely adequate for the needs of the population, and this chronic state of food shortage has been regularly converted to outright famine by wars, floods, and other disasters. It is the purpose of this chapter to describe the pattern and picture of nutrition in East Bengal during the decade before the disruptions which culminated in the independence of Bangladesh. Only against this background, which reflects the food and nutrition status of this region for decades, if not centuries, can the problems facing this new nation be understood. This discussion will draw heavily on data generated from a comprehensive survey of nutrition conducted in Bangladesh from 1962 to 1964.

AGRICULTURE AND FOOD PRODUCTION

Climatically, Bangladesh is one of the monsoon lands of Asia. The monsoons begin in June and continue to September, during which time more than three-quarters of the yearly rainfall occurs. The abundant rainfall and the rich soil make agriculture the dominant economic activity. With the exception of the relatively small area of the Chittagong Hill Tracts, most of Bangladesh is an alluvial, flat plain draining three large rivers. From the point of

IRWIN H. ROSENBERG was one of the organizers and a participant in the Nutrition Survey of East Pakistan, March 1962 to January 1964, sponsored by the Governments of Pakistan and the United States and the Department of Biochemistry, Dacca University (K. Ahmad, Chairman).

view of food production and consumption the region is rather homogeneous.

The land is cultivated intensively. Most farms are less than three acres, and 90 per cent of them are less than eight acres in size. Fragmentation of farms is a dominant pattern; 53 per cent of the farms of less than half an acre consists of two or more disconnected pieces of land. Over half of the farms with a total of five to seven acres consists of ten or more separate plots. Fragmentation adds to the difficulty the farmer finds in efficiently cultivating his total acreage, but it also enables him to have access to lands of different elevation and crop suitability, and thus to diversify his cropping patterns.

The most important food source is rice (Figure 4.1). There are three agricultural seasons in Bangladesh for rice: the *aus* season (April to July), the *badio-aman* season (July to December), and the *rabi-boro* season (December to April). Trends in rice production have been generally favorable, but their beneficial impact has been virtually eliminated by rapid population growth. With the rice crop of 1947–48 used as an index of 100 for comparison, total rice production increased to 152 in 1963–64. An increase of more than 50 per cent in 16 years is spectacular indeed, but one must realize that during this same time period the population increased by at least 35 per cent. The Third Five-Year Plan target was for an increase of 25 per cent between 1965 and 1970. Actual production increased only 15 per cent (Figure 4.2), and the continuing growth of population necessitated a nearly twofold increase in foodgrain imports during this period.

Sources of animal protein (fish and livestock) have also failed to keep pace with population growth. Although there are numerous waterways in Bangladesh, independent studies have concluded that fish consumption has remained rather modest. There are two reasons for the low consumption of fish. First, yields from inland waterways are limited and development of fishpond (tank) cultivation is immature. Second, the inland population is not accustomed

---

FIGURE 4.1. Rice Field and Village in Bangladesh (courtesy of Dr. R. Northrup)

to saltwater fish or seafoods from the Bay of Bengal. Dietary preferences are for freshwater fish and many seafoods (especially shrimp) are exported to generate foreign exchange.

The availability of livestock animal protein is even more modest. Although the livestock population (cattle, buffalo, sheep, goats, fowl) is considerable, its size is small in comparison to the needs of the large population. Moreover, certain livestock provide the primary source of power for agriculture and transportation and are too precious to be eaten as food. Milk yields per animal are poor (3–15 pounds per day), and milk consumption is believed to be low.

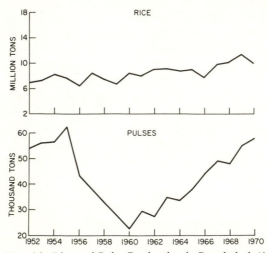

FIGURE 4.2. Trend in Rice and Pulse Production in Bangladesh (1952–1970)

Quantitatively, pulses (lentils, seed-legumes) constitute the most important source of non-animal proteins in the diet. Their importance is underscored by the fact that the amino acid content of pulses complements the proteins available from rice. Yet the production of pulses in Bangladesh decreased considerably from 1950 to 1960 (Figure 4.2). This was probably due to low incentive for the farmer. Pulse crops are mainly grown in the *rabi-boro* season and farmers have preferred to grow other crops such as wheat for a surer and more profitable market. Fortunately, considerable recovery of pulse production was achieved in the decade of the sixties.

Other sources of nutrients include fruits, vegetables, fats, and oils. Fruits and vegetables of all kinds are produced but they are entirely seasonal. Although some are nutritionally desirable, others such as gourds and cucumbers possess little nutritional value. Yields of vegetable oils per acre are low, and fats and oils (*ghee, mustard oil,* and *rapeseed oil*) are consumed in small quantities.

FOOD INTAKE AND DIETARY PATTERNS

In technically and economically advanced nations, food production, food distribution, and dietary patterns are closely interwoven. This is not, however, the case in the developing agricultural economy of Bangladesh where local food production and local food costs determine the dietary pattern to a greater extent. Food distribution and marketing on a countrywide scale are usually of lesser importance. The food supply and dietary pattern of the average farmer and his family are for the large part determined by what he produces himself. What he cannot produce (salt, sugar, fats, and oils) he must purchase. Yet what he is able to buy depends not only on local availability but also on how much he can sell. For the most part, farmers sell fish, meat, eggs, rice, wheat, and perishable products, such as fruits and vegetables. The sale of nutritionally valuable food is hazardous, but the farmer must sell in order to purchase the necessities of life.

The pattern of food intake in rural regions is different from the pattern in urban centers (Table 1). Per capita income is higher in the urban centers, and although food costs are higher there than they are in the rural areas, a smaller percentage of income is directed toward food costs by the average city dweller. Thus the townsman can afford a more balanced diet of essential nutrients than his counterpart in the countryside can.

There are several reasons for considering the findings from urban and rural areas separately. Urbanization is a characteristic feature of population shifts in Bangladesh. Shifts of this nature can be expected to produce changes in the dietary habits of the population through changes in price and availability of foodstuffs. Proper examination for the effects of such changes, as well as estimation of future food needs, requires a baseline evaluation of present nutritional conditions in urban and rural areas. The differing food consumption patterns also produces an unequal distribution of nutritional deficiencies, and this imbalance has important implications for nutrition, agricultural, and public health planners.

TABLE 1

Intake of Food by Food Groups in
Urban and Rural Locations

Food Groups	Intake Grams per Person per Day Rural	Urban
Cereals	536.9	363.7
Starchy Roots	55.5	31.6
Sugar and Sweets	7.4	11.7
Pulses and Nuts	28.0	26.5
Vegetables	134.6	134.4
(Leafy Green Vegetables)		(8.0)
Fruits	15.8	17.5
Meat	5.7	19.4
Eggs	1.6	2.5
Fish	32.8	41.9
Milk and Cheese	17.3	53.2
Fats and Oils	6.2	13.7
Miscellaneous Mixed Spices	4.6	10.0
Total	840.7	726.1

(The subgroup of leafy vegetables is included in the figure for total vegetable intake.)

Finally, since 94 per cent of Bangladesh's population is rural, the rural figures better reflect the state of the population as a whole.

The average Bengali eats two to three meals per day. Rice (puffed rice, rice cakes, or boiled rice) is eaten at breakfast. Bengalis ask "Have you taken rice?" instead of "Have you eaten?" because a meal is considered incomplete if rice is not consumed. Often, rice left over from the previous day is soaked in water overnight and taken at breakfast. Pulses may be mixed and cooked with rice into a thick soup called *kitchuri*. Curry left over from the evening meal may also be consumed with rice at breakfast. Gram powder eaten with molasses is sometimes substituted for rice. *Data,* a leafy green vegetable chopped into a paste, highly spiced and fried in mustard oil, is also taken at breakfast. Wheat is eaten in the form of *chapatti,* a pancake made of flour, water, and salt and fried in a dry pan. Less commonly, *parathas,* rich fried pancakes made of wheat flour and fat, are consumed. Consumption of bread is uncommon in village areas.

The mid-day meal generally consists of a large quantity of boiled rice eaten with fish or vegetable curry. Less often, meat curries (beef, mutton, or poultry) are served with the rice. Chilies and onions, mixed in the curry or eaten raw, are invariable items in the daily diet. The combination of rice with some form of curry is basic to the mid-day meal. The evening meal differs little in composition from the mid-day meal; often it consists of leftovers from the mid-day meal.

As shown in Figure 4.3 the bulk of calories and proteins comes from cereal grains. Over three-quarters of dietary calories comes

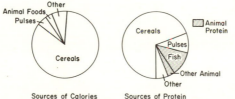

FIGURE 4.3. Food Sources of Calories and Proteins

from rice, and approximately two-thirds of the protein in the diet consists of rice. Smaller quantities of proteins are provided by curries made from vegetables, fish, and pulses (in the form of *dal*). Cereal protein is inferior in biologic value to proteins derived from animal sources. Yet milk, eggs, meats, and fish are consumed only in small quantities. Fruit intake is almost entirely seasonal (May–July), and cooking fats and oils make a negligible contribution to nutritional requirements.

Table 2 shows the per capita nutrient intake levels as compared with "acceptable" or recommended levels. Although the essentials of a good, balanced diet are present, the nutritious foods are eaten in such small amounts that they seldom make any substantial contribution to total nutrient intake. Moreover, a lack of knowledge of sound nutritional practices exacerbates the situation. Many foods

TABLE 2
Per Capita Nutrient Intake in
Rural and Urban Areas

Nutrient	Observed Intake Per Person Per Day		("Acceptable") Intake Recommended[a]
	Rural	Urban	
Calories	2,251[b]	1,732	2,150
Protein (gm)	57.5	49.5[c]	61.5
Fat (gm)	17.7	25.0	—
Carbohydrate (gm)	446.0	327.0	—
Calcium (mg)	304.0	226.0	494.0
Iron (mg)	9.7	8.5	12.1
Vitamin A (I.U.)	1,590	1,795	3,057
Thiamine (mg)	1.47	1.03	0.86
Riboflavin (mg)	0.53	0.54	0.86
Niacin (mg)	22.8	14.3	14.2
Vitamin C (mg)	39.6	38.5	28.5

a. The recommended or desirable intakes were calculated by standard methods.
b. This figure has been challenged as too high relative to food balance data. Small underestimates in family size in the survey could account for this discrepancy.
c. Although the per capita quantity of protein consumed in the urban area is less than the rural area, the urban diet is better because of the larger proportion of proteins of high biologic value.

are not taken in their natural forms and cooking practices often lead to considerable loss of nutrients, especially vitamin C, thiamine, and niacin. (It is fortunate that the bulk of rice consumed is parboiled and thus retains a portion of its thiamine and niacin even after cooking in excess water.) There is little knowledge of the special needs of growing children and pregnant or lactating women. Due to social customs, much of the best food is reserved for the men, and the women and children receive the remaining food.

Beliefs derived from the *ayurvedic* or ancient Hindu medicine may exert a considerable impact on dietary patterns. These beliefs are rather elaborate and in many cases resemble the Hippocratic attitude toward medicine. Foods are classified according to their "heating" or "cooling" effect on the body. Such foods as meat, eggs, *ghee,* fish, honey, and some oils are considered hot. Vegetables and fruits are thought of as cold. Illnesses are also classified as hot or cold. A hot illness is treated with cold foods and vice versa.

A person suffering from fever is bathed in cold water and given cold foods. In general, it is thought that a weak person should limit his consumption of hot foods because he is incapable of digesting them. For several days after childbirth, women rarely eat meat, eggs, fish, or hot curries which are believed to cause indigestion; their diet chiefly consists of rice, bread, tea, and cumin seeds. Their supply of breast milk is thought to be increased by eating certain kinds of fish (*koi, magur,* and *shing*). The first meal of a newborn child is honey and mustard oil. These are "heating" foods which give the child strength and keep it free of colds.

It is thought that hot foods should be eaten in cold weather and cold foods in summer. For example, *panta bhat,* a cold wet rice dish, is suitable for summer mornings, but dry foods such as *cirra* (beaten rice) and *muri* (puffed rice) are preferred in winter. Other beliefs concerning the effects of food are that sour foods irritate wounds and tamarind causes loss of sexual power.

NUTRITION AND HEALTH

The pattern described in the previous section was one of subsistence farming and inadequate dietary intake of proteins and vitamins. In this section, we will concentrate on the impact of these deficiencies on the nutritional health of the population. The special nutritional needs and increased vulnerability of preschool-age children and pregnant or lactating women merit special consideration. Because overt deficiencies usually manifest themselves earlier in these groups than in the general population, these individuals serve as an important index of the problems common to all groups.

The combined number of growing children under 5 years old and of pregnant or lactating mothers makes up 35 per cent of the total population. Of the two groups, children are at highest risk of experiencing severe malnutrition. One measure of the high prevalence of malnutrition among children is their appalling death rate; 16 per cent of all liveborn children die within their first year and 26 per cent die before their fifth birthday (Table 3). Those who survive suffer considerable growth retardation. When Bengali children are compared to their Western counterparts, the differences of height and weight are minimal at birth, but a striking disparity develops between 9 and 24 months of age (Figure 4.4). While the relative effects of genetic factors in producing such differences cannot be ascertained precisely, the available evidence suggests that nutritional status may influence growth rate considerably within the limits of genetic potential.

TABLE 3
Mortality Rate of Liveborn Children[a]

	Below 1 Month	1–6 Months	7–12 Months	1 Year	2 Years	3 Years[b]
Per Cent Mortality	8.7	5.3	2.7	3.3	3.2	2.6
Culmulative Per Cent	8.7	14.0	16.7	20.0	23.2	25.8

a. Data were obtained from random sampling but agree well with other sources.
b. The cumulative per cent died increased by 3 per cent each year thereafter.

Nutritional demands are increased during pregnancy to meet needs for growth of the fetus, and during nursing to replace nutrients provided to the infant in breast milk. In Bangladesh, 75 per cent of all women between 20 and 40 years of age are either pregnant or lactating at any one time, and they constitute 10 percent of the total population. Successive and frequent cycles of pregnancy and lactation create a drain on maternal tissue. As a result, the prevalence of malnutrition is greater among women who are either pregnant or lactating than among their female counterparts who are in neither condition (Table 4). The higher prevalence of malnutrition is also conducive to a higher mortality rate among women. The age-specific death rate for women in the child-bearing years exceeds that of men of comparable ages.

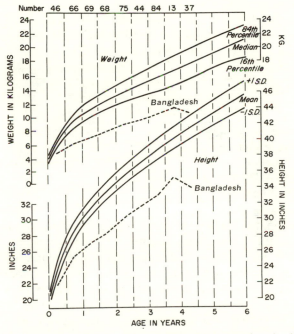

FIGURE 4.4. Height and Weight of Rural Boys 4 Years and under in Bangladesh Compared with Children of North European Ancestry

PROTEIN-CALORIE MALNUTRITION

The most common nutritional deficiency encountered in Bangladesh is protein-calorie malnutrition. This multi-symptom disease complex primarily affects children. According to standard anthropometric measurements such as weight to height, 50 per cent of all preschool-age children are malnourished. Severe malnutrition affects 3 per cent of all children in this age group. Far advanced clinical deficiency is manifested by either kwashiorkor or marasmus. These two conditions constitute opposite ends of the spectrum: if the deficiency is primarily one of protein, the child will develop kwashiorkor; if calories are the major deficiency, marasmus will result. Most cases observed in Bengal possess both caloric and protein deficiency and are difficult to classify as purely kwashiorkor or marasmus per se.

TABLE 4
Major Clinical and Biochemical Findings
in Adult Women

| | Percentage Prevalence | | | |
| | Pregnant or Lactating | | Nonpregnant, Nonlactating | |
	Urban	Rural	Urban	Rural
Clinical Goiter	40.4	40.5	29.2	33.6
Low Plasma Albumen	63.6	45.3	30.4	41.5
Low Hemoglobin	96.6	95.0	95.8	91.6
Low Plasma Vitamin A	31.2	41.7	26.7	25.5
Low Serum Vitamin C	18.5	24.4	11.1	11.7

It is estimated that 46 per cent of the population consume inadequate quantities of calories despite the heavy dietary dependence on cereals. Rice is the most important single source of calories and the availability of rice determines the levels of caloric intake. During early winter the prevalence of malnutrition rises sharply (Figure 4.5). This seasonal variation has been found to parallel changes in caloric and protein intake. During the early winter months, the largest rice crop (aman) has not yet been harvested and foodstocks are at their lowest annual level.

The heavy reliance on rice in the diet also provides a clue to certain vitamin deficiencies. Rice is lacking in vitamin A and vitamin C and is low in riboflavin. A heavy rice diet without other nutritionally important foods will thus inevitably result in these specific vitamin deficiencies.

The most widespread and serious nutritional problem in Bangladesh is protein deficiency. It has been shown that protein intake is inadequate in the two lowest income ranges (family monthly earnings less than 200 *rupees*), which is 85 per cent of the rural population. Sixty per cent of the households consume an amount of protein that is below the acceptable level. Because proteins are essential for tissue building and are necessary for growth and development, protein malnutrition primarily affects children. Kwashiorkor or severe protein deprivation is a disease which character-

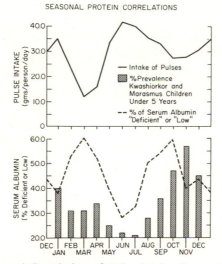

FIGURE 4.5. Seasonal Correlation of Pulse Intake, Serum Albumen Levels, and Prevalence of Kwashiorkor and Marasmus in Children under Five Years

istically affects the very young, 6 months to 2 years old. It typically affects the child whose post-weaning diet is insufficient in proteins. This disease may also be present in breast-fed children who are older than 6 months. Breast feeding provides sufficient proteins only for the first six months of life; thereafter supplementary foods are required. In Bangladesh, breast feeding is almost universal and is usually continued beyond 2 years (Table 5). However, supplementary protein foods are rarely given in sufficient quantity.

Protein deficiency is also found widely in the adult population, as determined by biochemical abnormalities (Table 4). Such subclinical deficiency may lower the physical and mental efficiency, the resistance to disease, and the work capacity of almost half of the productive segment of the population.

Figure 4.5 illustrates the importance of the quality of the proteins consumed in the diet. The pattern of amino acid content varies according to the food consumed; certain foods such as meat, fish, eggs, and milk products have amino acid patterns which most closely approximate human requirements. Proteins from a vegetable source, while itself incomplete, may complement protein from a second plant source to provide good protection. Most dietary protein, however, is obtained from cereals which are low in biologic value, and sources of animal proteins make a negligible contribution. Thus, protective protein appears to be provided by

TABLE 5
Age of Weaning
(Cessation of Breast Feeding)

Age of Child (months)	Per Cent of Mothers	Per Cent Cumulative
0	1.0[a]	1.0
6	0.6	1.6
9	0.8	2.4
12	1.4	3.8
15	3.4	7.2
18	2.4	9.6
21	6.8	16.4
24	28.4	44.8
Over 24	56.2	100.0

[a] Per cent not breast feeding.

pulses; when pulse intake drops, protein deficiency becomes more prevalent. Pulse consumption in Bangladesh is small but critical, for pulse protein is virtually the only complement to basic rice protein. The implications of the relationship between the two need special emphasis, for pulses are a popular and relatively inexpensive source of protein of high biologic value. As previously stated, agricultural production of pulses in the region has increased somewhat over the past ten years. This trend could have important consequences for the future health of the population. There is also a need to increase the availability of fish, which is another popular source of protein of high biologic value.

Food and agricultural planners should take into account the potential results of better balance in food production. The quest for continued adequacy of caloric supply (rice production) should be coordinated with efforts to supply other badly needed nutrients. Some good sources of protein, for example, are also good sources of calories; pulses are as high in caloric value as rice and three times as high as potatoes; they have three to four times as much protein as rice, ten to fifteen times as much protein as potatoes.

VITAMIN A DEFICIENCY

Vitamin A deficiency, leading to keratomalacia, ranks with protein malnutrition in its effect on health in Bangladesh. Several studies have shown that three out of four victims of keratomalacia either die or are partially or totally blind. The disease occurs most commonly and is most severe in children under 5 years of age, especially boys. Of every five hundred boys in Bangladesh under age 5, three to four may have it.

The average intake of vitamin A in Bangladesh is approximately half of the usually recommended value of 3,500 International Units (IU) per person per day. Low intakes of vitamin A are primarily owing to lack of knowledge of its source and importance. Low levels of fat intake (7 per cent of total calories in the average diet) further aggravate the situation in that the body needs fats in order to absorb vitamin A from the intestines.

The population's dependence on fruits and green leafy vegetables for protection from vitamin A deficiency is illustrated in Figure 4.6. Because over 90 per cent of the vitamin A intake is obtained from the carotene in these foods, there is a close correlation between the seasons and vitamin A levels. In the fruit season (May-July) only 11 per cent of the population show low plasma concentrations of vitamin A. During the period when fruits are not readily available, this proportion slowly rises to 40 per cent. Keratomalacia is found throughout the year, but its prevalence varies seasonally. A review of the 1962–64 records at the Dacca

Medical College Eye Clinic shows that 3.0 per cent of the people examined during the post-monsoon period and only 0.5 per cent of those examined during the fruit season were diagnosed as having keratomalacia.

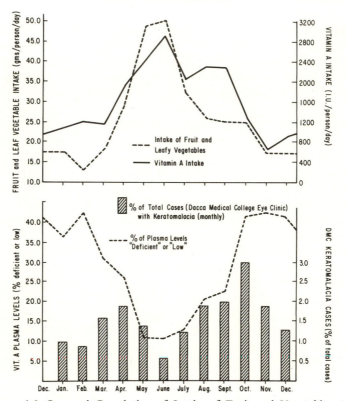

FIGURE 4.6. Seasonal Correlation of Intake of Fruit and Vegetables, Vitamin A Intake, Plasma Levels of Vitamin A, and Total Monthly Cases of Keratomalacia

These findings lead us to conclude that there is little awareness in the population of the sources or the importance of vitamin A. There is no understanding of the consequences of vitamin A deficiency, the prevention of keratomalacia, or the special needs of preschool children and adult women. The foods necessary for the prevention of the problem are inexpensive. Educating the population, however, is a long-term process. Interim measures—such as the development of incentives to spur production and consumption of fruits and vegetables and the development of vitamin-rich food supplements—are badly needed.

In a population existing on an inadequate diet, multiple deficiencies are more common than lack of any single nutrient. Keratomalacia, for example, is often found in association with kwashiorkor. The prognosis of children with protein malnutrition is significantly worse in the presence of keratomalacia, and children with both are far less likely to recover than those with either condition alone. Comparison, by season, of the prevalence of kwashiorkor and marasmus (Figure 4.5) with the prevalence of keratomalacia (Figure 4.6) illustrates the nature of most nutritional problems: diets deficient in one nutrient are likely to be deficient in other nutrients as well. The prevalence of deficiencies of both vitamin A and protein follows a closely associated seasonal pattern, and the prevalence of diarrheal disease in children follows the same seasonal pattern. Interactions between malnutrition and infectious diseases are extremely important; while it is likely that malnutrition increases susceptibility to infectious diseases, infection itself may be an important precipitating factor in the development of overt nutritional deficiency.

OTHER NUTRITIONAL DEFICIENCIES

Riboflavin

Riboflavin is essential for cell respiration and metabolism. While some of the manifestations of riboflavin deficiency are known, our present state of knowledge does not permit us to recognize all the consequences of riboflavin deficiency in man. Food of animal origin, especially dairy products, is the best source of riboflavin. Green leafy vegetables and ripe fruits, though not the richest sources of riboflavin, contribute significantly to the amount available to the average Bengali. Almost half of the population has "deficient" or "low" levels of urinary riboflavin excretion, suggesting that riboflavin deficiency is widely prevalent. Inflammation of

the angles of the mouth and other lesions associated with this vitamin deficiency are among the most common clinical findings in
Bangladesh. Riboflavin intake is low in all seasons and among all
income groups.

There is an urgent need to correct this deficiency among the
people of Bangladesh. The most effective corrective measures center on a more varied diet, for almost all of the other foods available have a higher riboflavin content than an equal dry weight of
rice. Measures aimed at correcting protein deficiency, such as increasing pulse production and consumption, could concomitantly
improve riboflavin nutriture.

Anemia

Over a third of the population of Bangladesh suffers from anemia. The great majority of these anemias are iron deficient in
type. The relative roles of insufficient intake and improper absorption of iron, excessive blood loss, and parasitic infestations in
causing anemia are not known. It is clear from pragmatic therapeutic trials, however, that additional iron taken in readily absorb-
able form can greatly diminish the degree of anemia in this population. The most anemic segments of the population are women of
child-bearing age and growing children. Food supplements
containing iron, given to these vulnerable groups, would help to
alleviate this condition. Ultimate long-term improvement may require greater attention to sanitation and to the control of intestinal
infections and parasitic infestations.

Goiter

Approximately one-fourth of the people of Bangladesh have a visible goiter. This proportion is higher than would be expected in a
population living in a non-mountainous area close to the sea.
Studies on urinary iodine excretions in a pocket of high goiter
prevalence in the Mymensingh District indicated that iodine deficiency is clearly a problem. Other data also suggest that the etiology may be more than simply iodine deficiency. Mustard oil, the
major cooking oil, contains goiter-producing agents, but it has not
been proven that the oil as used in the kitchens of Bangladesh retains its goitrogenic properties when heated. There is a lack of

competent studies on this matter but studies are not necessary for corrective measures to provide sufficient iodine to the population. Increased iodine intake can prevent the development of endemic goiter regardless of other etiologic considerations.

Vitamin C

Dietary data indicate that there is sufficient vitamin C in the raw (uncooked) diet in Bangladesh to prevent clinical deficiency. There is biochemical and clinical evidence, however, that some 10 per cent of the population has a subclinical (biochemical) deficiency and 3 to 4 per cent has early clinical signs of deficiency. Full-blown scurvy is rarely reported. Nutrition education aimed at instructing the population in ways to preserve the available vitamin C in the diet is needed.

Rickets and Osteomalacia

In the Nutrition Survey of East Pakistan (1962–64), skeletal abnormalities indicative of rickets were found in only one child. The population's supply of vitamin D, then, can be considered adequate. Clinical determination of osteomalacia requires x-rays and this has not been undertaken. Indirect evidence suggests that this condition may be a problem in adult females, but its scope is unknown. Dietary data suggest that calcium intake is low, and subclinical deficiency may be present.

Beriberi

Clinical signs suggestive of thiamine deficiency (bilateral edema of the legs, loss of ankle jerk, calf tenderness) are rarely found in the population. Thiamine deficiency is not a serious problem in Bangladesh, at present, but as milled rice which results in a loss of thiamine becomes more generally available, thiamine intake may fall to levels low enough to represent a health threat.

Pellagra

Niacin deficiency is found almost exclusively in populations subsisting on maize diets. The rice-eating people of Bangladesh show no clinical evidence of pellagra.

CONCLUSION

The magnitude of the problem of malnutrition in Bangladesh is sufficiently great that its effects can be seen in all sectors of life. No program of economic development can fail to recognize the importance of meeting the problems posed by malnutrition. Some of the problems documented in this chapter may be alleviated in the course of general economic development but such improvements must await the over-all process of economic growth, with all its delays. While these long-term goals are being achieved, Bangladesh will need to address itself with considerable urgency to the problems which face the country at this time. Food and nutrition programs, when implemented, will have an extensive and tangible impact on the problems of malnutrition and disease. In addition, an attack on malnutrition may in itself make a significant contribution (by increasing productivity) to the process of economic development.

It is axiomatic that a rigorous approach to the problem of population control is basic to the success of any program designed to improve nutritional status. All programs designed to increase the availability of proper foodstuffs can be vitiated by the counteracting effect of rapid population growth.

References

1. *Nutrition Survey of East Pakistan March 1962–January 1964.* A Report by the Ministry of Health, Government of Pakistan, in collaboration with the University of Dacca and the Nutrition Section, Office of International Research, National Institute of Health, U.S. Department of Health, Education, and Welfare, May 1966.
2. Wilbur, D. N. *Pakistan, Yesterday and Today.* Holt, Rinehart and Winston, Inc. New York, 1964.
3. *Age, Sex and Marital Status, Population Census of Pakistan, 1961.* Census Bulletin No. 3, Office of the Census Commissioner, Home Affairs Division, Karachi, May 1962.

4. *Pakistan Statistical Yearbook, 1963.* Central Statistical Office, Economic Affairs Division, Government of Pakistan, Karachi, 1964.
5. *Report of the Food and Agriculture Commission.* Ministry of Food and Agriculture, Government of Pakistan, November 1960.
6. *Demographic Yearbook, 1963.* United Nations.
7. *Economic Survey of East Pakistan, 1963–64.* Finance Department, Government of East Pakistan, 1964.
8. *Economic Survey of Pakistan, 1963–64.* Economic Adviser to the Government of Pakistan, Ministry of Finance, Rawalpindi, 1964.
9. *Pakistan.* International Economic Survey, Chemical Bank of New York Trust Company, No. 147, March 1965.
10. *Statistical Bulletin* Vol. 13, No. 2, February 1965. Central Statistical Office, Economic Affairs Division, Government of Pakistan, Karachi, 1965.
11. Corsa, L., Jr. Family Planning in Pakistan. *Am. J. Public Health,* 55:400 (1965).
12. 1960 Pakistan Census of Agriculture, Vol. 1, *East Pakistan.* Agricultural Census Organization, Ministry of Food and Agriculture, Government of Pakistan, October 1962.
13. Organization and Development of Food Research and Technology in the Laboratories of the PCSIR, FAO-ETAP Report No. 1180.
14. *Report of the FAO Regional Seminar on Food Technology for Asia and the Far East,* Mysore, 1959.
15. U.S. Department of Agriculture, *Indices of Agriculture Production for East Asia and South Asia,* April 1972.

(5) NUTRITION:
ROLE OF MALABSORPTION

John Lindenbaum

INTRODUCTION

The small intestine is vital in man and other animals because it is the primary organ for the absorption of all essential nutrients. Studies performed in Bangladesh during the past decade indicate that most of the people may have an intestinal disorder which is usually asymptomatic (subclinical) and is manifested by abnormalities of small intestinal morphologic appearance, often associated with impairment of absorptive function. I will briefly review here the evidence for the existence of this subclinical small intestinal disorder, examine its possible causes and relations to other conditions, such as the syndrome referred to as "tropical sprue," and consider its implications for the nutritional status and well-being of residents of Bangladesh.

INCIDENCE OF SUBCLINICAL MALABSORPTION

Intestinal absorptive capacity was studied in a randomly selected group of 106 employees of the Cholera Research Laboratory in Dacca (1). They represented a cross-section of the total employee group, with a wide range in occupation and economic status (from sweepers, guards, and bottle-washers to nurses and physicians). All were symptom-free and considered themselves in good health. The ability to absorb the five-carbon sugar, xylose, was impaired in 42 (or 39.4 per cent) of the employees. Absorptive capacity for

JOHN LINDENBAUM was formerly Assistant Chief and Chief, Clinical Research Section, Cholera Research Laboratory, Dacca, Bangladesh (1963–1966).

vitamin B_{12}, as measured by the urinary excretion test of Schilling, was subnormal in 20 per cent of those studied. Fat absorption, measured as the fecal excretion of lipid over a 72-hour period, was normal in 14 of 15 Bengalis tested. Standards of "normality" for the intestinal absorption tests were based on the ranges observed in healthy American volunteers studied in New York City. Since xylose is primarily absorbed in the duodenum and jejunum, and vitamin B_{12} in the ileum, the findings suggested impairment of mucosal function involving the entire small intestine. The presence of malabsorption could not be correlated with factors such as age, economic status, body weight, prior history of diarrhea, or the presence of anemia or eosinophilia. The values for urinary xylose excretion after the oral-test dose for the entire employee group followed a bell-shaped distribution curve. In addition, repeat studies after nine- to twelve-month intervals revealed in many individuals significant improvement in their ability to absorb xylose, while others who were normal at first testing became abnormal, despite the absence of weight loss or gastrointestinal symptoms in individuals in either category. Rigorous collection of urine under metabolic ward conditions as well as measurements of serum xylose levels during the absorption tests ruled out the possibility that variations in renal function or accuracy of urine collection could account for these results, which indicate that marked unexplained differences in absorptive capacity were occurring in the population studied. These observations suggested that small intestinal injury or insult was occurring in the entire population tested rather than a subgroup of abnormals (2).

Further evidence of a widespread intestinal disorder was provided by studies of jejunal mucosal biopsy specimens obtained from over 200 Bengalis (including both hospital employees and patients admitted to hospital for a variety of intestinal and non-intestinal disorders). None of the biopsy specimens was entirely normal by American standards (1, 3). The most frequent abnormalities noted were the presence of villi, which when viewed under the dissecting microscope had the architectural appearance of broad leaves, ridges, and convolutions, and the presence in histologic sections of increased inflammatory infiltrate (predominately lymphocytes and plasma cells) in the epithelium, lamina propria, and

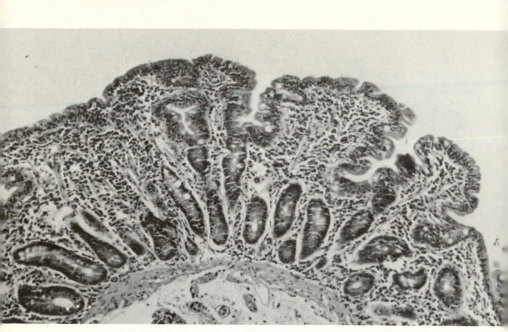

FIGURE 5.1. Histologic section of jejunal mucosa obtained from a 26-year-old Bengali engineer 5 months after arrival in New York City from India. He denied any gastrointestinal symptoms at any time in his life. Reduction in villus height, increase in crypt length, and moderate chronic inflammatory cell infiltrate are present in the lamina propria and epithelium. (Hematoxylin and eosin, X 80.) *Source:* From Gerson, *et al.,* 1971.

submucosa as well as lengthened crypt areas. Some normal individuals also had varying degrees of reduction of the height of villi (Figure 5.1).

The finding of impaired absorptive function and abnormal small intestinal mucosal morphologic appearance under the dissecting microscopy or in histologic sections is not limited to the people of Bangladesh. Similar findings have been reported by others in asymptomatic native-born individuals in India, West Pakistan, and in every other developing nation of the world where the problem has been studied, including countries in Southeast Asia, the Caribbean, South America, Africa, and the Middle East (4).

ACQUISITION OF INTESTINAL ABNORMALITIES
BY VISITORS TO BANGLADESH

It is of interest that the abnormalities of intestinal structure and function in Bangladesh are not limited to native-born Bengalis. Peace Corps volunteers resident in the area for 6 to 24 months also showed a high incidence of malabsorption and abnormal intestinal morphology (5). Abnormal intestinal absorption has been documented in this group within a few weeks of arrival in the country. In contrast to the Bengali laboratory workers, most of the Peace Corps volunteers had recurrent bouts of mild diarrhea while in Bangladesh. They also experienced significant weight loss. The intestinal symptoms and impaired absorption are rapidly reversible in most Peace Corps volunteers after return to the United States.

REVERSIBILITY OF THE SUBCLINICAL DISORDER

While the acquisition of similar intestinal abnormalities by Americans resident in Bangladesh and the return to normal of the Americans after repatriation suggested that the changes seen in Bengalis were of an acquired nature, it was possible that the intestinal changes seen in the Peace Corps volunteers were of a different etiology, since the jejunitis on biopsy and the impairment of absorptive function are non-specific findings. We therefore studied a group of Indians and Pakistanis (including a number of individuals previously studied in Bangladesh) who had moved to New York City. Most were university students. All had been symptom-free, both before and after arrival in the United States. Almost 40 per cent of those studied within two years of arrival in New York continued to have impaired carbohydrate absorption (6), though absorption improved with increasing periods of residence in the U.S. (Figure 5.2). In serially studied individuals, improvement in absorptive function occurred over periods of one to two years in the absence of therapy (Figure 5.3). Subjects whose xylose absorption was normal when first tested in New York, did not show depression of absorptive capacity when retested one to two years later (unlike Bengalis who were retested while resident in Bangladesh). In a few subjects, xylose absorption had not yet returned to the normal range even after three years away from the subcontinent. There was no correlation between persistence of malabsorption and continued ingestion of curried foods while in the U.S. Intestinal morphology showed the same tendency to improve the longer the individual was away from the subcontinent.

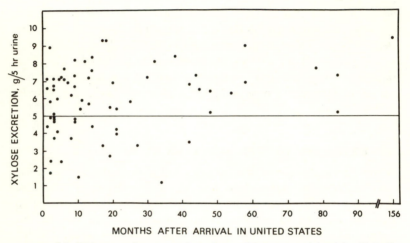

FIGURE 5.2. Urinary xylose excretion after a 25 gram oral load in 68 Indians and Pakistanis when first studied after they arrived in the United States. *Source:* From Gerson, *et al.,* 1971.

Ridges and convolutions were much more commonly seen at dissecting microscopy in specimens obtained within two years of arrival (13 of 21 biopsies) than in those taken more than two years after arrival (1 of 10). In five subjects in New York City who had two intestinal biopsies over approximately a nine-month period, there were more than six times as many finger villi present on the second specimen than the first. The majority of specimens obtained were histologically normal (Figure 5.4), suggesting that histologic recovery precedes normalization of the villus architectural pattern (6).

Regardless of whether malabsorption or jejunal morphologic

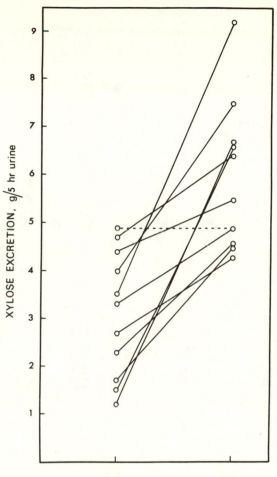

FIGURE 5.3. Initial and final xylose excretion in 11 subjects in whom the test was repeated on one or more occasions during residence in New York City. *Source:* From Gerson, *et al.,* 1971.

abnormalities were present, the Indians and Pakistanis studied appeared to be in good health. The hemoglobin, prothrombin, serum B_{12}, and folate concentrations were normal in all 68 subjects studied except for one vegetarian with a low serum B_{12} level. Of interest was the finding that hyperlipemia (elevated serum triglyceride, cholesterol, or both) was observed only in subjects with normal

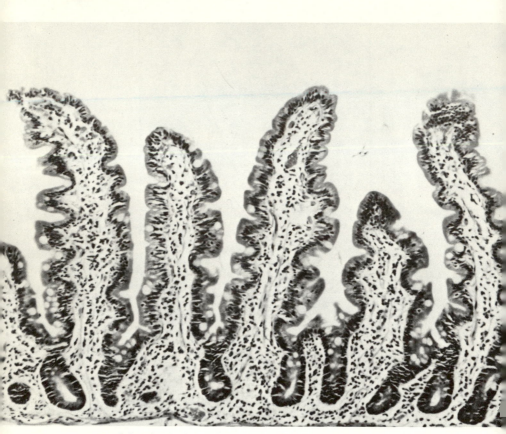

FIGURE 5.4. Histologic section of jejunal mucosa obtained from a 30-year-old asymptomatic engineer in New York City, 19 months after arrival from Bangladesh. The histologic appearance is similar to that seen in normal North American controls. (Hematoxylin and eosin, X 80.) *Source:* From Gerson, *et al.,* 1971.

xylose absorption. In addition, in 12 subjects whose xylose absorption improved with time during residence in New York City, serum triglyceride levels rose concurrently (Figure 5.5). The possible implications of these observations will be discussed later.

ONSET IN EARLY CHILDHOOD

A number of observations in other countries have suggested that the subclinical malabsorptive disorder of people of developing countries begins early in life. Investigators in India, Uganda, and Iran have observed ridged and convoluted villi in intestinal biopsy or autopsy specimens obtained from infants or small children without clinical intestinal disorders. These abnormalities were not present on examination of the small bowel of fetuses dying *in utero* in India or Uganda. Also, the incidence of xylose malabsorption in Liberia was as high in children as in adults. Two un-

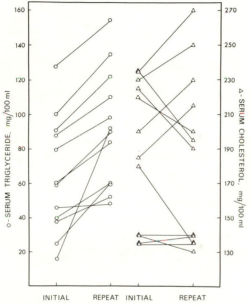

FIGURE 5.5. Changes in serum triglyceride and cholesterol concentrations in 12 Indian or Pakistani subjects resident in New York City whose xylose excretion improved 1.0 gm or more between initial and repeat studies. Serum triglyceride rose in every subject, while no significant change in serum cholesterol occurred. *Source:* From Gerson, *et al.*, 1971.

published studies from Bangladesh indicate a high incidence of malabsorption early in life. Einstein, in a study of the children of tea workers from South Sylhet, found that mean xylose absorption in the first six months of life was within the normal range published for American infants but was below the American normal between one and five years of life (L. Peter Einstein, unpublished observations). Harper demonstrated a high incidence of subnormal xylose absorption in three-year-old Hindu children in a village near Dacca (Gordon Harper, unpublished observations). Both Harper and Einstein found an association between growth retardation and xylose malabsorption.

ETIOLOGY

Since the jejunitis found on intestinal biopsy in asymptomatic residents of developing countries is morphologically similar to that found in patients with the symptomatic clinical syndrome known as tropical sprue, Klipstein has speculated that the subclinical disorder is a mild form of tropical sprue and that the clinically symptomatic cases represent merely the tip of an iceberg. The currently existing evidence, however, points away from such a hypothesis. The subclinical disorder is found in many countries of the world where clinical tropical sprue does not occur; none of our Bengali subjects with subclinical malabsorption has come down with clinical sprue after several years of observation; tropical sprue is not typically a disease of childhood; short-term therapy with folic acid and tetracycline did not lead to improvement in xylose malabsorption (as it usually does in patients with symptomatic sprue); and the biopsy findings and abnormal absorption tests in both the clinical and subclinical disorders are highly nonspecific and appear to represent a common pattern of the small intestinal response to a wide variety of noxious stimuli. On the other hand, symptom-free patients with quiescent tropical sprue certainly exist, and it is possible that some asymptomatic individuals with malabsorption in countries where tropical sprue is common have subclinical sprue. The hypothesis cannot be further tested until the cause of tropical sprue (which is probably not a single disorder in any case) is determined (7).

The worldwide distribution of the subclinical disorder makes it unlikely that it is due to a food toxin, as does the documented recovery of absorptive function in Bengalis living in New York who continue to ingest curries. Since parasitic infestation of the gastrointestinal tract is nearly universal in Bengal, and is common in the first years of life, and since experimental round worm infestation in animals results in jejunal atrophy and malabsorption, the notion that parasites cause the subclinical disorder deserves consideration. In fact, the presence of parasites on stool examination was significantly more common in our Dacca subjects with impaired xylose absorption than in those with normal absorption (1) and the difference was statistically significant for infestation with the round worm, *Ascaris lumbricodes*. On the other hand, studies in humans to date have not demonstrated improvement in absorptive function after eradication of *Ascaris*. Furthermore, Bengalis in New York City with continued malabsorption and abnormal intestinal biopsies for several years after arrival are free of parasitic infestation (6). The only parasites proven to cause malabsorption in man (*Giardia, Strongyloides, Capillaria* and, possibly, *Coccidia*) are absent or only rarely present in individuals with subclinical malabsorption. The small bowel, however, despite the rapid turnover of its epithelium in a matter of days, characteristically returns to normal quite slowly after injury (as has been documented by serial study of patients with celiac disease treated with gluten restriction), and the absence of parasites in an adult with subclinical malabsorption does not rule out the possibility of remote injury related to parasitism. A controlled trial of antihelminthic therapy in small children with malabsorption in Bangladesh would resolve this question.

Children with kwashiorkor and marasmus frequently have marked impairment of absorptive function and a severe jejunitis with loss of villi, and similar findings have been reported in adults with protein malnutrition. Could mild malnutrition be responsible for the subclinical malabsorptive state? This seems unlikely in the majority of cases, since subclinical malabsorption is not associated with hypoalbuminemia, and occurs in well-to-do Bengalis, in individuals who are above average for height and weight, and in Peace Corps volunteers resident in Bangladesh on a protein-and-vitamin-supplemented diet. In other countries, such as Haiti or parts of Africa where hypoalbuminemia is more common in the general population, it is possible that malnutrition plays a primary role.

In patients with disordered peristalsis (for example, with multiple jejunal diverticulae or surgically created blind loops) bacterial overgrowth occurs in the upper small bowel, commonly resulting in malabsorption, and occasionally in a histologically demonstrable jejunitis. Few studies of the jejunal flora of normal inhabitants of developing countries have been reported. Recently, Gorbach and colleagues reported that the intestinal flora of normal Bengali control subjects in Calcutta, including some with xylose malabsorption, was indistinguishable from that of the inhabitants of Western countries (8). On the other hand, Bhat and associates from Vellore reported increased numbers of fecal type microorganisms in the upper small bowel of normal Indian subjects, some of whom had malabsorption (9). The discrepancy between the two studies may have been related to differences in nutrient intake. Even in the Vellore subjects, however, there was no correlation between the results of xylose test and the bacteriologic findings. Tetracycline therapy given to Bengali subjects with malabsorption did not affect absorptive capacity for xylose (1). Furthermore, Bengali subjects with subclinical malabsorption show no evidence of disordered peristalsis on small intestinal x-rays, which are characteristically normal.

If a continuous state of small bowel microbial overgrowth similar to the blind loop syndrome seems an unlikely cause of the subclinical intestinal disorder, the possibility of recurrent, transient small bowel infection should be considered. Repeated exposure to an environmental agent or agents would help explain the variations in absorptive function in the same individual and would be consistent with the findings that malabsorption can be demonstrated within the first year or two of life and persists well into adulthood, yet is reversed by emigration to a Western country. It is thus likely that continuing or recurrent small intestinal injury which is not clinically apparent is occurring throughout adult life. There is a high incidence of recurrent diarrheal episodes in Bengali infants and children (as well as in Peace Corps volunteers shortly after arrival in Bangladesh) that is presumably the result of fecal contamination of food and water. These repeated episodes of symptomatic intestinal infection, such as the traveler's diarrhea syndrome, which may be caused by certain strains of *E. coli* previously not thought to be enteric pathogens, are typically clinically self-limited. Such mild enteritides may be associated with profound transient impairment of absorptive function and with an inflammatory jejunitis (3,10). Both in Einstein's study of children in South Sylhet and in our investigation of adults in rural Liberia (in collaboration with Dr. John Harmon) a correlation was apparent between contamination of water supplies and the presence of asymptomatic malabsorption. It is possible that after repeated exposure to contaminated water as residents of Bangladesh and other developing countries grow to adulthood, clinical symptoms no longer occur with each episode of infection, but the process of subclinical small bowel injury is perpetuated.

NUTRITIONAL IMPLICATIONS

The etiology of the subclinical intestinal disorder widespread in Bangladesh is clearly unknown and the above remarks remain highly speculative at this time. The existence of the subclinical state is well documented, however, as is its onset soon after birth. What are the implications of the presence of malabsorption, at least intermittently, throughout life in Bangladesh? Does impairment of absorptive function contribute to the short stature and low body weight of Bengalis over 1 year old compared to those of their American counterparts beyond the first year of life? Does the presence of subclinical malabsorption play a role in precipitating frank malnutrition syndromes in children with borderline nutrient intake?

No data at present provide a reliable answer to any of these questions. Yet several observations may be worth making here. First, the subclinical disorder is characteristically mild from the standpoint of impairment of mucosal function. The jejunitis is manifested histologically primarily by the presence of inflammatory infiltrate, and major loss of villus cells is unusual; the so-called "flat" mucosal morphology, with complete loss of villi as in celiac disease, is not seen.

Second, the xylose test, while unquestionably useful in the diagnosis of clinical disorders, may be too sensitive a test of mucosal function. As the 25 gram xylose test is performed, it represents a maximal "stress" to the reserve absorptive capacity of the small bowel; no individual, no matter how normal, can absorb the entire 25 grams (which may be why the test can cause diarrhea even in persons with normal absorption). Furthermore, xylose is not an essential nutrient and it does not necessarily follow that an individual with impairment of xylose transport will have difficulty assimilating glucose, amino acids, or vitamins. Therefore, in future studies it would be advisable to evaluate absorptive capacity for some crucial nutrient, such as an amino acid, rather than (or in addition to) xylose. The only important nutrient so far shown to be poorly absorbed by normal Bengalis has been vitamin B_{12} (1) and impaired absorption was not as prevalent as with xylose. Body stores are so extensive that it may take many years to develop significant B_{12} deficiency, except in infants born of B_{12} deficient mothers (as may occur in some Hindu communities).

Third, it has not been established that the subclinical malabsorptive state is necessarily an undesirable or pernicious one. The jejunal morphologic and functional changes could be viewed as adaptations to increased exposure to fecal contamination, similar to the adjustments in mucosal morphology that occur in germ-free animals after exposure to "normal flora." The findings of significant weight gain and an increase in serum triglyceride with recovery of absorptive function in Bengalis who have moved to New York City, and the presence of hyperlipemia only in those who have achieved normal absorption, may even indicate that the subclinical malabsorptive state plays a role in protecting Bengalis from lipid overload and its possible deleterious cardiovascular consequences. This cannot be stated with certainty since factors other than improvement in mucosal function may have contributed to the weight gain and hyperlipemia seen in Bengalis after arrival in the United States (6). It is also possible that subclinical malabsorption may be of trivial or even protective significance in most people but contribute to morbidity in children whose food intake is quite marginal.

SUMMARY

Studies of normal adults and children in Bangladesh indicate a high incidence of impaired intestinal absorption and of inflammatory changes on small intestinal biopsy. These changes appear to occur very early in life and are perpetuated in some manner into adulthood but are ultimately reversible. They are also acquired by foreigners who come to live in Bangladesh. Their etiology in unknown, but they do not appear to be due primarily to malnutrition, food toxins, tropical sprue, or a state of constant bacterial overgrowth. That parasitic infestation plays an etiologic role seems unlikely but has not been ruled out. It is postulated that repeated clinical and subclinical exposure to fecal microorganisms may result in the perpetuation of small bowel injury, but this remains to be proved. It is uncertain whether the mild malabsorptive state contributes to impaired nutritional status, is of no significance, or even protects against "overnutrition." Further studies of absorptive function in Bengali children are required and should include tests of assimilation of essential nutrients.

References

1. Lindenbaum, J., Alam, A. K. J., and Kent, T. H. Subclinical Small Intestinal Disease in East Pakistan. *Brit. Med. J.* 2:1616 (1966).
2. Lindenbaum, J. Small Intestine Dysfunction in Pakistanis and Americans Resident in Pakistan. *Am. J. Clin. Nutrition* 21:1023 (1968).
3. Kent, T. H., and Lindenbaum, J. Correlation of Jejunal Function and Morphology in Patients with Acute and Chronic Diarrhea in East Pakistan. *Gastroenterology* 52:972 (1967).
4. Klipstein, F. A. Recent Advances in Tropical Malabsorption. *Scand. J. Gastroenterology*, Suppl. 6:93 (1970).
5. Lindenbaum, J., Kent, T. H., and Sprinz, H. Malabsorption and Jejunitis in American Peace Corps Volunteers in Pakistan. *Annals of Int. Med.* 65:1201 (1966).
6. Gerson, C. D., Kent, T. H., Saha, J. R., Siddiqi, N., and Lindenbaum, J. Recovery of Small Intestinal Structure and Function after Residence in the Tropics. II. Studies in Indians and Pakistanis Living in New York City. *Annals of Int. Med.* 745:41 (1971).
7. Klipstein, F. A., and Baker, S. J. Regarding the Definition of Tropical Sprue. *Gastroenterology* 58:717, 1970.

8. Gorbach, S. L., Banwell, J. G., Jacobs, B., Chatterjee, B. D., Mitra, R., Sen, N. N., and Guha Muzumder, D. N. Tropical Sprue and Malnutrition in West Bengal. I. Intestinal Microflora and Absorption. *Am. J. Clin. Nutrition* 23:1545 (1970).
9. Bhat, P. Shantakumari, S., Rajan, D., Mathan, V. I., Kapadia, C. R., Swarnabi, C., and Baker, S. J. Bacterial Flora of the Gastrointestinal Tract in Southern Indian Control Subjects and Patients with Tropical Sprue. *Gastroenterology* 62:11 (1972).
10. Lindenbaum, J. Malabsorption During and After Recovery from Acute Intestinal Infection. *Brit. Med. J.* 2:326 (1965).

(6) INFECTIOUS DISEASES: THEIR SPREAD AND CONTROL

William M. McCormack and George T. Curlin

INTRODUCTION

Acute infectious diseases are not the major health problems in Bangladesh. Although epidemics of smallpox and cholera attract the attention of the press and although these and other communicable diseases take an immense toll, problems which relate more directly to socio-economic development—overpopulation, overcrowding, and malnutrition—pose the greatest health threat. Immense effort will be required to solve these difficult socio-medical problems. For the immediate future, however, it is also essential to direct attention toward certain infectious diseases which can be controlled with existing knowledge and technology. In this chapter, we shall examine the more prevalent infectious diseases in Bangladesh with emphasis on those diseases for which control measures are available.

Morbidity and mortality resulting from acute infectious diseases in Bangladesh cannot be accurately estimated as there have been no reliable nationwide systems for reporting the incidence of infectious disease or for recording deaths and causes of death. Limited information is available from the cholera-vaccine field-trial area in Matlab Bazaar of Comilla District, where births, deaths, and probable causes of deaths have been recorded since

WILLIAM M. MCCORMACK was formerly Epidemiologist, Cholera Research Laboratory, Dacca, Bangladesh. Dr. McCormack is a recipient of United States Public Health Service Post-Doctoral Fellowship 1 F02 AI44394-02. This work was supported in part by research grant HD-03693 from the National Institute of Child Health and Human Development and training grant T01 AI-00068 from the National Institute of Allergy and Infectious Diseases.

1966 (1,2). As most deaths in Matlab are reported by non-medical personnel, it is often not possible to obtain an accurate definition of the cause of death. Table 1 lists by age and reported cause of death the 1,906 persons who died during the 12-month period beginning May 1967. As one might predict, most of the deaths occurred at the extremes of age. Although the reported causes of deaths are imprecise, it is evident that infection was responsible for a substantial proportion of total deaths.

TABLE 1

Persons Who Died Between May 1967 and April 1968 in the Cholera Vaccine Field Trial Area in Comilla District According to Age and Reported Cause of Death[a]

Cause	Age[b]					
	Under 1	1–4	5–14	15–39	40+	All Ages
Fever (all forms)	101	76	25	24	72	298
Acute Diarrhea	8	5	4	4	3	24
Other G.I. Disease	12	75	16	8	91	202
Respiratory Disease	56	25	4	13	65	163
Measles & Smallpox	25	83	27	11	8	154
Accidents	8	39	18	13	13	91
Unknown	343	16	1	8	11	379
Others	100	108	45	64	278	595
All Causes	653	427	140	145	541	1,906

a. The surveillance was conducted on a total population of 114,561.
b. The age structure of the population (nearly half of the population is under age 15) should be considered in viewing the age distribution of deaths (Figure 2.2).

CHOLERA

Cholera is a diarrheal disease endemic in the deltaic regions of Bengal and is caused by the gram negative bacillus *Vibrio cholerae*. The disease is spread by the ingestion of the causative organism, usually by drinking water which has been contaminated with fecal matter from an infected individual. The organism elaborates an enterotoxin which causes massive outpouring of fluid and electrolytes into the small intestine. The resulting dehydration and electrolyte imbalance are responsible for all of the signs and symptoms of cholera.

Cholera, like most of the other infectious diseases in Bengal, is primarily a disease of children. Attack rates are highest among 1 to 4 year olds and decline with increasing age (Table 2) (3). The relatively low attack rate among older age groups can be corre-

TABLE 2
Age Specific Attack Rates
for Cholera in Matlab,
Bangladesh (1969–1970)

Age	No. of Cases	Attack Rate Per 1,000
Under 1	0	0
1–4	132	9.0
5–14	87	2.3
15–44	83	1.9
45 and above	16	1.0

Source: From Mosley, Bart and Sommer, 1972

TABLE 3
Number of Cholera Cases Hospitalized
at Matlab Hospital by Month (1969–1970)

Month	No. of Cases	Month	No. of Cases
July	0	January	49
August	0	February	9
September	0	March	10
October	7	April	15
November	28	May	5
December	185	June	10

Source: From Mosley, Bart and Sommer, 1972

lated with increasing vibriocidal antibody titers (4) and is presumed to be due to immunity acquired through exposure to cholera vibrios and through cholera vaccination. When cholera occurs in a non-endemic area, all age groups have similar attack rates (5).

Cholera has a striking seasonal pattern in Bangladesh. The disease appears in North Bengal in September and October and proceeds southward, reaching its peak in Dacca in November and December. In Matlab, which is about 40 miles south of Dacca, the peak incidence of cholera occurs about four weeks later than in Dacca (Table 3). In Khulna, Jessore, and Calcutta, most of the cholera occurs during March, April, and May (W. M. McCormack, unpublished observation). There is no satisfactory explanation for this seasonal pattern.

In the rural regions of Bangladesh, cholera affects over half of all villages each year. It usually occurs in small sporadic village outbreaks, two-thirds of which subside spontaneously before five cases are noted. In the remainder of the villages, large outbreaks may precipitate many deaths. Cholera is largely an "iceberg" disease: mild diarrheas and totally asymptomatic infections far outnumber clinically recognizable cases (6,7). Case-fatality ratios among untreated individuals will vary depending on the spectrum of illness considered. If only severely ill patients are included, the case-fatality ratios among untreated patients may be over 50 per cent. The inclusion of patients with milder illness will decrease the case-fatality ratio. During recent epidemics in Bangladesh, district hospitals where modern treatment could not be provided had a case-fatality ratio of about 20 per cent (W. M. McCormack, unpublished observation).

Cholera has a profound impact on mortality in Bangladesh even though the over-all case rate is 2.7 cases per 1,000. Assuming a case fatality ratio of 50 per cent, the over-all death rate due to cholera is 1.4 per 1,000. Although this cholera death rate would increase the crude mortality rate by only 9 per cent, the age-specific nature of cholera attack rates indicates a considerably greater impact. Attack rates are highest in those over 1 year of age and under middle age, an age group of low mortality. In this group, the deaths due to cholera would contribute 20 to 40 per cent of the mortality rate (13).

Modern treatment consists primarily of the intravenous or oral replacement of the diarrheal water and electrolyte losses. Tetracycline and other antibiotics to which the vibrios are susceptible reduce the duration and volume of the diarrhea, thus reducing the volume of fluid which must be replaced. Experience has shown that cholera patients treated in this manner have a case-fatality rate of less than 1 per cent (8).

There has been some discussion in recent years about the optimal approach to cholera control in developing countries. All agree that the ultimate solution will come through improved sanitation, as it did in western Europe and the United States, but there has been some disagreement as to where major emphasis should be placed during the time that it will take to implement satisfactory improvements in sanitation.

TABLE 4
Effectiveness of Cholera Vaccine (13)

Age Group	Control Vaccine[a]		
	No. Injected	No. of Cholera Cases	Attack Rate per 1,000
0–4	3,793	37	9.8
5–14	6,130	29	4.7
	Cholera Vaccine[b]		
	No. Injected	No. of Cholera Cases	Attack Rate per 1,000
0–4	3,818	25	6.6
5–14	6,202	5	0.8
	Per Cent Reduction in Case Rate by Cholera Vaccine[c]		
0–4	33		
5–14	83		
Total	55		

Source: From Mosley, Bart and Sommer, 1972
a. Diphtheria and tetanus toxoid was used as the control vaccine.
b. Cholera vaccine was administered annually over three years.
c. Per cent reduction in cholera cases provides an estimate of vaccine effectiveness.

The classical approach to control has been through regular vaccination. Killed-whole-cell cholera vaccine is one of the least effective vaccines in regular use today; its protection is incomplete (46 to 93 per cent) and short lived (three to six months) (9–12) (Table 4). Mosley, Bart, and Sommer have urged that cholera control efforts be re-directed toward establishment of treatment centers (13). A rural hospital in Matlab *Thana* serving 750,000 people within a fifteen-mile radius treated 6,432 cases of diarrheal illness from 1963 to 1970. This included 1,743 cholera cases. Not only was the case fatality rate of treated patients successfully reduced to 1 per cent, but the total cost was only 287,000 *rupees*. A vaccine campaign covering the same population would have cost approximately 204,000 *rupees* (Table 5). Since the vaccine is only partially effective, however, only half of the cholera cases would

TABLE 5

Summary of the Operations of Two Rural Cholera
Hospitals with a Comparison of the Costs for an
Immunization Program to Cover the Same Population

	Permanent Hospital (*Matlab*)	Temporary Hospital (*Rangpur*)
Estimated Population Served	750,000	180,000
Duration of Operation	12 months	3 months
Number of Beds	15–50	5–15
Ambulance Support	14 speed boats	2 vehicles
Total Cases Treated	6,432	642
Cholera Cases	1,743	399
Non-cholera Diarrheas	4,689	243
Cholera Deaths	4	4
Cost of Operation	Rs. 287,000	Rs. 34,000
Estimated Cost of Vaccine Program (one injection per year at Rs. 0.27 per injection)	Rs. 204,000	Rs. 49,000

Source: From Mosley, Bart and Sommer, 1972.

have been prevented by immunization, and treatment centers would still be required to treat the vaccine failures. Treatment centers were also able to treat the 4,689 cases of severe non-cholera diarrhea.

Permanent facilities are not essential to the concept of treatment centers. In 1970 a temporary treatment center cared for 642 cases of diarrheal illness (399 cholera cases) over a three-month period in Rangpur District. This hospital served approximately 180,000 people and the cost of the temporary center was estimated to be 30 per cent less than a vaccine campaign (Table 5). Mosley and his colleagues therefore concluded that until such time that a truly effective vaccine or improved sanitation facilities are available, treatment centers should be more effective and less expensive in preventing deaths from cholera than vaccination.

While few can argue with these estimations and projections, some workers are concerned that the establishment, maintenance, and supervision of a network of treatment centers may be beyond the immediate capability of some of the developing nations where cholera is now endemic. In such countries, routine vaccination as an adjunct to control probably will have to be continued until properly functioning treatment centers can be established.

SMALLPOX

Smallpox is an acute exanthematous disease caused by variola virus. The disease is spread by inhalation of airborne droplets from an infected individual. A two-week incubation period and a three-day prodrome of fever and other constitutional symptoms usually precede the development of the characteristic centrifugal eruption. Variola major, the disease type prevalent on the Asian subcontinent, carries with it a case-fatality ratio of 15 to 25 per cent. Case-fatality ratios are higher among infants.

In Bangladesh, the large cities form the most important reservoir of variola virus. Smallpox is introduced into rural villages primarily by adult male villagers returning from jobs in the large cities. Following introduction, the disease spreads slowly and usually dies out within a few generations even in the absence of containment measures and without reaching all susceptible individuals (14,15).

Unlike cholera, smallpox can be easily controlled through vaccination with vaccinia (cowpox) virus. This vaccine provides durable immunity, protecting most recipients against infection for upwards of five years and protecting against death from smallpox among those who do become infected for a much longer period of time.

A global program for smallpox eradication has been under way since 1958. This program places major emphasis on early recognition, reporting, isolation of cases, and vaccination of susceptible contacts. It has succeeded in rendering many nations free of smallpox. Bangladesh, then East Pakistan, was reportedly on the verge of eradicating smallpox in 1970, but the events of 1971 precluded further efforts. In 1972, a major smallpox epidemic erupted in Bangladesh, spread mainly by refugees returning to their homes from camps in India. This is described in Chapter 15.

Our knowledge of the epidemiology of smallpox in Bangladesh suggests that the primary thrust of an eradication program should be directed toward the large cities. In the rural areas that have been studied, smallpox was almost always introduced from outside, usually from Dacca and Narayanganj. Furthermore, the disease was apparently unable to sustain itself in these rural areas, usually dying out after a few generations (14,15). Thus, elimination of smallpox from large cities should also prevent a high proportion of rural cases. As only about 5 per cent of the population of Bangladesh resides in such urban centers, they should be given the highest priority in any eradication program.

PREVENTABLE CHILDHOOD ILLNESSES: DIPHTHERIA, PERTUSSIS, TETANUS, MEASLES, POLIOMYELITIS

The exact incidence of these diseases in Bangladesh is not known and the information that is available is largely anecdotal or conjectural. Mitford Hospital in Dacca, when visited in 1967, had entire wards filled with children who had diphtheria or tetanus (W. M. McCormack, unpublished observation). Tetanus was responsible for 8 per cent of the 150 deaths that Martin reviewed in Comilla District (16). Deaths associated with rigidity and convulsions are attributed by villagers in this area to an evil spirit called "Takuria." These deaths usually occur during the first month of life and most are probably due to neonatal tetanus, presumably related to unsanitary care of the umbilical cord after birth. During one year of observation in the cholera vaccine field trial area, almost 10 per cent of the deaths of children under 1 year of age were attributed to *"Takuria"* (1).

Measles is seen most often among 1- to 5-year-old children and is also a common cause of death. Martin listed measles as the cause of death in 5 per cent of the 150 deaths that he reviewed (16). In the cholera vaccine field trial area, "measles and small-pox" accounted for 5 to 10 per cent of deaths among 1- to 5-year-old children. There are few data on the incidence of polio-myelitis. Presumably most individuals are infected with wild strains of polio virus while they are infants and the resulting asymptomatic or mild infection induces durable immunity. Poliomyelitis can be expected to become a more serious problem when standards of sanitation improve and children first become exposed to the polio virus later in life when they are more prone to develop paralytic disease.

Although little is known about the prevalence of these diseases, we do know that they are preventable. Diphtheria toxoid, pertussis vaccine, tetanus toxoid (usually given in combined form called DPT or triple antigen), measles vaccine, and oral polio vaccine are all highly effective and form the mainstay of well-child care in more developed countries. There are, however, several problems that must be solved before these agents can be used to control disease in Bangladesh. Domestic production of these immunizing preparations should be initiated. Reliance on imported products tends to retard their widespread use. Furthermore, the concept of well-child care must be introduced. This will require the education of health workers and parents alike and a major reorganization of health care delivery will be needed if children are to be immunized several times during the first year of life.

TUBERCULOSIS

Tuberculosis is contracted by inhalation of the causative organism *Mycobacterium tuberculosis*. Crowding is a major determinant of the spread of this disease. In Bangladesh, over 80 per cent of adults have positive tuberculin skin tests and it has been estimated that the incidence of active disease is likely to be as high as 500 per 100,000 population (17). One can only speculate as to what proportion of "respiratory" deaths are due to tuberculosis. Several effective chemotherapeutic agents are available for the treatment of tuberculosis. However, the cost of these drugs and the logistical problems involved in diagnosis and treatment would seem to suggest that initial control efforts should be directed toward prevention through vaccination with Bacille Calmette Guerin (B.C.G.), ideally as a part of well-child care.

OTHER ENTERIC INFECTIONS

Diarrhea is a very common symptom in Bangladesh. In Rayer Bazaar, a community on the outskirts of Dacca which was surveyed prospectively by Khan and Mosley in 1965 and 1966, there were 310 episodes of diarrhea per 1,000 persons per year (18). The etiology of the vast majority of these diarrheal illnesses could not be defined. Shigella, the most commonly isolated pathogen, was found in the patient's stool in only 4.4 per cent of diarrheal episodes (19). Salmonellosis, other than typhoid fever, is unusual since it is primarily a disease of more developed nations where mass processing and distribution of poultry and other food predisposes to its spread. Vibrios, other than *Vibrio cholerae,* are responsible for some diarrheal illnesses, presumably through the elaboration of an enterotoxin. *Non-cholera vibrios* were isolated from 34 of 1,120 patients hospitalized with diarrhea at the Cholera Research Laboratory Hospital in Dacca (20). Two types of diarrheal diseases have recently been attributed to the ubiquitous coliform, *Escherichia coli* (21). This suggests that some of the previously unidentified causes of diarrhea may be due to *E. coli.*

Intestinal parasites are ubiquitous. Ascaris infestation is common and the hookworm is an important cause of anemia due to intestinal blood loss. *Entameba histolyticum* can be found in the stools of many individuals, some of whom are asymptomatic while others have clinical amebiasis with symptoms ranging from mild diarrhea to life-threatening colitis.

Viral hepatitis is prevalent in most of Asia and studies of American missionaries (22) and British Voluntary Service Overseas (V.S.O.) recruits (23) have shown that the risk of contracting viral hepatitis approaches 2 per cent per year of residence in an endemic area. Presumably most Bengalis are infected with hepatitis virus early in life when the disease is more likely to be mild or asymptomatic. Thus, hepatitis, like poliomyelitis, will become a more important health problem as the nation becomes more developed.

Most of the enteric diseases are spread by the ingestion of food or water which has been contaminated with fecal matter containing the causative microorganism. Effective chemotherapeutic agents are available for many of these diseases (hepatitis is an exception) and preventive measures exist for a few of them (gamma globulin for viral hepatitis; typhoid vaccine; oral shigella vaccine). Cost and logistical difficulties will severely limit the widespread application of these therapeutic and preventive measures. The ultimate control of these disorders will come with improvement in the standard of living and adequate sanitation.

OTHER INFECTIOUS DISEASES

Those infections usually considered "tropical diseases" are less of a problem from a public health viewpoint than some of the aforementioned disorders. The incidence of malaria has been greatly reduced through the malaria eradication program. Spraying of houses with DDT to eliminate the mosquito vector, surveillance to detect new cases through periodic examination of blood smears for the causative parasite and treatment with effective antimalarials are the major elements of this program. Malaria has recently reappeared in some countries where surveillance has been relaxed following a successful eradication program. This could also occur in Bangladesh.

Filariasis, another mosquito-borne disease, is endemic to North Bengal. Fourteen per cent of the people examined in Dinajpur District had microfilariae of *Wuchereria bancrofti* in their blood and many infected adult men had hydroceles. Elephantiasis was unusual (24). Leprosy and Kala Azar are chronic debilitating diseases which affect few people.

CONCLUSION

Infectious diseases figure heavily in the over-all moribidity and mortality statistics of Bangladesh. The young and aged are at highest risk. In a situation where improvement in the health sector may be dominated by complex socio-economic goals, one must not fail to recognize and utilize existing technical capacity to control the communicable diseases. There is an increased awareness among Bengali villagers of the technological capability of modern health measures. To the affected population, the illnesses and deaths caused by infections are a major health issue.

References

1. Mosley, W. H., Chowdhury, A. K. M. A., Aziz, K. M. A., Islam, S., and Fahimuddin, Md. *Demographic Studies in Rural East Pakistan, 1966–1967,* Pakistan-SEATO Cholera Research Laboratory, Dacca, East Pakistan, 1968.
2. Chowdhury, A. K. M. A., Aziz, K. M. A., and Mosley, W. H. *Demographic Studies in Rural East Pakistan, Second year, May, 1967–April, 1968,* Pakistan-SEATO Cholera Research Laboratory, Dacca, East Pakistan, 1969.
3. McCormack, W. M., Mosley, W. H., Fahimuddin, Md., and Benenson, A. S. Endemic Cholera in Rural East Pakistan. *Am. J. Epidemiol.* 89:393–404, 1969.
4. Mosley, W. H., Benenson, A. S., and Barui, R. A Serological Survey for Cholera Antibodies in Rural East Pakistan. *Bull. Wld. Hlth. Org.* 38:327–334, 1968.
5. Mosley, W. H. The Role of Immunity in Cholera a Review of Epidemiological and Serological Studies. *Tex. Rep. Biol. Med.* 27:227–241, 1969.
6. McCormack, W. M., Islam, M. S., Fahimuddin, Md., and Mosley, W. H. A Community Study of Inapparent Cholera Infections. *Am. J. Epidemiol.* 89:658–664, 1969.
7. Woodward, W. E., Mosley, W. H., and McCormack, W. M. The

Spectrum of Cholera in Rural East Pakistan. I. Correlation of Bacteriologic and Serologic Results. *J. Infect. Dis.* 121:Suppl:S10–16, 1970.

8. Cash, R. A., Nalin, D. R., Rochat, R., Reller, L. B., Haque, Z. A., and Rahman, A. S. M. M. A Clinical Trial of Oral Therapy in a Rural Cholera-Treatment Center. *Am. J. Trop. Med. Hyg.* 19:653–656, 1970.

9. Oseasohn, R. O., Benenson, A. S., and Fahumuddin, Md. Field Trial of Cholera Vaccine in Rural East Pakistan. *Lancet* 1:450–453, 1965.

10. Benenson, A. S., Mosley, W. H., Fahimuddin, Md., and Oseasohn, R. O. Cholera Vaccine Field Trials in East Pakistan. *Bull. Wld. Hlth. Org.* 38:359–372, 1968.

11. Mosley, W. H., McCormack, W. M., Fahimuddin, Md., Aziz, K. M. A., Rahman, A. S. M. M., Chowdhury, A. K. M. A., Martin, A. R., Feeley, J. C., and Phillips, R. A. Report of the 1966–67 Cholera Vaccine Field Trial in Rural East Pakistan. *Bull. Wld. Hlth. Org.* 40:177–185, 1969.

12. Mosley, W. H., Woodward, W. E., Aziz, K. M. A., Rahman, A. S. M. M., Chowdhury, A. K. M. A., Ahmed, A., and Feeley, J. C. The 1968–1969 Cholera Vaccine Field Trial in Rural East Pakistan. *J. Infect. Dis.* 121:Suppl:S1–9, 1970.

13. Mosley, W. H., Bart, K. J., and Sommer, A. An Epidemiological Assessment of Cholera Control Programs in Rural East Pakistan. *International J. Epidemiol.* 1:5, 1972.

14. Thomas, D. B., McCormack, W. M., Arita, I., Khan, M. M., Islam, M. S., and Mack, T. M. Endemic Smallpox in Rural East Pakistan. I: Methodology, Clinical and Epidemiologic Characteristics of Cases, and Intervillage Transmission. *Am. J. Epidemiol.* 93:361–372, 1971.

15. Thomas, D. B., Arita, I., McCormack, W. M., Khan, M. M., Islam, Md. S., and Mack, T. M. Endemic Smallpox in Rural East Pakistan. II: Intravillage Transmission and Infectiousness. *Am. J. Epidemiol.* 93:373–383, 1971.

16. Martin, A. R. Preventive Aspects of Rural Medicine. *E. Pakistan Med. J.* 12:132–134, 1968.

17. Hirschhorn, N. *Health in Bangladesh.* Hearings before the Subcommittee to Investigate Problems Connected with Refugees and Escapees, Committee of the Judiciary, U.S. Senate. Appendix VII. February 2, 1972. U.S. Government Printing Office, Washington.

18. Khan, M., and Mosley, W. H. Contrasting Epidemiologic Patterns

of Diarrhea and Cholera in a Semi-urban Community. *J. Pakistan Med. Assn.* 19:380–385, 1969.

19. Khan, M., and Mosley, W. H. The Significance of Shigella as a Cause of Diarrhea in a Low Economic Urban Community in Dacca. *E. Pakistan Med. J.* 12:45–50, 1968.

20. McIntyre, O. R., Feeley, J. C., Greenough, W. B. III, Benenson, A. S., Hassan, S. I., and Saad, A. Diarrhea Caused by *Non-cholera Vibrios. Am. J. Trop. Med. Hyg.* 14:412–418, 1965.

21. DuPont, H. L., Formal, S. B., Hornick, R. B., Snyder, M. J., Libronati, J. P., Sheahan, D. B., LaBrec, E. H., and Kalas, J. P. Pathogenesis of *Escherichia Coli* Diarrhea. *New. Engl. J. Med.* 285:1–9, 1971.

22. Cline, A. L., Mosley, J. W., and Scovel, F. G. Viral Hepatitis Among American Missionaries Abroad. *J. Am. Med. Assn.* 199:551–553, 1967.

23. Pollock, T. M., and Reid, D. Immunoglobulin for the Prevention of Infectious Hepatitis in Persons Working Overseas. *Lancet* 1:281–283 (1969).

24. Wolfe, M. S., and Aslamkhan, M. Bancroftian Filariasis in Two Villages in Dinajpur District, East Pakistan. I. Infections in Man. *Am. J. Trop. Med. Hyg.* 21:22–29, 1972.

(7) INFECTIOUS DISEASE: TREATMENT OF CHOLERA AND OTHER DIARRHEAL ILLNESSES

Richard L. Guerrant and Richard A. Cash

INTRODUCTION

As in other developing regions of the world, in Bangladesh diarrhea is a major cause of mortality among infants and children and morbidity in all age groups. Although precise nationwide statistics are unavailable, a recent survey in rural Bangladesh revealed more than 17 cases of severe diarrheal illness per 1,000 population annually (1). Since the mortality rate of untreated severe cases is approximately 20 to 60 per cent, a projection of over a quarter of a million deaths per year seems a reasonable estimate of the death toll from diarrheal illness. But as is the case with many diseases, mortality represents only a small fraction of the total cases. The submerged mass of morbidity due to debilitating but non-lethal diarrhea may impose an even greater burden on society. The same survey, for example, recorded more than one episode of diarrhea per person annually. Furthermore, diarrhea may adversely affect other health problems. It is one of the leading factors precipitating severe malnutrition in marginally nourished children and is often the terminal event associated with severe malnutrition.

This chapter will review the infectious diarrheas common to Bangladesh. More specifically, it will: (a) discuss etiologies of acute diarrheas, (b) review their clinical presentation, (c) present therapeutic approaches, and (d) focus on the impact of diarrhea on nutrition.

ORGANISMS

The bulk of all diarrheal illnesses in Bangladesh is associated with infectious organisms. The most commonly identified offending agents are *Vibrio cholerae, Escherichia coli, Non-cholera vibrios, Shigella,* and *Salmonella.* The largest number of diarrheas is due to unknown pathogens and is classified as "undifferentiated." The epidemiologic pattern of these diseases, however, strongly suggests an infectious etiology, and recent studies have demonstrated that many hospital cases are caused by enterotoxin-producing strains of *E. coli* (2, 3). Table 1 summarizes the common diarrheal illnesses of Bangladesh, their mechanism of action, and their epidemiologic characteristics.

The pathogens seem to act by one of two mechanisms: elaboration of an enterotoxin or tissue invasion. The enterotoxin-producing organisms colonize and multiply within the small intestine and elaborate an enterotoxic substance. Diarrhea results from the ability of these enterotoxins to interfere with the transport of water and electrolytes across intestinal epithelium (4). The histologic appearance of the intestine remains unaltered, and neither enterotoxin nor organism invades the systemic circulation. Fluid losses associated with these diarrheas are usually acute and may be massive. For those who survive, full recovery can be anticipated as the diseases are self-limiting.

The invasive organisms physically damage the intestinal tissue of the large bowel. A local anti-inflammatory response is generated, and infection may be accompanied by release of toxin(s) into the blood stream. Although the illness lasts longer than enterotoxic diseases, fluid losses are not as severe. Untreated patients have a lower mortality rate than those with untreated enterotoxin-induced diarrheas.

The prototype of enterotoxin-induced diarrhea is cholera, which is endemic to Bengal. Bengal is the only area of the world where cholera is principally caused by the classical biotype. The recent spread of cholera into Africa, the Middle East, and eastern Europe has been due to the El Tor biotype. In Bangladesh, cholera has a seasonal incidence. It is primarily a disease of children: 60 per cent of cases are under 10 years and 35 per cent are under 5 years of age.

A cholera-like syndrome has been observed in the absence of *V. cholerae.* Recent studies suggest that a major cause of diarrhea may be an enterotoxin-producing, non-invasive *E. coli* (2,3).

TABLE 1

Diarrheal Illness in Bangladesh

Primary Pathology:	Enterotoxin				Invasive		
Organism	V. cholerae	Undifferentiated		"NCV"[b]	Shigella	Salmonella	Invasive E. coli
		Hospital[a]	Community				
Peak Season	Oct.–Jan.	unknown	unknown	none	June–Oct.	none	
Peak Age (years)	1–9	0–1	0–1	0–2	0–5	adults	adults
Incidence per 1000 Population	2.6–6.1	projected 14.6	300–1000	est. 3–12	7.1	est. 8–15	unknown
Per Cent of Hospital Cases	20–50	50	—	2.1–4.9	1.4	1.4	unknown
Per Cent of Community Cases	5.8	—	90	2.5	4–13	5.5	unknown
Transmission	Water			Water, seafood	direct contact	food and direct contact	direct contact

a. Over 50 per cent of undifferentiated hospital diarrhea has been found to be associated with homogenous enterotoxin-producing Escherichia coli (3).

b. "Non-cholera vibrios" includes Vibrio parahemolyticus and "non-agglutinable vibrios."

Since these organisms were not previously recognized as pathogens, their importance has not been widely appreciated. A recent study in Calcutta showed that a striking 50 per cent of cholera-like diarrheas were due to enterotoxin-producing *E. coli* (3). This and other studies suggest that these *E. coli* may be the most common cause of diarrhea in Bengal. This observation parallels findings in many other regions of the world where certain strains of *E. coli* are being increasingly identified as causes of diarrhea, especially among infants and children.

The commonest invasive organisms that cause diarrhea are *Shigella, Salmonella,* and certain strains of *E. coli*. In the past *Shigella* has accounted for fewer than 5 per cent of hospitalized diarrheas in Bangladesh (5,6). It can be isolated from asymptomatic individuals, however, and family contacts of *Shigella* positive cases have significantly more diarrhea than controls. This suggests that *Shigella* may play a greater role in community diarrheas than suspected. In the fall of 1972 a large outbreak of *Shiga* dysentery associated with a high mortality rate was reported in Dacca. *Salmonella* is less important than *Shigella* as a pathogen. Invasive *E. coli* has not yet been adequately studied.

CLINICAL PRESENTATION

Table 2 summarizes the clinical aspects of the major diarrheal diseases in Bengal. Patients with enterotoxin-induced diarrheas experience the onset of watery diarrhea without prodromal symptoms. The composition of the stool is low to isotonic in sodium and chloride but with excess bicarbonate and potassium. It contains no white blood cells and little protein. Its appearance ranges from light brown-green to rice watery, and may have a "fishy" odor. The degree and composition of the massive fluid loss associated with diarrhea account for the entire clinical presentation (7).

Severe fluid loss causes dehydration, inadequate circulatory volume, and compromised renal function. Hypovolemic shock is the commonest cause of death. The severely ill patients who reach a hospital have low or unobtainable blood pressure, thready or absent pulse, dry tongue, sunken eyeballs, and poor skin turgor. Fever and other constitutional symptoms are rare, although pa-

TABLE 2
Clinical Aspects of Diarrheal Illnesses in Bangladesh

Organism	V. cholerae	Undifferentiated	"NVC"	Shigella	Salmonella	Invasive E. coli
Incubation Period (hours)	48–72	48–72	48–72	48–72	12–36 48–72	48–72
Abdominal Pain	0	±	+	+	±	+
Vomiting	±	0	±	+	±	+
Stool	no odor green-brown to rice water	no odor green-brown to watery	may be bloody	blood with mucus foul odor	occasionally bloody	often bloody foul odor
Duration (untreated)	5–7 days	1–2 days	1–4 days	4–12 days	4–12 days	4–12 days
Complication	dehydration and shock			systemic symptoms and dehydration		
Therapy	adequate fluid replacement and antibiotics			supportive, appropriate antibiotic		
Primary Location	upper small bowel			colon	colon and small bowel	

tients may be nauseated, drowsy, or even unconscious. Vomiting and tenesmus are common. There is usually a profound derangement of electrolyte metabolism. Loss of bicarbonate leads to a metabolic acidosis, and patients often have compensatory hyperventilation with a respiratory rate in excess of 30 per minute. Although serum potassium concentrations may be normal or high (due to acidosis), patients have a depletion of total body potassium. Hypokalemia may lead to poor muscle tone and ileus. If significant hyponatremia occurs, muscle cramping may be observed.

Complications occur more commonly in infants, children, and pregnant women. The dangers of hypokalemia are greater in children because many have experienced additional losses due to chronic diarrhea or malnutrition. Aspiration pneumonia, especially in infants may further complicate the clinical picture. Seizures may develop in children because of hypoglycemia. The mechanism of this hypoglycemia is unknown but may be due to the stress on an undernourished child with low liver glycogen stores. In pregnant women miscarriage is common during the third trimester if severe dehydration is present.

Patients with diarrhea due to invasive organisms usually experience significant constitutional symptoms of fever, anorexia, headaches, vomiting and, tenemus. Diarrhea is not as voluminous, and acute dehydration is not as great. The stool is filled with white cells, is often bloody, and may have an extremely foul odor. Complications are due to both intestinal involvement and systemic infection. The mortality rate of untreated cases is much lower than with cholera.

THERAPY

Recently, major advances have been made in the therapy of enterotoxic diarrheal diseases. This section, therefore, will focus on the treatment of cholera which can be applied to all dehydrating diarrheas (8). Replacement of fluid and electrolytes by intravenous or oral solutions forms the cornerstone of cholera therapy. Management is divided into two phases: rehydration and maintenance. Rehydration is the replacement of the water and electrolytes lost before admission to a treatment center. Maintenance is the replacement of continuing stool losses during hospitalization.

Rehydration requires a rapid clinical evaluation of the patient's level of hydration. If he is severely dehydrated, lethargic, or comatose, an intravenous solution should be infused immediately into the patient. A good rule to follow in a lean individual is to give 10 per cent of total body weight (kilograms) within the first one to two hours to severely dehydrated patients. Moderately dehydrated patients require 5 to 7 per cent replacement immediately. A number of effective intravenous solutions have been employed; a convenient solution, with a long-shelf life, is the Dacca solution which has the following composition: sodium 134, potassium 13, chloride 98, and acetate (or bicarbonate) 48 milli-equivalents per liter. For a moderately dehydrated and alert patient, rehydration with an oral solution may be sufficient. Regardless of the state of initial hydration, it is essential that hypotension and oliguria be promptly corrected by infusion of adequate volume.

After the patient is hydrated, continuing stool losses must be replaced. Most in-hospital cholera deaths are due to inadequate replacement of continuing stool losses. The quantity of maintenance fluid required is determined by measuring stool losses. Regular and frequent measurements of fluid input and output must be recorded for each patient. Accurate stool measurements are easily accomplished by the use of a cholera cot (Figure 7.1). This canvas or jute cot has a six-inch aperture beneath the patient's buttocks; a rubber sheet with a central sleeve passes through the hole into a clear plastic bucket calibrated to enable health personnel to monitor stool volume accurately. If plastic buckets are not available, a calibrated dip stick may be used. Adequacy of fluid replacement is assessed by constantly checking the following: physical signs of hydration, pulse, blood pressure, and urine output.

Tetracycline or furazolidone are effective adjuncts to fluid therapy but they are no substitute for adequate replacement of water and electrolytes. Antibiotics readily kill the bacteria and thus shorten the duration of diarrhea from five to two days. There is no need to limit food intake. Indeed adequate caloric intake is mandatory after initial rehydration as glucose stores may be low in poorly nourished children. Pediatric cases are treated using the same guidelines as adults, except greater care must be observed in their fluid and electrolyte management.

There are a number of therapeutic regimens which have little place in dehydrating diarrheas. These include opiates and absorbing preparations such as kaolin. Pressor agents should not be used in treating shock associated with cholera. Bacteriophages have no place in either the prophylaxis or the therapy of cholera.

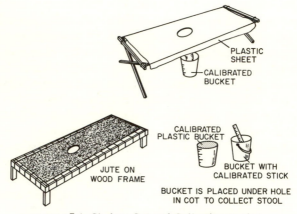

FIGURE 7.1. Cholera Cot and Collecting Bucket

Utilization of these simple guidelines can reduce cholera mortality to less than 1 per cent. Therapy is simple, effective, and inexpensive. Therapy has significant advantages over the present cholera vaccine. When cholera epidemics occur, there is always a great temptation to institute massive vaccination programs. Yet the present vaccine for cholera has been shown to be only partially protective and relatively short-lasting (9). Moreover, vaccines must be given at least one week prior to the onset of the index cases to offer any immunity to the community in the event of an epidemic. Under most circumstances, morbidity and mortality from cholera can be better combated by the establishment of treatment centers.

ORAL THERAPY

A separate discussion of oral therapy is being presented as it has important implications for the treatment of diarrhea in rural and inaccessible regions. Though intravenous solutions have been standard therapy, its use poses difficult problems for regions such as Bangladesh. Little intravenous fluid is made in the country; most must be imported. Because of its bulk, it is difficult to transport to outlying villages. Some have suggested stockpiling intravenous fluids in strategic locations throughout the countryside; unfortunately, because cholera usually strikes quickly and communications are primitive, most deaths occur before intravenous solutions can be delivered to a village. Another major disadvantage of parenteral therapy is its cost. A liter of intravenous fluid now costs 30 to 60 *taka* in Bangladesh when available. Since a cholera patient requires an average of 10 liters during the course of his illness (if antibiotics are administered), 300 to 600 *taka*s are required to finance therapy. Yet the average family income in Bangladesh is only 200 *takas* per month. Moreover, intravenous therapy requires skilled personnel and expensive supportive equipment such as needles and sterile intravenous tubing.

These handicaps of unavailability and high cost have been significantly reduced by the introduction of oral therapy (9–12). Because oral therapy requires only drinking water and ingredients which can be purchased at any local bazaar, it is within the reach of every village in Bangladesh. Moreover, its cost is less than one one-hundredth that of intravenous fluid.

The composition of the oral solution is similar to that of cholera stool except that glucose is added (Table 3). Inclusion of glucose and/or glycine is necessary to enhance the intestinal absorption of sodium. This solution is effective for all age groups and all forms of enterotoxin-induced diarrheas. It is preferable to weigh the salts if possible. However, even a simple teaspoon is sufficient to ensure a sufficiently accurate composition of the oral solution.

Oral therapy may be used in all patients except those with

shock or lethargy. Under these circumstances, initial rehydration is accomplished by intravenous solutions, and maintenance is continued with oral solutions. For moderately severe illnesses, initial rehydration and maintenance can be achieved with oral solutions alone. Even more important, oral therapy may be initiated before the patient goes to a hospital, while he is still in his village. In this way, deaths and complications due to hypovolemic shock may be

TABLE 3
Composition of Oral Solutions for Cholera
and Cholera-like Diarrheas

	Millimoles per liter	*Gms*[a]	*Level Teaspoons*[b]
Glucose	110	20	8
Sodium Chloride	72	4	1
Sodium Bicarbonate	48	3.5	¾
Potassium Chloride	25	2.0[c]	
Potassium Citrate		1.6	½

a. Weight of these various salts added to 1 liter of drinking water will provide equivalent glucose and electrolyte content of oral solution.
b. If scales are unavailable, a teaspoon measure is sufficient. It should be a *level* teaspoon.
c. Either potassium chloride or potassium citrate (but not both) may be used to provide potassium and alkali.

minimized. Most patients drink the oral solution but it can be conveniently delivered by nasogastric tube as well. For those administering therapy, only a short period of training is required; the necessary skills do not require sophisticated formal education.

DIARRHEA AND MALNUTRITION

As in other developing regions, there is a strong inter-relationship between diarrheal illnesses and malnutrition in Bangladesh. In Bangladesh, this relationship is particularly evident because of the high prevalence of both conditions, especially among the pediatric population (Figure 7.2). There are at least four deleterious effects of diarrheal disease on nutritional status. First, anorexia and vomiting associated with diarrhea leads to diminished oral food intake. Second, food that is ingested is poorly absorbed by the intestine. More than 90 per cent of hospitalized diarrheal patients in Bangladesh exhibit some form of intestinal malabsorption during the acute phase of their illness. Three, the stress of illness (especially if fever is present) imposes additional metabolic demands upon the body depleting caloric and protein reserves. Four, in Bangladesh, there are folk customs associated with the treatment of diarrhea that affect nutrition. The giving or withholding of food is considered by social and cultural tradition to be an integral part of the treatment process. The following observation has been made:

Foods are regarded as "hot" or "cold" according to allegedly inherent properties. Illnesses and body states are also classified as "hot" and "cold," the distinction providing a framework of do's and don't's for the maintenance of good health. A "hot" illness or body state should be treated with "cold" foods and a "cold" illness with "hot" foods.

An infant suffering from loose motions is believed to have a "hot" stomach, so it is given a diet of "cool" foods which lessen the heat and allow the stool to harden. It is therefore given barley water or glucose water with a little lemon. And if the mother is still breast feeding the child, she, too, restricts her diet to vegetarian non-heating foods (14).

An infant with diarrhea thus receives food of little caloric or electrolyte value. Borderline nourished children under such a regimen may be pushed into acute malnutrition. For those already malnourished, diarrhea may exacerbate and prolong the duration and severity of disease. Dietary restrictions may also extend to the mother. These practices have deleterious nutritional effects on the two most nutritionally vulnerable groups. Not only are these practices highly prevalent among Bengali villagers, but, even more important, their acceptance is all too common among local physicians.

Does malnutrition also have a direct impact on diarrheal illness? Certainly, mortality and morbidity of diarrheal illnesses are enhanced by the simultaneous presence of malnutrition. But the question of increased susceptibility of the malnourished to infec-

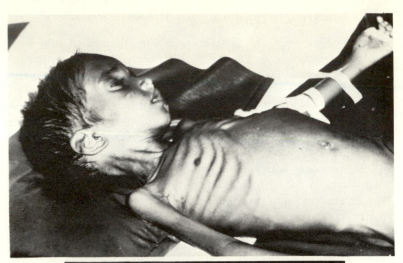

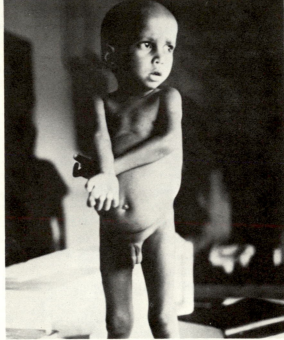

FIGURE 7.2A. Five-Year-Old Child with Acute Cholera and Severe Malnutrition (courtesy of Dr. R. Northrup)
FIGURE 7.2B. Three Months Later After Rehydration and Feeding

tious diarrheas is more difficult to answer. The malnourished child has depressed protein synthesis, depressed phagocytic activity, disruption of tissue integrity, and decreased mucous secretions, all likely to enhance susceptibility to infections (15). But preliminary studies in Bengal have failed to conclusively demonstrate an increased incidence of diarrhea among malnourished children. No differences were noted in thiamine, ascorbic acid, vitamin B_{12} levels in patients with cholera and normal controls.

CONCLUSION

Acute infectious diarrhea is a major cause of mortality and morbidity in Bangladesh. It is conservatively estimated that over 250,000 people, mostly children, die each year from dehydration and other complications associated with diarrheal illness. Furthermore, diarrheal illnesses impose an enormous "sickness" burden upon the society. The impact of these diseases is all the more devastating because of the simultaneous high prevalence of malnutrition.

Diarrhea exists where sanitation and potable water are inadequate. It will be difficult to improve current sanitation conditions sufficiently in the immediate future to reduce the high incidence of diarrhea in Bangladesh. Present vaccines are technically inadequate. If effectively applied, however, recent advances in therapy can significantly reduce mortality and morbidity. The greatest potential at the moment rests with oral therapy, which is effective, inexpensive, and accessible to rural regions. Barring revolutionary scientific breakthroughs, the most urgent priority for the present is the establishment of treatment centers.

References

1. Oseasohn, R. O., Benenson, A. S., and Fahimuddin, M. Field Trial of Cholera Vaccine in Rural East Pakistan—First Year of Observation. *Lancet* 1:450 (1965).
2. Gorbach, S. L. Acute Diarrhea—A Toxin Disease? *New Eng. J. Med.* 283:44 (1970).

3. Gorbach, S. L., Banwell, J. G., Chatterjee, B. D., Jacobs, B., and Sack, R. B. *Escherichia coli* from Patients with *Non-vibrio Cholera. J. Clin. Invest.* 50:881 (1971).

4. Carpenter, C. C. J. Cholera Enterotoxin—Recent Investigations Yield Insights into Transport Processes. *Am. J. Med.* 50:1 (1971).

5. Khan, M., and Mosley, W. H. The Significance of Shigella as a Cause of Diarrhea in a Low Economic Urban Community in Dacca. *E. Pakistan Med. J.* 12:45 (1968).

6. Nalin, D. R. Mortality from Cholera and Other Diarrheal Diseases at a Cholera Hospital. *Trop. Geographic Med.* 24:101 (1972).

7. Carpenter, C. C. J. Cholera: Diagnosis and Treatment. *New York Acad. Med.* 47:1192 (1971).

8. Hare, W. K., Nalin, D. R., Northrup, R. S., Rahaman, M. R., Cash, R. A., and Phillips, R. A. Cholera. In: *Current Therapy—1970,* W. B. Saunders Co., Philadelphia.

9. Mosley, W. H. The Role of Immunity in Cholera. A Review of Epidemiological and Serological Studies. *Texas Rep. Biol. Med.* 27:227 (1969).

10. Nalin, D. R., and Cash, R. A. Oral or Nasogastric Maintenance Therapy for Cholera in Adults. *Lancet* 2:370 (1968).

11. Pierce, N. F., Sack, R. B., Mitra, R. C., Banwell, J. G., Brigham, K. L., Fedson, D. S., and Mondal, A. Replacement of Water and Electrolyte Losses in Cholera by an Oral Glucose-Electrolyte Solution. *Annals Intern. Med.* 70:1173 (1969).

12. Cash, R. A., Nalin, D. R., Rochat, R., Reller, L. B., Haque, A. Z., and Rahman, A. S. M. M. A Clinical Trial of Oral Therapy in a Rural Cholera Treatment Center. *Am. J. Trop. Med. Hyg.* 19:653 (1970).

13. Nalin, D. R. and Cash, R. A. Oral Maintenance Therapy for Cholera for All Age Groups. *Bull. World Health Organization,* 1971.

14. Lindenbaum, S. Infant Care in Rural East Pakistan. Report of the Pakistan-SEATO Cholera Research Laboratory, 1965 (unpublished).

15. Scrimshaw, N. S., Taylor, C. E., and Gordon, J. E. *Interactions of Nutrition and Infections.* World Health Organization Monograph Series No. 57, Geneva, 1968.

(8) HEALTH MANPOWER AND ORGANIZATION

Robert S. Northrup

INTRODUCTION

Medicine at its simplest is a skilled service that one human being performs for another (1). Thus, the people, the manpower comprising a health-care system, are its most important element, and their training and skill, their dedication and sense of responsibility, their inter-relationships within the system, are the major determinants of its success.

This chapter discusses medical manpower in Bangladesh prior to March 1971, analyzes related factors contributing to the success or failure of this manpower in bringing health to the people, and suggests an approach to health manpower needs and utilization in the new country.

AVAILABLE HEALTH MANPOWER AND FACILITIES

The health manpower and facilities estimated to be available in Bangladesh are listed in Tables 1-4. Because of the recent war with Pakistan, present resources are very likely less, as these figures were gathered from reports or surveys prepared no later than 1970 (2–6). A post-war estimate obtained by an American relief worker from the Bangladesh Health Ministry in late April 1972 suggests that approximately one-third fewer doctors and nurses were available than before the war. A survey to obtain accurate current data regarding personnel and facilities would be useful. Yet the tremendous shortages which existed even in 1970 indicate clearly where attention is needed.

Doctors. Following partition from India, the training of physicians received high priority in the Pakistan health budget. This

TABLE 1

Trained Health Manpower in Bangladesh

Type	Number Available	Starting Salary (approx.) Rupees per Month	Education (years) Prior to Training	Specific Training	Approximate Cost of Specific Training (Rupees)	Average Output per Year
Doctor	8,052		12	5	60,000[a]	
MBBS[e]	4,500	325				400
Licentiates	7,000		10	4	30,000[d]	0
Nurse	700	175+	10	4	10,000	50
LHV[e]	262	175	10	2½	3,200	<20
Health Technician	0	220	10	2½	3,200	0
Dresser-Dispenser Compounder	>2,100	60	?	on-the-job to 1 yr	0– 1,000	?
Trained Midwife	286	115	10	1½	1,000	<20
Trained Dai	1,300	15+	?	1	1,000	290
LFPV[e]	400	135+	10	1½	2,700	70
FP Dai[e]	20,000	15	?	few weeks	100[d]	thousands
Sanitary Inspector	118[b]	125	10	1½	1,000	10–40
Other Technical[c]	Several thousand	125–300	10	¼–2	200–3,000[d]	hundreds

Sources: From Furst, 1970 and Planning Commission, Government of Pakistan, 1970.
a. estimated at Rs. 164,000 by Chowdhuri (3)
b. estimated at 928 by Fourth Five-year plan (6)
c. malaria microscopists and technicians; FP officers, supervisors, and technicians; general laboratory technicians.
d. approximate cost (estimated)
e. See the text for meaning of abbreviations.

priority was effected largely through the influence of a series of critical appraisals of medical and health progress, beginning with the Bhore Report of 1946 (7) and continuing until recent times with reports from planning commissions of the Pakistan central government and assessments by outside groups such as the American Association of Medical Colleges (2). These study groups con-

TABLE 2

Healers in Private Practice in Rural Bangladesh, 1969

Type	Number per Survey Population[a]	Per Cent of Total	Healer / Population Ratio
Adequately Trained			
Qualified Doctors	10		1:57,000
Nurses	1		1:570,000
Lady Health Visitors	1	6	1:570,000
Health Technician	0		
Trained *Dais*	4		1:142,500
Poorly Trained or Untrained			
Untrained *Dais*	101		
Dispensers	30	49	1:4400
Non-scientific			
Homeopath	44		
Hakims	11	45	1:4800
Faith Healers and Others	64		
	266	100	

Source: From Awan, A. H., 1969.
a. total population of surveyed unions—567,961

sisted almost exclusively of physicians, and concluded, perhaps predictably, "in favor of one grade of doctor—the highest" (7). The "licentiate," a less extensively trained doctor (see Table 1) was to be gradually phased out of existence, while the MBBS (Bachelor of Medicine, Bachelor of Surgery) degree programs were to be promoted.

Since that time stress has been placed on providing high-caliber training for physicians. Medical "schools" previously graduating licentiates were upgraded to medical colleges and, within the medical colleges, standards were set so that graduates would be the equivalent of their counterparts in Britain and other Western countries.

TABLE 3
Health Facilities in Bangladesh[a]

	Total
Hospitals	155[b]
Beds	9,723[c]
Rural Health (R.H.) Center	160[c]
R.H. sub-centers and units	150
R.H. dispensaries	2,100[d]
Family Planning clinics	
Full Time	
Urban	37
Rural	284
Part Time	
Urban	88
Rural	541
Maternal Child Health Centers[e]	
Independent	56
Connected to F.P. Clinics	100

a. figures primarily from Furst (4)
b. as of 1966 (4)   d. estimate by Furst (4)
c. as of 1970 (6)   e. as of 1968 (4)

These programs have, over 25 year, resulted in a supply of between 8,000 and 12,000 "doctors" (see Table 1), including both MBBS doctors and licentiates. The Fourth Five-Year Plan figure of 8,052 doctors (6) suggests that the ratio of doctors to population is approximately 1:10,000, while the more generous figures of the Furst study (9) suggest a ratio of 1:7,000. In rural areas the situation is even worse. As indicated in Table 2, the doctor:population ratio in 40 rural unions was only 1:60,000 (8).

Medical training, although generally good, is poorly adapted to the needs of the country. The medical professors teach hospital-oriented curative medicine. There is emphasis on diseases of high incidence in Western countries—heart and renal disease, metabolic disorders, other primarily adult medical conditions—disproportionate to their importance in Bangladesh. There is only minimal emphasis on those aspects of medicine which would

TABLE 4
Health Training Facilities in Bangladesh

Type	Number	Yearly Output
Medical Colleges	6	400
Nurse Training Centers	5	50
Lady Health Visitor Training Center	3	26[a]
Midwife Training Centers	11[b]	<20[c]
Paramedical Training Institute (Sanit. Insp., Hlth Tech., Lab Tech., etc.)	1	50 or less
Malaria Eradication Training Center (microscopists, inspectors, etc.)	1	181

a. average 1965–67 (Chowdhuri (3));
b. Chowdhuri—1968 (3); Furst (4) claims only 4 training centers for Bangladesh as of 1970, with 27 in training in 1967 as per UNICEF figures.
c. estimate is based on refs. (3) and (4)

equip the MBBS graduate to lead a health team—epidemiology, preventive medicine, statistics, education and motivation techniques, administration. There is no opportunity given for rural experience during training.

The result is a competent physician suited better for practice in Western countries than at home, as indicated by the fact that half the graduates leave the country (3). Those that remain, as the figures suggest, avoid rural practice and congregate in the urban areas.

The output from the six medical colleges in Bangladesh is low, probably about 400 per year in 1970, and the maximum admission capacity is only 640 per year, were all faculties and seats to be filled (3). The cost per graduate is staggering in relation to the scanty health budgetary allocation likely to be available in Bangladesh—up to Rs. 160,000 (U.S. $32,000) [1] per graduate, or Rs. 18 million (U.S. $3.6 million) for all six colleges (3). There is almost no economically feasible possibility of producing enough physicians to provide primary health care for all the people. If one doubled the present number of medical colleges to twelve each graduating 100 doctors per year, it would take until at least the year 2000 to bring the ratio of doctors to the *present* population to 1:2,000—and by that time the population would have more than doubled in size.

Nurses. There are many fewer nurses than doctors. This has been attributed in the past to poor salaries, particularly in relation to their extended training; long and irregular working hours; cultural distaste for nursing activities such as handling blood and excrement; and the lack of an image in society of nursing as a desirable profession for educated young ladies (5, 6). Nurses have been thought of as subservient to doctors rather than as having their own role on a team of health professionals. Training facilities are few (Table 4), and there are not enough faculty members. This may contribute to the high failure and drop-out rate—over 50 per cent of admissions—which in turn represents a tremendous waste of scarce teaching time and effort. Most three-year graduates go on for an additional year of midwifery and become nurse-midwives.

Nursing in Bangladesh is primarily oriented toward the care of hospitalized patients. Whether hospital medicine should be emphasized at present is debatable. Yet the potential role of nurses in hospital-based *out*patient medicine is unrealized, and the effectiveness of those physicians caring for hospitalized *in*patients is severely hampered by the lack of trained nurses.

Training for a nurse, although prolonged, is substantially less expensive than that of a physician (Table 1), and yet nurses could multiply the effectiveness of the doctor many times over.

---

1. The currency used in Bangladesh at present is the *taka*. Prior to independence the Pakistan *rupee* was the official currency.

Other trained generalists

Lady Health Visitors (LHV's) and Health Technicians. These two categories represent the female and male counterparts of the health paraprofessional called the "medical assistant" by other countries and the WHO (9) or "clinical officers" in Malawi (1). These workers are broadly trained in the recognition and treatment of diseases common in rural areas; in hygiene, family planning, and other preventive measures; and in the case of the LHV, midwifery and pre-partum and post-partum care of mother and child. Despite early recognition of the potential importance of the LHV in the health plans for Pakistan (9), implementation was minimal (Table 1). During the period 1960–66, a total of only 79 women from the three training schools in East Pakistan were qualified to be LHV's (3), and only 142 were registered by June 1969 (4). No Health Technicians had ever been graduated from the Training Institute for Paramedical Personnel in Dacca by late 1969 (6). The relative brevity and inexpensiveness of training, the broad capabilities of the trainees in dealing with the common diseases in both preventive and curative ways, and the greater likelihood of inducing these less-internationally interchangeable personnel to work in rural areas, all indicate that the medical assistant would ideally meet the pressing rural health needs of Bangladesh. Yet present numbers are negligible, and major efforts (and expenditure) would be required to attract, train, and utilize enough workers to begin to satisfy the needs of the country.

Dressers-Compounders-Dispensers. Sources in Dacca estimated that there were over 3,000 dressers-compounders-dispensers in Bangladesh as of December 1971. These men help with dressing wounds, compound and dispense medications, and perform other auxiliary tasks. Their training is limited, however, often being confined to on-the-job experience; their knowledge is usually primarily of curative medicine, either simple surgery or medical treatment; and their lack of pre-technical education (completion of secondary school is often not required) makes continued self-education, so necessary for any medical practitioner, difficult or unlikely. Table 2 suggests that these individuals are willing to live in rural areas, and they doutless serve as primary-care sources there. Yet official utilization of these individuals as practitioners would be suitable only if their training were substantially improved and broadened. At present the dresser or dispenser should not function without constant supervision. With such supervision he can be a valuable member of the health team.

Others. Below these workers in training and scientific ability are the other general "healers" mentioned in Table 2—hakims, practicing a folk medicine based on indigenous herbs, homeopaths, faith healers, and quacks. With modern medicines available without prescription, these practitioners may often employ useful scientific medications and do provide strong psychological support for their patients, much like the "witch doctors" of Africa. In the absence of adequate numbers of scientifically trained personnel, these individuals often represent the only health resource for the majority of the people.

Health workers in the area of gynecology

Several types of workers are available to treat women during pregnancy and delivery and to help in family planning. As noted in Tables 1 and 2, they range, in decreasing order of training, as follows:

a. Nurse-midwife (see above).

b. Trained midwife: a matriculate with 18 months' further practical and classroom training in midwifery.

c. Trained *dai:* an indigenous village midwife, often illiterate or with less than matriculate background, with one year's training in child as well as maternal health.

d. Family Planning Visitor: trained as part of the crash Family Planning Program, this woman received instruction in basic hygiene, in motivational training techniques, and in the practical aspects of contraception techniques, particularly IUD insertion (9).

e. Family planning *dai:* a village midwife with very brief training in family planning techniques. Often illiterate, this woman was trained primarily to "sell" contraception to the village women, and get them to go to the family planning clinics. She is probably only slightly more informed than the untrained *dai.*

f. Untrained *dai:* traditional village midwife who helps mothers during delivery. She has no formal training.

The long tradition of the use of the midwife will doubtless persist, as it has in many areas in Europe where adequate numbers of doctors are available. Furthermore, the population structure in Bangladesh, with its predominance of children and young adults, ensures that the number of pregnant mothers needing care will continue to be large. Thus, it seems desirable to pursue this type of service. Nevertheless, as documented in Tables 1 and 2, the number of well-trained personnel is low, and past training programs have not combined midwifery and family planning.

Other health auxiliaries

Other personnel trained exclusively in preventive aspects of health care or in laboratory or supervisory roles are available. These include a relatively few sanitary inspectors, whose task has been to promote good public health measures, particularly regarding water and sewage, food handling, and the like; microscopists and technicians trained for laboratory and field control work in the Malaria Eradication Program; family planning personnel, often university graduates trained briefly in principles of family planning and occupying administrative positions in that program; and technicians trained for work in clinically oriented hospital or health laboratories. Such personnel have provided technical and administrative support for both preventive and curative health programs. In general, as with nurses, their numbers are few relative to the number of doctors available.

Training facilities

The major training facilities for health manpower are outlined in Table 4, together with approximations of the numbers of graduates per year. The approximate cost per graduate is noted in Table 1. With the exception of the training programs for *dai*s and family planning administrators, the yearly output of all medical personnel other than doctors is barely equal to the output of doctors. Even without considering cost, this is deplorable. When cost is considered, the situation seems even more unreasonable—Chowdhuri (3) estimates that the total annual expenditure for doctor education is upward of Rs. 17 million (U.S. $3.4 million). From the figures of Table 1, it appears that only Rs. 2–3 million are being spent for the training of all other health personnel.

Health facilities

Health personnel require facilities, whether they be a spread-out cloth covered with bottles of medicine under an umbrella at a bazaar, an individual practitioner's office with little more than a desk and an examining table, or a hospital with wards, laboratories, operating rooms, and x-ray. *Proper* facilities and tools obviously increase both the efficiency and capability of health workers but their availability is minimal in Bangladesh.

Table 3 outlines the governmental or semi-governmental facilities extant in Bangladesh before 1970. The few hospitals are concentrated primarily in urban areas. District hospitals, those associated with medical colleges, comprise the majority of the largest. Other hospitals are either specialty hospitals (e.g., Chest Hospital, Dacca), or smaller general hospitals of 20–25 beds (5). The ratio of available beds is about 1 per 10,000 population, compared with ratios of 1 bed per 100–200 population in highly developed countries, or 1 to 175 in Poland (4). Hospitals, like doctors, are generally in the cities in Bangladesh, and, lacking efficient referral techniques and transportation facilities, benefit primarily the nearby urban dweller. Also, many hospitals were set up initially by government institutions such as the railroads or police and are used by their "entitled" employees. Those which were designed to serve the general public frequently include "private cabins" or other beds more readily available to those who can pay, particularly the private patients of the professor. Thus, the high priority given hospital care in Bangladesh has only further increased the imbalance in facilities available to the vast majority of the people, i.e., the poor, the rural, and the jobless.

General rural health centers and sub-centers have lagged far behind development goals. These units were originally conceived of as functioning with a doctor and some auxiliary personnel and later were divided into centers with a doctor and sub-centers or units with only sub-doctorate professionals and auxiliaries. Only 310 of either were available before the war.

Rural health dispensaries, usually little more than simple offices, are estimated to be fairly numerous in comparison to other facilities but are in general poorly equipped and are likely to add little to the practitioner's capabilities other than a modicum of privacy. A dresser or dispenser is usually the only staff in such a unit (4).

Family Planning and Maternal-Child Health centers, usually involving only sub-doctorate personnel, have provided preventive as well as some therapeutic services in the past, but are few in number.

An accurate estimate of the number or extent of private health facilities in Bangladesh is not available. With the exception of some mission hospitals, Mirzapur hospital (a large charity hospital), and a few charitable clinics, most private facilities are small and minimally equipped.

Supplies and instruments for all health facilities, including the private practitioner's office are scarce and expensive. Often they are available only from outside the country. This lack of needed items has severely handicapped health personnel, particularly the private practitioner, who is often unable to afford even simple items. Making essential equipment and supplies available would substantially enhance the efficiency and capability of the existing health manpower.

Planning goals for the country (6) included expansion of both hospital and rural health facilities. Implementation of these plans was minimal, however, and resulted in the present severe lack of facilities, particularly in rural areas. Major efforts will be needed to "catch up" even to goals based on the present population.

SUMMARY OF THE HEALTH MANPOWER SITUATION

From this brief consideration of available manpower and facilities, a number of points are apparent:

1. Available trained personnel and health facilities are too few overall to meet the present health needs of Bangladesh, and are even scarcer in rural areas where the majority of the population lives.

2. The rapidly expanding population of Bangladesh demands a

similarly rapid expansion in the health staff and facilities
merely to maintain existing levels of health services. Improving
these services will require even more rapid expansion.

3. Past concentration on physician education has produced doctors of high quality but poorly suited for the work needed in
their own country. The number of doctors is small, and the
high cost of doctorate-level education makes it impossible to
consider attempting to meet health needs by increasing substantially the output of doctors.

4. The lack of emphasis on training sub-doctorate professionals
and auxiliaries has resulted in an extreme shortage of these
personnel, both in absolute numbers and also relative to the
number of doctors. This in turn has exaggerated the lack of
doctors by reducing the efficiency of those that are available.

5. Facilities in which health personnel can work are scarce, particularly in rural areas. Hospital care has been emphasized in
the past, while outpatient clinics and rural centers have lagged
behind.

6. The availability and output of various types of training facilities
reflect the previous emphasis on curative health care by physicians in hospitals.

7. An organizational system for effectively coordinating all portions of the health program for the delivery of care, both preventive and curative, public and private, is lacking.

AN APPROACH TO FUTURE HEALTH MANPOWER NEEDS

The way to improve the existing manpower situation in
Bangladesh seems clear—by giving maximum priority to the
training of sub-doctorate personnel, both professional and auxiliary, and the provision of facilities in which they can work with
maximum efficiency.

The World Health Organization defines professionals as "health
workers trained to the generally accepted level for that discipline
in a particular country" (9) and includes as examples physicians,
nurses, midwives, and sanitarians. Auxiliary workers are technical
workers in a particular field, usually with less than full professional qualifications, who work as auxiliaries to professionals in

their fields, usually under supervision by the professional. Drawn often from a less highly educated group, trained for a briefer period at lower cost, designed to serve a specific function in a health team, paid a lower salary than the full professional, and usually willing to serve in rural areas, the auxiliary health worker has admirably met the long-term needs and the budgets of many developing countries (10–11) and some developed ones, such as the USSR (12). The long-term health needs and present manpower resources of Bangladesh, and an extremely limited health budget, indicate that this approach would be ideal for Bangladesh in the future.

Such a reordering of priorities might require a reduction in the extent of physician training programs for budgetary reasons, and this course could be interpreted as leading to a reduction in the quality of medicine in Bangladesh. In fact, such an approach is more likely to lead to an increase in the over-all quality of medical care. The well-trained auxiliary can perform many simple technical tasks as well as the professional, including diagnosing and treating many common and easily recognizable diseases, taking temperatures, keeping nursing records, assisting at uncomplicated deliveries, and taking water samples and vaccinating. Within the framework of a *health team,* the auxiliary can refer to the professional those more complex problems demanding greater competence. Such division of labor would ensure that the professional's skills are maximally utilized, and thus would raise the *quality* of the *total output* of the health team.

In addition, the low cost of training auxiliaries would allow for expansion of the health care team relative to the population. This would be impossibly expensive if doctors were to continue as the only member of the team engaged in diagnosis and treatment. Such an increase in the over-all *quantity* of care available would bring scientific medicine to a population previously dependent on non-scientific healers or folk remedies, for them a definite increase in the quality of their medical care.

Bangladesh should certainly retain professional training programs of the highest quality. Indeed, expansion and strengthening of training programs for sub-doctorate professionals—nurses, midwives, and sanitarians—are particularly needed. Such programs, however, will in no way overcome the pressing need for auxiliaries.

SPECIFIC SUGGESTIONS FOR IMPLEMENTATION

This chapter cannot explore thoroughly the training of health auxiliaries and their most effective utilization. Successful programs in countries as diverse as Russia, Kenya, Burma, Venezuela, Fiji, and the United States have been described in detail in many books and articles by WHO committees (9, 13), symposiasts (14–16), and individual experts in the field (17). Some comments regarding the specific situation in Bangladesh do seem appropriate, however.

The target area for health services improvement in Bangladesh is the rural population. Current health manpower there is very meager. Facilities consist of a few rural health centers and family planning clinics and a few dispensaries. Organization of these units into a system for delivering a range of health services is lacking.

The organizational concept of graduated facilities, from many rural health units staffed only by auxiliaries to fewer rural health centers staffed by some professionals as well as auxiliaries, then small- and medium-sized hospitals, and finally the six major medical centers, each with its medical college hospital, for referral of the most difficult cases, would effectively encompass both present facilities and personnel and those needed for the future. The rural health units and centers at the periphery could handle the diagnosis and treatment of most common diseases, as well as family planning, public health, and preventive medical programs, while more difficult problems would be referred toward the center. Effective organization of all components, however, with careful supervision of each level by those higher up, would be essential if the system were to work *as a system,* and not to break up into individual units, each operating independently in a void.

Focusing on the rural health units and centers, staffing could be arranged as suggested in Table 5. A "clinical officer" (medical assistant, health technician) would head the team of each unit and be responsible for the unit, as well as diagnose and treat common diseases and minor surgical problems. He would be assisted by a "comprehensive nurse" capable of community as well as individual patient nursing, family planning, maternal child-health care, and midwifery; a "trained nurse-midwife" trained in midwifery and simple patient nursing; and a "health assistant" trained to be a combination of dresser, compounder, dispenser, and clerk.

TABLE 5

Health Manpower Needs by Year 2000 for Rural
Health Units (1 unit / 10,000 population)

Type	No. Per Rural Center	Total Needed for 160 Million pop. (year 2000)	Duration of Training (years)	Yearly Output[a]
Auxiliaries				
Clinical officer[b]	1	16,000	3	700
Comprehensive Nurse[c]	1	16,000	2½	700
Trained midwife / nurse	1	16,000	1½	700
Health assistant[d]	1	16,000	½ + on the job	700
Professionals				
Doctor[e]	¼	4,000	5 +	175
Sanitary inspector[e]	¼	4,000	1	175

a. allows for 5 per cent retirement / yr
b. other names: medical assistant, health technician
c. other names: lady health visitor, family planning worker, maternal child health worker, etc.
d. other names: dresser, dispenser, compounder, clerk
e. one per R.H. center—one of four R.H. units to be a center

Those problems unable to be handled by this team would be referred to a more highly trained "senior clinical officer," or a doctor if available, at the rural health center, and referred by him, if necessary, to a hospital. At the present population density in Bangladesh of about 1,350 persons per square mile, a rural health unit would be no more than 1 to 2 miles from any individual; a center would be no more than 4 miles away.

Experience in other countries has indicated that a large volume of clinical patients makes it difficult for the clinical officer himself to be much involved in public health and preventive work (17). In order to ensure that this work is done, a sanitary inspector at each center would be primarily responsible for carrying out such activities, and would in addition have had sufficient training in family planning to supervise the activities of the comprehensive nurse in that area. The effectiveness of the sanitary inspector is severely hampered unless he has the legal power to enforce the sanitary regulations. Such power should be given to these men to ensure progress in this crucial area.

The "health assistant" at each unit or center would receive only minimal formal training. For him to become a valuable team member, all personnel must believe in the importance of constant teaching as a way of passing tasks along to those less skilled (15).

TRAINING PROGRAMS FOR AUXILIARIES

Previous admission requirements for medical auxiliaries in Bangladesh have demanded the completion of secondary school (matriculation) for admission to most training programs (Table 1). Although this represents a desirable ideal, the past failure of these programs to attract many candidates (4) may be attributed in part to the fact that matriculates are few (over-all literacy is only 8 per cent (6)), needs for personnel in areas other than health care are great, and the nature of health care work does not have broad appeal. For these reasons, reducing admission standards in order to attract more candidates, as is done in other countries (10, 17), is recommended. Most auxiliary training programs include an introductory course of up to one year to bring their students up to a common level in reading, writing, mathematics, and basic science (9, 12, 13, 17). In Bangladesh, where even matriculates can vary widely in ability, inclusion of such an introductory course would ensure competence despite lowered admission requirements.

Past crash health programs in Pakistan (family planning, malaria eradication) trained large numbers of personnel, but within a limited and specific curriculum. The "graduates" have been unable to shift to different roles because they do not have a broad background. Although specifically trained personnel are of course useful, it would be preferable to design future training programs to produce manpower able to do a variety of work. Combining mid-wifery and family planning training and functions would be particularly beneficial, as birth control information could be given to women at the time of delivery, thus reaching women during a time of high motivation toward acceptance of contraceptives. The specifically trained health workers presently available in Bangladesh are ideal candidates for "upgrading," through further training, to clinical officers, comprehensive nurses, etc.

A major problem in the past has been retaining health workers in rural areas. In order to overcome this problem in the future, the recruitment of candidates from rural areas would be desirable. Additionally, training programs should be located in rural areas, as in China (18), or at least should include substantial practical experience in rural areas. At least three months in a rural health clinic under the supervision of an experienced practitioner would be a reasonable portion of a three-year program (17). In this way, training would acquaint the graduate with the practical problems as well as the rewards of rural practice.

A further step to ensure that graduates remain in rural jobs would be to restrict all clinical officers or other auxiliaries to salaried positions—either with government or with private parties, such as mission programs, charitable organizations, and private businesses. This step would reduce the financial appeal of private practice in cities, where the wealthier patients reside. Many countries do not allow private practice at any time, and even restrict the acceptance of gifts by their clinical officers. Others allow private practice after a service period of five years (17). Such regulations would ensure a high degree of government control over the placement of personnel in appropriate locations.

Finally, postgraduate training of auxiliaries is of great importance. It is essential for the maintenance of skills. Such teaching can take the form of review, criticism, and instruction on the job by regular supervisors, and also of intermittent courses at training centers. In addition, a few particularly capable auxiliaries could be allowed to progress into formal professional training programs after a period of service. This would provide an incentive to work.

Manpower needs demand longer than five years of planning, as programs require time to start up and personnel needs increase with increases in population. I have estimated in Table 5 the approximate number of health personnel needed *only for the rural health units and centers* by the year 2000, along with the yearly output of graduates required to reach target numbers by that time. Obviously, except for doctors, the numbers demanded are greatly in excess of the present output. They require substantial investment in training facilities and substantial recurrent expenditure in adequate provision of faculty, subsidization of students, and salaries of graduates. Looking at relative costs, however, one can estimate that for the previous cost of training 400–500 doctors per year (Rs. 17 million), one could train, at a cost of 4000 *taka*s (U.S. $555) each, 4,250 clinical officers. Proportionate costs for other auxiliaries and professionals hold. Faced with minimal funds for health and a rising population, present health-spending patterns could be continued only with acceptance of the inevitability of a further reduction in the services and facilities available to the common man.

THE ROLE OF THE PROFESSIONAL

The priority of professional education and the future role of the doctor in particular are obvious questions demanding answers. Should the same number of physicians continue to be educated? Should postgraduate and specialty programs for doctors be strengthened? Should hospitals be expanded and their professional staffs augmented?

Bangladesh has a unique advantage among newer nations in having a strong corps of doctors and numbers of other professionals. Such men and women could be the teachers and leaders in an expanded cadre of health workers deepened and enriched by expansion at the sub-doctorate level. As mentioned before, the professional's capacities could be substantially enhanced by having less demanding tasks done by less trained personnel, thus allowing the professional to exercise his broader skills and knowledge to the utmost.

Yet this change in the role of the doctor or nurse or other professional must coincide with a change in training. Inclusion of instruction in administrative techniques, teaching methods, health education and motivation skills, and, in particular, training and experience in working with auxiliaries are essential as the basis for assumption of new roles. With such changes, professional and auxiliary alike may participate in a revolution in health care in Bangladesh through which good health could become an attainable goal for every citizen.

ROLE OF OUTSIDE ASSISTANCE

How can other countries best contribute to health in Bangladesh? Recent efforts receiving foreign assistance have been primarily concentrated in specific crash health programs, while over-all health care has been ignored. Certainly, containment of the population increase is crucial to Bangladesh, and the programs for the eradication of malaria and smallpox have been valuable. The long-range view, however, demands that a system for health services down to the local level be established, both to ensure the maintenance of advances made in short-term crash programs and to make some provision for the large number of health problems not yet approached by recent programs, such as diarrheal diseases, parasite infestations, and nutrition. In addition, many preventive and public health measures can best be "sold" by those who are providing curative services, combining a visit to the clinic with health education or a vaccination. The essential elements of such a system have been described: trained manpower; an effective organizational structure; and functional facilities, including supplies and equipment, both for training and for operation. Other nations could help to provide all of these elements: (a) in planning the system; in determining practical interrelationships between personnel working at the same level and also between levels in the referral chain; in working out a practical over-all time scale of progressive steps; perhaps most usefully, in setting up model systems in limited areas of 100,000–200,000 population; (b) in training personnel, by providing teachers; by giving equipment for training or constructing well-designed training centers; by providing advice based on practical experience in other countries as to curriculum design, texts, laboratory aids, and teaching methods (it is as difficult to choose and to teach well a limited body of knowledge as to try to cover everything known); (c) in provision of facilities, by providing advice regarding practical and efficient units, based on experience gained in other countries; by actually constructing, or funding the construction, of the many units and centers needed; and by providing the equipment and supplies which would enable a unit to function above a bare minimum level of care. Such assistance would "crank up" the over-all health program, which has to achieve quick progress if it is not to fall inexorably behind the growth of population. Assistance from outside could perhaps also allow Bangladesh to retain her high-quality but expensive physician and other professional educational programs while pursuing the proposed massive expansion at the subprofessional level.

SUMMARY AND CONCLUSIONS

Available health manpower in Bangladesh is limited and unbalanced, both in geographic distribution and in the ratio of physicians to other professionals and auxiliaries. There are few health facilities avaliable and those that exist are poorly distributed. A major stress on the training and effective utilization of medical auxiliaries is recommended as the only economically feasible solution to the manpower problem. Outside assistance could substantially hasten progress in this area. Physicians and other professionals are essential as teachers and leaders in the development effort.

References

1. King, M. The Auxiliary—His Role and Training. *J. Med. Educ.* 45:336–354, 1970.
2. *Medical Education in East Pakistan.* Report to USAID, Amer. Assn. Med. Colleges, Washington, D.C., 1964.
3. Chowdhuri, A. Subhan. *Brief Review of Medical Manpower and Its Utilization in Pakistan.* Health section, Planning Division, Rawalpindi, 1968.
4. Furst, Barbara G. *Medical Manpower and Training and Clinical Facilities in Pakistan.* USAID, Rawalpindi, 1970.
5. Superintendent of Nursing, Government of East Pakistan, and

Nurse Advisor, USAID, Dacca. *Report on Nursing Needs and Resources in East Pakistan.* Dacca, 1964.

6. Planning Commission, Government of Pakistan. *The Fourth Five-Year Plan (1970–75),* Rawalpindi, 1970.

7. *Report of the Health Survey and Development Committee* (Bhore Report) Government of India, 1946.

8. Awan, Akhtar H. *The System of Local Health Services in Rural Pakistan,* Public Health Assn. Pak. (Lahore, 1969).

9. WHO Technical Report #112. *The Use and Training of Auxiliary Personnel in Medicine, Nursing, Midwifery and Sanitation,* World Health Organization, Geneva, 1961.

10. Jensen, Robert J. The Primary Medical Case Worker in Developing Countries—A Review. *Medical Care* 5:382–400, 1967.

11. Vaughan, J. P. A Review of the Need for the Medical Assistant in Developing Countries. *J. Trop. Med. Hyg.* 74:265–271, 1971.

12. Sidel, Victor. Feldshers and Feldsherism—The Role and Training of the Feldsher in the USSR. *New Eng. J. Med.* 278:934–992, 1968.

13. WHO Expert Comm. on Professional and Technical Education of Medical and Auxiliary Personnel. 17th Report. *Training of Medical Assistants and Similar Personnel.* WHO Technical Report #385. Geneva, 1968.

14. King, Maurice, *in Ciba Symposium. Teamwork for World Health.* edited by G. Wolstenholme and M. O'Connor, J & A Churchill, London, 1971, pp. 25–36.

15. King, M. ed. *Medical Care in Developing Countries—A Symposium from Makerere.* Oxford University Press. Nairobi, 1966.

16. Institute on International Medical Education, March 1966, (edited by H. vanZile Hyde). Manpower for the World's Health. *J. Med. Educ.* 41. Part 2, September 1966.

17. Rosinski, R. F., and F. J. Spencer. *The Assistant Medical Officer: The Training of the Medical Auxiliary in Developing Countries.* University of North Carolina Press, Chapel Hill, 1965. Also "The Training and Duties of the Medical Auxiliary Known as the Assistant Medical Officer." *Am. J. Pub. Hlth.* 57:1663–1669, 1967.

18. Horn, J. S. Experiments in Expanding the Rural Health Service in People's China, *in Ciba Symposium*—"Teamwork for World Health" Churchill, London, 1971.

19. Winslow, C. *The Cost of Sickness and the Price of Health,* World Health Organization, Geneva, 1951.

20. Taylor, C. E., and Hall, M. F. Health, Population and Economic Development. *Science,* 157:651–657, 1967.

Part Two

DISASTERS IN BANGLADESH

(9) THE CYCLONE: MEDICAL ASSESSMENT AND DETERMINATION OF RELIEF AND REHABILITATION NEEDS

Alfred Sommer and W. Henry Mosley

INTRODUCTION

Within the past several years, Bangladesh has been the victim of two disasters of unprecedented proportions. In November 1970, a cyclone and tidal bore swept across the southern coast of Bangladesh leaving countless deaths and hundreds of thousands of destitute survivors in its wake. In 1971 Bangladesh achieved independence after a tragic civil war. With each disaster, precipitated by man or nature, emergency relief requirements were enormous. Concerned governments, international organizations, and voluntary agencies contributed large quantities of relief materials, personnel, and supportive equipment to aid the victims. Yet, those anxious to assist often lacked even minimal information on the nature of the disaster and the character of relief requirements. This chapter discribes an assessment and survey technique employed after the cyclone of November 1970, which was effectively utilized to assist and direct relief efforts. Such an assessment can be performed rapidly, efficiently, and at low cost. Similar approaches should be implemented for more effective relief and rehabilitation activities after future disasters.

The help of Colonel Rex Davis (MC) U.S. Stricom; Drs. Paul B. Dean, John N. Lewis, John M. Leonard, Matthew S. Loewenstein, Kenneth J. Bart of the Epidemiology Program, Center for Disease Control; and Messrs. K. M. A. Aziz and Alauddin Chowdhury of the Cholera Research Laboratory is gratefully acknowledged.

ALFRED SOMMER was formerly Medical Epidemiologist, Cholera Research Laboratory, Dacca, Bangladesh, from May 1970 to September 1971. W. HENRY MOSLEY was formerly head, Epidemiology Division, Cholera Research Laboratory, Dacca, Bangladesh, 1965 to 1971.

BACKGROUND

Bangladesh is one of the most densely populated nations of the developing world. Trapped between a rapidly growing population and a limited amount of land, the average Bengali has been forced to feed his family from progressively smaller plots of paddy. This has greatly increased his vulnerability, to the point that even minor fluctuations in climatic conditions can seriously affect his family's already marginal existence (1).

While adequacy of the food supply is an annual uncertainty, the loss of thousands of lives and hundreds of villages to the monsoon rains is not. The same press of humanity that forced villagers to build their homes in areas subject to recurring flooding also sowed the seeds of one of the worst and certainly swiftest natural disasters of all times. For the past 60 years land hunger has forced villagers southward, to clear and settle the Sunderban Forest. Once the home of the Bengal tiger, it was transformed in two generations into a relatively prosperous rice surplus area, but one constantly exposed to the vagaries of the Bay of Bengal.

Like most of Bangladesh, the cyclone-affected area is a flat deltaic plain eminently suited for the cultivation of rice, the main dietary staple. Eighty per cent of the workers are farmers, 10 per cent are fishermen, and the rest are traders, clerks, day laborers, and professionals. Over 85 per cent are Moslem, the remainder primarily Hindu. More than 90 per cent of the population live in rural villages where sanitation is primitive at best, and where defecation is usually along the banks of the rivers and ponds, which serve as the primary sources of water for drinking, cooking, laundering, and bathing. It is therefore not surprising that there are a host of endemic diarrheal diseases, including cholera, whose historical home has been the Ganges Delta.

Houses are generally one-room structures of woven bamboo and jute stick, with either thatch or, rarely, corrugated iron roofs. They sit on elevated dirt mounds, which raise them above the lower-lying paddy and offer some protection from the summer monsoon floods. Most homes are grouped into family-related compounds or *bari*s opening on a common courtyard. Most of the trees (banana, date and coconut palm, bamboo, etc.) are found in close proximity to these *baris*.

The cyclone area is divided administratively into villages, unions (2–20 villages), and *thanas* (2–20 unions).

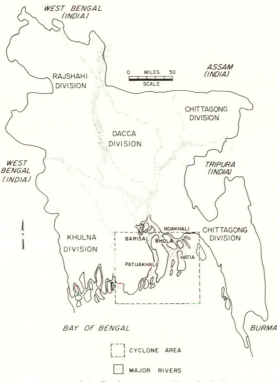

FIGURE 9.1. Cyclone Area, Bangladesh

THE CYCLONE

On the night of November 12–13, 1970, tragedy—in the form of a cyclone and massive tidal bore—struck this southern coastal region of Bangladesh (Figure 9.1). With the resulting disruption in communication, the devastation was for days not even suspected outside the disaster area. But within weeks the major airport in

Dacca and the docks of Chittagong and Narayanganj were awash with food, medicine, and international relief teams. To document the extent of the tragedy and to help define emergency relief needs and future requirements for rehabilitation, the Epidemiology Division of the Cholera Research Laboratory in Dacca conducted two medical assessments of the 2,000-square-mile affected area. In the first, carried out between November 24 and 28, 1970, four two-man teams visited 18 sites by helicopter, addressing themselves to the urgent questions of post-cyclone morbidity and incidence of epidemic diseases. The second more detailed survey, aimed at establishing baseline information for planning further relief and rehabilitation efforts, was carried out by ten two-man teams between February 10 and March 4, 1971; these teams studied 72 sites in the nine most affected *thana*s (Table 1), and 8 sites in a nonaffected control *thana* for comparison. A total of 3,500 families, representing 22,000 people or 1.4 per cent of the area's precyclone population (1.4 million in 1970) were studied.

FINDINGS

Cyclone Mortality

Villagers described the flooding in one of two ways, depending on their location: either as a gradual process increasing over hours until it reached a height of 8 to 20 feet, or as a sudden thunderous roar followed by a massive wall of water. Whichever the onset, the results were the same: huge numbers of deaths, all within the brief period of a single night. Where the water rose gradually, people scrambled on to roofs of their houses or scaled trees. But the houses frequently gave way, and only the strongest could maintain their grip on the wet and slippery tree trunks in the face of the 90-mile-per-hour winds. In areas where the tidal bore struck suddenly, there was even less hope of withstanding the force of the waves. After the water receded, those not washed out to sea were often found miles inland, caught in the branches of some distant tree.

The mortality was appalling. Almost 17 per cent of the population of the surveyed area, at least 225,000 people in all, were lost in the storm. This is far from the total. We had no accurate way

TABLE 1
Surveyed Unions
Map References Numbers

Ramgati Thana

1. Char Kalkini
2. Char Lawrence
3. Char Falcon
4. Char Jangalia
5. Char Kadira
6. Char Alexander
7. Char Abdulla
8. Char Algi
9. Char Ramiz
10. Barakheri
11. Char Gazi
12. Char Badama

Sudharam Thana

13. Char Jabbar
14. Char Bata

Tazumuddin Thana

15. Sonapur
16. Chandpur
17. Chanchra
18. Manpura

Lalmohan Thana

19. Bodarpur
20. Okalma
21. Dhali Gaurnagar
22. Char Lalmohan
23. Char Lord Hardinge

24. Char Bhuta
25. Char Umed

Char Fasson Thana

26. Osmanganj
27. Aslampur
28. Jinnagar
29. Char Madras
30. Hazarganj
31. Aminabad
32. Char Nilkamal
33. Char
34. Char Kalmi
35. Char Manika

Galachipa Thana

36. Rangobali
37. Bora Baisdia
38. Choto Baisdia
39. Char Kajal
40. Panpatti
41. Galachipa
42. Dakua
43. Ratandi Taltali
44. Rango Paldi
45. Chiknikandi
46. Bakulbaria
47. Alipur
48. Dasmina

49. Betagi Sankipura
50. Golekhali
51. Amkhola
52. Auliapur

Amtali Thana

53. Dankhali
54. Karaibaria
55. Bara Bagi

Kalapara Thana

56. Lata Chapli
57. Khaprabanga
58. Mithaganj
59. Nilganj
60. Tiakhali
61. Lalua
62. Chakamala

Hatiya Thana

63. Harni
64. Chanandi
65. Suk Char
66. Nalchira
67. Char King
68. Char Iswar
69. Char Tamoruddin
70. Sonadu
71. Burir Char
72. Jahajmara

Source: From Sommer and Mosley, 1972.

of estimating the losses among migrant workers, between 100,000 and 500,000 of whom had come south to help with the harvest, and all of whom slept in the low-lying fields without benefit of houses or trees.

Mortality varied considerably with geography. On such off-

shore islands as Char Hare and Sonar Char it reached 100 per
cent, and all that remained of large pre-cyclone settlements were
some trees and an occasional dirt mound. Among the *thana*s, mortality ranged from a low of 4.7 per cent in Amtali to a high of
46.3 per cent in Tazumuddin. Mortality is mapped by union in
Figure 9.2. The areas of highest mortality, lying along the coast of

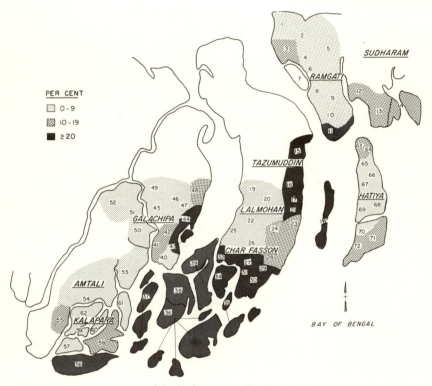

FIGURE 9.2. Cyclone Mortality by Unions

the Bay of Bengal and skirting Hatiya Island, probably indicate
the path of the tidal bore itself.

Age-specific mortality ranged from a high of 29.2 per cent for
those 0–4 years of age, and 20.7 per cent for those 70 years and
over, to a low of 6.1 per cent for those 35–39 years old. Females
fared worse than males in all but the youngest age groups. Adult

males between the ages of 15 and 49 had the highest rates of survival.

These findings confirmed our impression that it was those too young, too old, and too weak to hold on to the trees who were lost in the storm.

Post-cyclone Population Patterns

Post-cyclone morbidity was limited to lacerations, contusions, and occasional fractures. A common clinical finding, which we dubbed "cyclone syndrome," consisted of severe abrasions of the chest and medial aspects of the arms and thighs: grim evidence of the tenacity with which the survivors had clung to the trees to withstand the buffeting of the waves.

Post-cyclone mortality remained low for at least the three months immediately following the storm and compared favorably with that of the control area (0.5 per cent). The same was not true for migration patterns. Within the cyclone-affected region, we found large numbers of females in all age groups migrating into existing families. This probably represents remnants of family units that had lost their male heads seeking the security of kindred families—an example of the "extended families" function as the subcontinent's equivalent of Social Security.

Housing Losses

Fully 85 per cent of all families studied claimed that their homes had been severely damaged or destroyed by the cyclone, representing a loss of 176,121 houses (Figure 9.3). Objective measurements at the time of the second survey indicated that 53 per cent of all families in the cyclone region still lived in shelters deemed inadequate, even by Bengali standards, to withstand the summer monsoon rains. While the minimal amounts of bamboo distributed by the government were adequate for repairing the roof or sides of a house in the more northerly areas, they were wholly inadequate for rebuilding the entire structure, which was necessary in the more devastated coastal regions. The results were pathetic: tiny grass and straw huts, three or four feet wide and high and perhaps six feet long, each housing a family of two to eight persons.

FIGURE 9.3. A *Bari* Devastated by the Cyclone. The rice stalks hanging in the tree (upper right) indicate the height of the tidal wave.

Food Sources *

The villagers' private stores of rice were negligible. The cyclone had struck at the worst possible time, at the end of the traditional famine period when reserves were depleted and the new crop was ready for harvesting. The storm destroyed what little supplies still existed as well as most of the standing paddy. In the hardest hit areas, the tidal wave inundated the fields, destroying everything in its path. But even the more northerly regions were not spared; there we found the rice stalks standing tall and green when they should have been bending over under the weight of the grain. The latter, unfortunately, had been blown away by the 90-mile-per-hour winds that accompanied the storm.

* The results of the nutritional assessment conducted during these surveys are presented in the next chapter.

As a result of inadequate local food supplies, relief food was mandatory to avert starvation. By the time of the second survey, fully 75 per cent of the population were receiving free food on a regular basis, and 13.9 per cent (157,871 persons) were dependent on relief for more than half of their total food intake.

Agricultural Potential

While the land available for cultivation was three times larger on a per capita basis in the cyclone-affected region than in the control area, statistics on the land with newly planted rice at the time of the second survey were very different. Ranging from a low of 0 decimal (100 decimals equal 1 acre) in three *thana*s, Amtali, Hatiya, and Char Fasson, to a high of 2.12 in Lalmohan, the average for the cyclone-affected region as a whole was 0.48 decimal per survivor. This contrasts sharply with the 1.9 decimals per person planted with rice in the control area, a ratio of 1:4.

While many explanations were advanced by the villagers for this lack of cultivation, the most common was the lack of seeds, plows, and more important, bullocks and buffaloes. By comparing the total number of draft animals owned with the amount of land worked by each farmer, we derived area-wide ratios of bullocks and buffaloes available per 100 acres. This ranged from a low of 5.4 in Char Fasson to a high of 20.2 in Hatiya, with a mean of 12.8 for the cyclone area as a whole. This is approximately half the density of bullocks and buffaloes found in the control area, which stood at 25.1 per 100 acres.

Similar calculations indicated a mean density of 7.4 plows per 100 acres in the cyclone region, compared with 20.0 in the control area.

Relief and Rehabilitation

While it was impossible to assess the degree of rehabilitation achieved, since we lacked detailed data on the actual levels of destruction and dislocation at the time of the cyclone, it was clear that villagers in the less affected regions were busy reconstituting the fabric of their society. The same was not true in the more devastated coastal regions. There the men were usually found squatting despondently in the center of the village. They lacked all the implements basic to achieving self-sufficiency, and they had no money with which to buy them.

We attempted to gauge the amount and kind of relief received to date, but the effort was not overly successful. Except for money, amounts were either unquantifiable (bamboo, seed, etc.) or negligible (no one reported having received plows or draft animals). The major relief distributed, besides food, was in the form of *rupee* payments. Although these were dispensed for specific purposes (purchase of seed, building materials, etc.) they were in fact spent by the villagers for food. Among the 76 per cent of families who received some monetary relief, the average grant per family was 148 *rupees*.

RELIEF REQUIREMENTS

From the surveys, an estimation of relief and rehabilitation requirements for the entire cyclone-devastated region was made. These data, summarized in Table 2, represented an absolute minimum estimate of the area's needs.

1. Housing: 110,000 houses were needed to provide "adequate" shelter for over 500,000 people.
2. Food: almost 1,000,000 people were dependent on outside food relief for survival, although only 160,000 depended on relief for more than half their food at the time of the second survey.
3. Agriculture: to return the area to agricultural self-sufficiency, a minimum of 125,000 draft animals and 127,000 plows were needed.

These represented bare minimums—we did not survey the entire cyclone-affected region, only the hardest hit. While other areas may have been less affected, their total losses, because of their higher population base, may have been just as great. Yet with all this destruction and suffering, the impression that remained with us is of a determined and resilient people. Even as we prepared to return to Dacca after the survey, we encountered men setting out to establish themselves and their families on the

TABLE 2
Relief and Rehabilitation Requirements

	Houses Required	Persons Homeless	Persons On Food Relief	Persons Getting More Than ½ Their Food From Relief	Animals Required	Plows Required
Amtali (part)	5,210	26,050	29,918	5,507	25,093	25,730
Hatiya	16,710	85,221	102,030	5,051	6,576	12,750
Kalapara	9,789	52,861	78,535	11,162	12,660	13,375
Ramgati	9,798	60,748	97,548	5,366	4,020	7,112
Lalmohan	13,076	79,764	141,065	30,877	9,254	8,387
Galachipa	32,019	179,306	242,645	43,868	22,485	24,647
Sudharam (part)	2,497	13,734	26,856	12,556	8,445	6,678
Char Fasson	12,985	62,328	79,249	19,869	19,757	16,128
Tazumuddin	6,354	33,041	56,093	23,615	14,801	12,599
Total	108,438	593,053	853,939	157,871	123,091	127,406

Source: From Sommer and Mosley, 1972.

off-shore islands, the very same islands that only two months earlier had been swept, in one tragic night, of all signs of human habitation.

DISASTER SURVEYS AND SURVEILLANCE

While the international community has become increasingly involved in worldwide relief activities, too little attention has been given to the need for rapid, accurate assessment in support of such operations. Each new disaster is approached on an *ad hoc* theoretical basis, rather than a solid evaluation of actual conditions. As a result, huge amounts of money and effort are wasted on unnecessary activities. The Bangladesh cyclone and tidal bore is a recent example: a large number of countries and private relief organizations sent fully equipped field hospitals, including surgical teams, although there was little post-cyclone morbidity and almost no need of surgical care; emergency food supplies were often culturally unacceptable; medicines included large numbers of weight-reducing pills, birth control pills, and aspirin, the least appropriate items for a starving and homeless population; thousands of Bengalis were vaccinated against cholera when there was no indication of increased levels of cholera; and water-processing and storage facilities were erected to replace "saline-contaminated" sources which proved not to be contaminated after all. By documenting the absence of significant post-cyclone morbidity, the initial survey allowed the U.S. Government alone to save over $2 million earmarked for unnecessary field hospitals and to use that money for urgently needed clothing and shelter.

The cost of such surveys is insignificant (our detailed second survey cost under $10,000), nor do they delay relief operations appreciably (it took over two weeks for significant amounts of relief to arrive in Dacca; our initial survey took only four days).

When a disaster produces consequences necessitating relief activities that will last over months or years, as when there is an interruption in agricultural activities at planting or harvest time (Bangladesh cyclone disaster) or continuing civil strife (Biafra and Bangladesh), longitudinal surveillance is as important as the initial assessment. Only by closely monitoring indices of nutritional status, health, food availability, etc., can relief officials be certain that their efforts are being effective. All too often the various donor countries and their voluntary agencies are concerned with their small area of responsibility, to the neglect of the country at large (2). All too often, generalizations about the huge quantities of food donated obscure the fact that isolated communities or even whole regions with inadequate transportation facilities are not receiving their proportionate share, that selling cheap rice at ration shops does not benefit the penniless, that work relief projects do not aid the fatherless, and that feeding centers do not aid those too weak or sick to leave their huts (3). And the overemphasis on establishing sophisticated medical treatment centers at huge expense often benefits no one. The Nigerian experience showed that the people directly involved in providing relief are *least* capable of making such objective assessments.

With these considerations in mind, a three-phase survey and surveillance system can be used with great effectiveness for future disaster relief. The first phase would involve a rapid initial survey of randomly selected sites covering the entire disaster area. Such surveys can define the priority of relief materials (food, shelter, clothing, blankets, etc.) and identify outbreaks of communicable diseases and the physical extent of destruction. Information generated from the initial assessment can serve as guidelines for the first stage of relief activities. The logistical support for the survey should facilitate rapid evaluation. We used two helicopters and completed such a survey within four days. While a rapid survey may seem crude, we found that the first survey produced virtually the same results as the second more detailed assessment (4).

The second survey should be more detailed and more stringently structured. It should include an intensive study of sampling sites and should form the basis of a longitudinal surveillance system, which is the third phase. During the third phase selected families should be studied at regular intervals (one to two months). Data to be monitored should include births, deaths, illnesses, and status of housing, food stocks, and agricultural activities. Such an objective data-gathering system can provide a framework for future rehabilitation efforts and evaluate the adequacy of existing relief measures.

References

1. United States Agency for International Development. East Pakistan Civil Strife and Cyclone Victims, Disaster Relief Memo No. 4 (August 24, 1971).
2. Aall, C. Relief, Nutrition, and Health Problems in the Nigerian/Biafran War. *J. Trop. Peds.* 16:69–90, Monograph No. 2 (June 1970).
3. Woodham-Smith, C. *The Great Hunger,* Harper and Row, New York (1962).
4. Sommer, A., and Mosley, W. H. The East Bengal Cyclone of November 1970: Epidemiologic Approach to Disaster Assessment. *Lancet* 1:1029–1036 (1972).

(10) THE CYCLONE: NUTRITIONAL ASSESSMENT WITH THE QUAC STICK

Matthew S. Loewenstein

INTRODUCTION

There exists in much of the densely populated developing world a precarious balance between food supplies and requirements. In these areas large parts of the juvenile population are chronically malnourished, and even larger numbers of children are at borderline nutritional levels with only minimal caloric and/or protein reserve. Under such conditions, natural or manmade events disrupting the normal supply of food can quickly lead to large-scale epidemics of malnutrition. Two recent examples are the eastern region of Nigeria during and immediately following the Biafran rebellion and more recently Bangladesh.

The population of Bangladesh has been estimated at 75 million and that of Biafra as high as 15 million. Providing complete food rations to such populations is obviously far beyond the capacity of any relief organization now operating. It thus becomes imperative to utilize objective techniques for assigning geographic and often individual priorities to maximize the effectiveness of existing resources. If one considers food as medicine to treat the disease, malnutrition, then the problem of assigning priorities is resolved by the use of epidemiologic methods for determining disease severity and attack rates.

This chapter reviews one technique for conducting nutritional surveillance that has proved to be of great value, both in Nigeria

At the time of the cyclone, MATTHEW S. LOEWENSTEIN was a visiting epidemiologist with the Cholera Research Laboratory, Dacca, Bangladesh. After independence, the author returned to Bangladesh under the auspices of the United Nations to coordinate the Bangladesh National Health and Nutrition Survey.

and Bangladesh. The QUAC stick was first used during the Biafran crisis to classify individuals and groups according to nutritional status. The technique was also employed in Bangladesh following the cyclone of November 1970.

THE QUAC STICK METHOD

Objective evaluation of nutritional status is of crucial importance in assessing the current and long-term food needs of both individuals and populations. The use of clinical evaluation for this purpose has been criticized on the grounds that it is prey to observer subjectivity and does not lend itself to quantitation. Biochemical determinations have also been used but require relatively sophisticated laboratory support. For these reasons, nutritional epidemiologists have sought to develop simple, reproducible anthropometric measurements that can be used to locate those individuals requiring food supplementation (screening) as well as to characterize entire populations by reference to accepted "norms." Because children are most vulnerable to the effects of malnutrition, the development of anthropometric techniques has been aimed primarily at juvenile age groups.

Childhood growth prevents the use of a single anthropometric determinant. To evaluate nutritional status, one must make one measurement related to nutrition and compare it to another not related. The commonest comparison is weight (total body mass) to age. But accurate scales are necessary for direct weight measurements, and scales often break down under field conditions. Moreover, precise ages of children in developing regions of the world are frequently unobtainable. The QUAC stick was developed as a field alternative to weight-age ratios. This technique utilizes arm circumference (AC) and height as the dependent and independent variables, respectively. Arm circumference is an indirect determination of weight since the primary components of body mass (muscle and adipose tissue) are also the major constituents of arm bulk. Height is an acceptable alternative to age because it is only minimally affected by acute malnutrition; while it is true that linear growth is stunted by chronic food deprivation, it is still less affected than weight or AC.

Previous studies have shown that the AC-height ratio of the QUAC stick is a reliable indicator of nutritional status. A close correlation has been found between AC and weight for individuals and populations (Table 1) (7–10). Others have shown the close relationship between AC, clinical examination findings, and weight-height ratios as determinants of malnutrition (4,11). The use of AC-height ratios is advantageous because such determinations require only a trained observer and rudimentary non-breakable equipment: a tape measure and a measuring stick. The use of the QUAC stick also permits rapid nutritional evaluation of large numbers of individuals by non-professional personnel.

A schematic drawing of the QUAC stick designed for a rural Bengali population is shown in Figure 10.1. The QUAC stick is a

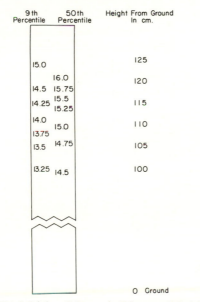

FIGURE 10.1. QUAC Stick—Schematic Diagram (Matlab Standards)

height-measuring rod on which is written at various height levels the specific AC found at any chosen percentile for that height. Its use is quite simple. Left mid-AC measurements are determined for children one to nine years of age. If a child's head reaches

TABLE 1

Studies Correlating Arm Circumference and Weight

Reference	Country	Location or Ethnic Group	No. Studied	Age (months)	Measurement	Coefficient of Correlation
(1)	Egypt				AC vs. Wt as Per Cent Normal	.59
(2)	Uganda	Bantu	55	13–36	AC vs. Wt/Ht	.67–.75
	Uganda	Nilotic	77	13–48	AC vs. Wt/Ht	.55–.79
	Uganda	Nilohamitic	191	13–48	AC vs. Wt/Ht	.70–.76
(3)	Uganda	Ankole	282	12–59	AC/Age vs. Wt/Age	.68–.78
(4)	Uganda	Busoga	156	25–33	AC vs. Wt	.79
(5)	Lebanon	Arab	1,049	3–48	AC vs. Wt	.79
(6)	Malaysia	Ulu Trengganu	183	17–48	AC vs. Wt	.60–.79

Source: From Lowenstein, 1973.

above the point on the stick where his AC measurement is written, then, in a sense, he is too tall for his arm: or, alternatively, his arm is too thin for his height. In actual practice, two scales representing different percentiles of malnutrition are employed, permitting immediate assignment to one of three percentile ranges. These may be designed to represent normal nutrition and mild or severe malnutrition.

Standards for these three categories of nutrition can be obtained from measurements of a control population. For the cyclone, measurements were conducted in a nearby, non-cyclone-devastated region. The QUAC stick permits the nutritionist: (a) to assign percentages of population to various degrees of malnutrition, (b) to rapidly screen for individuals requiring nutritional rehabilitation, (c) to identify geographic regions of nutritional need, and (d) to follow the nutritional status of populations longitudinally with time.

NIGERIAN WAR EXPERIENCE

The QUAC stick was developed by the Quaker Service Committee during the Nigerian civil war as a means of rapidly assigning individuals to specific nutritional categories (12). Since no "normal" AC standards for Eastern Nigerian children were available, the Wolanski mean AC-age data for Polish children was combined with Morley's height-age tables for Western Nigerian children to produce a new AC-height standard (13, 14). Arnhold found that the 85 per cent level of the newly defined AC-height standard agreed well with clinical separation between normal and all degrees of malnutrition (12). During the early stages of the war, Arnhold also successfully used the QUAC stick for village surveys and individual screenings. Davis surveyed 60 villages and found an excellent correlation between QUAC-stick-defined malnutrition rates and proximity to the war front (15).

The rapid collapse of Biafran forces and the subsequent surrender of the rebel government early in 1970 suddenly presented the Nigerian Red Cross with the task of providing immediate relief to millions of additional needy persons. The QUAC stick was then used to rapidly gather nutritional data in order to direct the very limited relief supplies to areas of greatest need. Within a six-day period, QUAC stick determinations were made on 200 children in each of 15 randomly selected villages. Village children were placed in a line and the first and last 100 were measured. No difference was noted between children at the beginning of the line as compared to those at the end. The entire process required less than one and a half hours per village.

Once geographical priorities were established, all children 1 to 9 years of age in certain areas were screened to identify those in need of special food rations or hospitalization. Nutritional scouts were appointed in each village. They were taught how to use the QUAC stick and asked to screen out those measuring less than 75 per cent of the QUAC stick standard. These selected children were individually examined by relief personnel and were either discharged, given a ration card entitling them to daily food supplements, or hospitalized in nutrition treatment centers. Within several weeks, an estimated 100,000 children were screened.

Finally, the QUAC stick was also employed to reassess the field situation to determine periodically the effectiveness of on-going relief programs. Initial and two-month follow-up data from villages are presented in Table 2. This shows that the level of severe malnutrition (QUAC stick less than 80 per cent) declined more than total malnutrition (QUAC stick less than 85 per cent). This was interpreted as demonstrating that the in- and out-patient programs for the severely malnourished were relatively more effective than the general food distribution aimed at all levels of malnutrition.

POST-CYCLONE EXPERIENCE

On the night of November 12, 1970, a massive cyclone and tidal wave devastated the southern coastal region of Bangladesh. An initial, rapid survey assessed the extent of damage to life and property and documented the absence of epidemics of communicable diseases.[1] Widespread loss of crops and food stocks brought fears of a major famine since the affected population was known to be

1. The methodology and results of the initial and second surveys are presented in the preceding chapter.

marginally nourished even during normal times. It was, therefore, decided to include nutritional assessment in the more detailed and comprehensive second survey conducted in February 1971. Since the QUAC stick had been so successful in Nigeria, it was used to assess the nutritional status of children residing in various parts of the cyclone-devastated region.

TABLE 2

Nigerian Towns QUAC Stick Surveyed
in January and March 1970

| Towns | QUAC Stick | | Edema Per Cent | Month of Survey |
	85 Per Cent	80 Per Cent		
Ubomiri, Egbeada Kindred	76	66	14	Jan.
	65	43	15	March
Ifakala	65	34	9	Jan.
	51	28	4	March
Amuburu (Orodo)	66	44	11	Jan.
	59	32	10	March
Mbieri	63	41	10	Jan.
	43	33	7	March
Ogwa	56	37	12	Jan.
	50	30	7	March

Source: From Lowenstein, 1973.

In preparation for this study, standards for rural Bengali children (newborn to age 9 years) were derived by measuring the AC and height of approximately 10,000 children living in Matlab Thana. Matlab Thana was chosen because it is the site of the cholera vaccine field trials. Years of surveillance by the Cholera Research Laboratory in Matlab provided accurate age data for all children up to 5 years old and close age estimates for older children. Two percentiles of AC to height were derived from the Matlab measurements. The fiftieth percentile (median) was chosen as the borderline between normal and all degrees of malnutrition. This percentile was chosen because it corresponded to about the second percentile for Western children and since shifts from it can best characterize changes in the population as a whole. The fiftieth percentile in Matlab corresponds to 84 per cent (not percentile) of the mean AC-age ratio of Western societies. A value of 75 per cent of the mean AC-age is virtually never encountered in Western countries and is considered by some as indicative of severe malnutrition. This level corresponded to the ninth percentile among Matlab children. Therefore, the ninth percentile of AC-height was chosen as the borderline between moderate to severe malnutrition. These standards are shown in Table 3.

These standards were used in February 1971, when nearly 13,000 children living in the cyclone-devastated region were surveyed with the QUAC stick. Over 2,000 children in Gazaria, a non-devastated area near the cyclone region, were studied as controls. The results from these studies are shown in Table 4. The most striking result is the better showing of the cyclone and Gazaria regions as compared to Matlab. Approximately 60 per cent of children from the cyclone and Gazaria regions were considered normally nourished as compared to 50 per cent of those residing in Matlab. Furthermore, the percentage of moderately or severely malnourished children in the cyclone and Gazaria regions was significantly lower than the percentage of malnourished in Matlab. There were no differences in the nutritional status of children who survived the cyclone as compared to those who lived in an adjacent, but non-cyclone-affected, region (Gazaria).

There seem to be two main reasons for the surprisingly better showing of children in the cyclone area as compared to those in Matlab. First, the cyclone-devastated region is a fertile, rice-surplus region with lower population densities. Thus, during normal times, one might expect children living in these regions to be better nourished than their Matlab counterparts. Second, there may have been a higher mortality rate among the weaker or more sickly malnourished children trapped in the path of the cyclone. Those who survived may have been the healthiest and fittest. It is unlikely that these differences are due to genetic variation between these populations. The deltaic plain of Bangladesh contains a relatively homogeneous population ethnically. Moreover, AC measurements obtained from school children of well-to-do families in Dacca, the capital, were only slightly lower than those of Western

TABLE 3
Measurements for QUAC Stick Construction
Based on "Normal" Levels for Rural Bangladesh

Scale A–50th Percentile[a]		Scale B–9th Percentile[b]	
Height	Arm Circumference	Height	Arm Circumference
62.0	12.5	63.0	11.0
65.0	12.75	65.0	11.25
68.0	13.00	68.0	11.50
71.5	13.25	71.0	11.75
75.0	13.50	74.0	12.00
79.5	13.75	77.5	12.25
85.0	14.00	82.0	12.50
91.5	14.25	85.0	12.75
100.0	14.50	94.0	13.00
107.0	14.75	101.0	13.25
110.0	15.00	105.0	13.50
114.0	15.25	108.5	13.75
116.0	15.50	112.0	14.00
118.5	15.75	115.5	14.25
121.0	16.00	118.5	14.50
123.5	16.25	121.5	14.75
126.0	16.50	124.0	15.00
128.5	16.75	127.0	15.25
130.0	17.00	129.0	15.50
132.5	17.25		15.75
			16.00

a. Children below the 50th percentile were classified moderately malnourished. This corresponds with the 2nd percentile among Western children.
b. Children below the 9th percentile were classified severely malnourished. This level is virtually never observed among Western children.

children. This seems to eliminate the possibility that genetic differences may have been responsible for the high malnutrition rates found in Matlab.

TABLE 4

QUAC Stick Assessment in Cyclone
and Other Regions

Thana (cyclone)	Children Measured	Normal Nutrition	Nutritional Status[a] (Per Cent)	
			Moderately Malnourished	Severely Malnourished
Amtali (part)	623	59.6	33.1	7.4
Hatiya	1,948	65.2	30.8	4.0
Kalapara	1,205	63.7	31.9	4.4
Ramgati	3,043	52.1	41.1	6.8
Lalmohan	769	59.4	33.6	7.0
Galachipa	3,267	60.9	34.3	4.7
Sudharam (part)	497	59.4	34.0	6.6
Char Fasson	1,227	60.0	36.8	3.3
Tazumuddin	—	—	—	—
Total	12,579	60.0	34.5	5.5
Gazaria (control)	2,134	60.3	33.0	6.7
Matlab	10,000	50.0	41.0	9.0

Source: From Sommer and Mosley, 1972.

a. 84 per cent of European standard for arm circumference ("normal"), 75–83 per cent ("moderately malnourished"), 75 per cent ("severely malnourished").

CONCLUSION

The civil war which erupted in March 1971 precluded extending of the QUAC stick assessment into a longitudinal nutritional evaluation mechanism. If it were not for this, geographic trends could have been followed and would have been extremely useful for the direction of food supplies. For critical regions, individual screening of children by the QUAC stick would have permitted identification of those in need of special nutritional consideration, either extra rations or hospital care.

Surveillance based on sound epidemiologic principles holds great promise for increasing the efficiency and effectiveness of all relief operations. Nutritional surveillance requires simple and reliable means of obtaining objective data for assessing individuals and populations. The QUAC stick has proven to be such a method, and its usefulness has been demonstrated in both Nigeria and Bangladesh. It promises to be a useful tool for future nutritional relief programs following disasters.

References

1. El Lozy, M. A Modification of Wolanski's Standards for the Arm Circumference. *J. Trop. Peds.* 15:193 (1969).
2. Ruithauser, I. H. E. Correlations of the Circumference of the Mid-Upper Arm with Weight and Weight-for-Height in Three Groups in Uganda. *J. Trop. Peds.* 15:196 (1969).
3. Cook, R. The Arm Circumference in a Field Survey in Ankole, Uganda. *J. Trop. Peds.* 15:198 (1969).
4. Robinow, M., and Jelliffe, D. B. The Use of Arm Circumference in a Field Survey of Early Childhood Malnutrition in Busoga, Uganda. *J. Trop. Peds.* 15:217 (1969).
5. Kanwati, A. A., Hadded, N., and McLaren, D. S. Preliminary Results with Mid-Arm and Mid-Arm Muscle Circumference Used as Nutritional Screening Procedures for Pre-school Children in Lebanon. *J. Trop. Peds.* 15:233 (1969).
6. McKay, D. A. Experience with the Mid-Arm Circumference as a Nutritional Indicator in Field Surveys in Malaysia. *J. Trop. Peds.* 15:213 (1969).
7. Blankhart, D. M. Experience in Sierra Leone and Zambia. *J. Trop. Peds.* 15:205 (1969).
8. Young, H. B. Arm Measurements as Indicators of Body Composition in Tunisian Children. *J. Trop. Peds.* 15:222 (1969).
9. Dodge, W. F., and West, E. F. Arm Circumference in School Children. *Lancet* 1:417 (1970).

10. Choovivanthanavanich, P., and Kanthavichitra, N. Arm Circumference in Children. *Lancet* 1:44 (1970).

11. Beghin, I. D. The Arm Circumference as a Public Health Index of Protein-Calorie Malnutrition of Early Childhood. *J. Trop. Peds.* 15:248 (1969).

12. Arnhold, R. The QUAC Stick: A Field Measure Used by the Quaker Service Team, Nigeria. *J. Trop. Peds.* 15:243 (1969).

13. Jelliffe, D. B. *The Assessment of the Nutritional Status of the Community.* World Health Organization Monograph Series No. 53, World Health Organization, Geneva, 1966, p. 228.

14. Morley, D. C., Woodland, M., Martin, W. J., and Allen, I. Height and Weight of West African Village Children from Birth to the Age of Five. *West Afr. Med. J.* 17:8 (1968).

15. Davis, L. E. Epidemiology of Famine in the Nigerian Crisis: Rapid Evaluation of Malnutrition by Height and Arm Circumference in Large Populations. *Am. J. Clin. Nutr.* 24:358 (1971).

16. Sommer, A., and Mosley, W. H. The East Bengal Cyclone of November 1970: Epidemiologic Approach to Disaster Assessment. *Lancet* 1:1029 (1972).

17. Loewenstein, M. S. Evaluation of Arm Circumference Measurement for Determining Nutritional Status of Children and Its Use in An Acute Epidemic of Malnutrition: Owerri, Nigeria, Following the Fall of Biafra. *Am. J. Clin. Nutrition,* in press, 1973.

(11) REFUGEES IN
INDIA: HEALTH PRIORITIES

Jon E. Rohde Lincoln C. Chen, and Pierce Gardner

INTRODUCTION

The Bangladesh crisis of 1971 stands as one of the greatest human tragedies of this century. In March of that year, a civil war erupted in East Bengal and as the hostilities escalated, millions of Bangladesh refugees fled from their homes into neighboring India. Most of these refugees were entirely dependent upon the Government of India for survival. Despite the energetic and capable relief efforts of the Indian Government, overcrowding, inadequate shelter, poor sanitation, and shortage of food created immense health problems.

This chapter reviews the refugee migration and describes selected aspects of refugee camp conditions which were hazardous to health. It also analyzes the significance of various medical survey and surveillance techniques that were employed to define the magnitude and nature of the health crisis. Finally, a few critical health problems are examined retrospectively to emphasize the importance of utilizing existing knowledge in the implementation of health programs under emergency situations, such as those found in the refugee camps.

REFUGEE INFLUX AND CAMPS

Every aspect of the refugee health problem was profoundly affected by the magnitude of the migration. Over a nine-month pe-

JON E. ROHDE'S and PIERCE GARDNER'S work in the refugee camps was sponsored by the International Rescue Committee and Oxfam-Canada. The authors are grateful to the Ministry of Relief and Rehabilitation, Government of India, for its cooperation during their studies.

riod, 10 million refugees from Bangladesh poured across the northeast frontier of India (1). The average daily influx was approximately 36,000 persons and during the peak flow months of May and June the migration rate often exceeded 100,000 daily (Figures 11.1 and 11.2). In the month of May alone, there were nearly 3 million new arrivals.

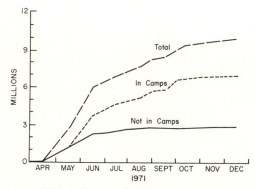

FIGURE 11.1. Refugee Influx into India During 1971

The Indian Government rapidly mobilized its administration and resources, and a relief operation was organized under its Ministry of Relief and Rehabilitation. At most border crossings, attempts were made to inoculate all refugees against cholera; most were also vaccinated against smallpox. Inoculation certificates enabled the refugees to acquire family ration cards which were used for record keeping and to determine relief allocations.

Initially most refugees fended for themselves or moved in with relatives (Figure 11.3), but the influx soon exceeded the absorptive capacity of the local society. Nearly all of those who arrived after mid-May (over 6 million) were settled into hastily constructed camps. By December, approximately 1,200 makeshift camps were operating along the 1,350 mile India-Bangladesh border.

The camps varied in size from 5,000 to 200,000 inhabitants. Conditions within individual camps depended to a large extent on their size, location, administration, and supplementary input (2,3).

FIGURE 11.2. Bullock Cart Transporting Entire Family Fleeing Bangladesh Near Bagdha, India, a Border Reception Point for Refugees (courtesy of UNICEF)

Rudimentary shelters were erected: small grass huts, tents, and huge bamboo sheds with tarpaulin or plastic sheet roofing that housed 250 to 300 people (Figure 11.4). Crowding was intense. Although most refugees had a roof over their heads, few slept on more than a few square feet of mud (Figure 11.5). In June the monsoon arrived, flooding many camps which were pitched on low pasture land. Exposure to the elements compounded with over-crowding greatly endangered the health of the refugees.

Sanitation was the most hazardous environmental condition. Bengali villagers traditionally use the open fields to absorb human wastes and have little concept of public sanitation in crowded situations. Latrines, where constructed, were often improperly used or they overflowed. Placed in low drainage areas, many were inundated by the monsoon floods. A crash tube-well program provided potable water to some camps; the number of wells was small, however, and all too often pumps broke down. Many wells were

FIGURE 11.4. A Refugee Camp in West Bengal (courtesy of the International Rescue Committee)

shallow and lacked concrete aprons permitting easy contamination. Poor sanitation and contaminated water contributed significantly to the spread of enteric diseases.

A standard food ration was allotted to each refugee (4). This consisted of 400 gms of rice, 100 gms of pulses, 30 gms of oil, and occasional vegetables and small quantities of salt. Children under eight years of age were given half-portions. It was indeed remarkable that throughout the crisis the daily rice ration (or wheat equivalent) was usually received by all refugees. Full quotas of pulses, oil, and vegetables, however, were rarely distributed because of shortage of supplies. Furthermore, deeply ingrained social customs often diverted food from women and children to adult men. Had each child actually consumed his allotted

FIGURE 11.3. With only an umbrella and straw-mat for shelter, a refugee family rests at a roadside on the Indian side of the frontier (courtesy of UNICEF).

FIGURE 11.5. Refugee Women and Children in a Shelter with Plastic Sheet Roofing. Overcrowding posed a major threat to health by permitting infectious diseases to spread more readily (courtesy of the International Rescue Committee).

ration of rice and pulses, it seems unlikely that the epidemic of protein-calorie malnutrition (PCM) would have been as severe.

HEALTH SURVEYS

In addition to inadequate food intake, the environmental hazards of poor sanitation, overcrowding, and exposure resulted in epidemics of malnutrition and communicable diseases. The nature and character of the health difficulties that prevailed were not unfamiliar to Bengal, where nutritional deficiencies and infectious diseases are endemic. The stress of the disaster, however, exacerbated the state of chronic poor health and precipitated a major health crisis.

Regardless of the nature or dimension of a health crisis, it has been demonstrated that an initial, accurate, and reliable field assessment can establish relief priorities and avoid costly and time-consuming errors.[1] Possession of sound statistical information on the character of the problems currently affecting a disaster-ridden

1. See Chapter 9.

population is an important step toward adequately meeting their needs. Surveys help to direct scarce resources to relevant health problems and to geographical regions where they are needed most. They can define and quantitate existing problems, can detect emergence of new diseases, and can establish priorities for optimal utilization of existing resources.

Eyewitness Impressions

The simplest type of survey, the eyewitness impression, was frequently and dramatically reported by journalists in the world press (5–7). Although these reporters were unacquainted with clinical diagnosis and treatment, the exposure of the public to news accounts of the catastrophe served an important function; they focused the attention of the world on the crisis that engulfed 10 million destitute people. These reports helped to stimulate concern among the general public and was responsible in part for the many donations from private groups and governments to the refugees.

A similar impact followed the visit and report of Dr. Nevin Scrimshaw, a nutrition expert who visited the camps in August as a consultant to the U.S. Senate Subcommittee for Refugees. Dr. Scrimshaw confirmed the alarming reports of malnutrition and infectious disease. His moving testimony to the Subcommittee in September (8) prompted a more rapid and substantial monetary response on the part of the U.S. Government to assist with refugee relief programs.

In August, Dr. F. Loven, World Health Organization (WHO) Representative in India, and Dr. C. V. Foll, WHO Regional Advisor of Communicable Diseases, visited a large number of refugee camps in southern West Bengal. Their report to WHO enumerated in detail the deplorable health conditions in the camps (9). They concluded: "It is difficult to see how much more can be done by WHO to relieve the present miserable situation nor for that matter is any solution envisaged. It may be summed up as human misery on an enormous scale." Its lack of constructive proposals was a disappointing contribution from an organization in a position of worldwide health leadership.

The Nutrition Survey

The nutrition survey conducted by Dr. V. Ramalingaswami and Dr. B. N. Tandon of the All India Institute of Medical Sciences was the first major attempt to quantitatively determine the prevalence of malnutrition in the refugee population (10). Utilizing pre-established clinical criteria and anthropometric standards, they studied the nutritional status of 800 children from 13 representative refugee camps in West Bengal. Their findings concluded that one-fifth of all children under 5 years of age were critically malnourished and nearly 50 per cent of children in this age group were suffering from moderate or severe PCM (Figure 11.6 and 11.7). While readily stating that the population surveyed was small and perhaps not statistically representative, they concluded that their results provided a "rough approximation" of the magnitude of the nutrition problem. This survey, therefore, identified a health problem, measured its severity, recognized its own methodological limitations, and provided the first step in the formulation and implementation of a practical program to contain and treat malnutrition.

A direct outgrowth of this survey was Operation Lifeline. The program called for the following:

1. Establishment of 1,000 large-scale milk-feeding stations for all infants and children under age 8, mainly as a measure for preventing further deterioration of nutritional status (code name, Lifeline Alpha). As rapidly as facilities, supplies, and personnel would permit, this program was to be extended to include all children under the age of 14 years as well as pregnant and lactating women.

2. Establishment of 500 nutrition therapy centers for all children under the age of 5 who exhibit signs of moderate and severe PCM (code name, Lifeline Beta). An extension of the survey data projected that 115,000 refugee children required intensive nutritional therapy.

FIGURE 11.6. A Refugee Child Showing the Ravages of Severe Malnutrition (courtesy of UNICEF)

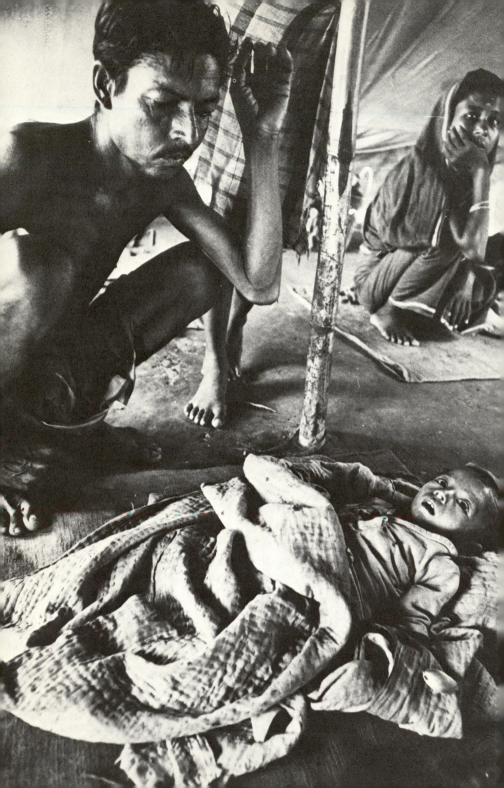

The strengths of the Lifeline programs lay not only in their statistical reliability, but also on their thoroughness, practicality, and applicability. Requirements for high-protein vegetable mixtures and milk were projected; the logistics of transport and distribution were formulated; staffing of the nutritional therapy centers was standardized; locations of the centers were chosen; and even the recipes and feeding schedules for each program were carefully spelled out to streamline operations. The proposal also strongly recommended the formation of a full-time, powerful Coordination and Policy Committee for Nutrition Relief with an able administrator. Part of the Committee's activities was to independently evaluate the performance of the program based on objective assessment of the nutritional situation in the field. These features of firm guidelines, strong coordination, and self-analysis completed the essential components of a unique and pragmatic nutrition program.

Broad-Spectrum Medical Surveys

A systematic survey of a broad-spectrum of medical problems in a randomly selected refugee population was conducted by two of the authors in October at Barasat Camp near Calcutta (11). Ninety-four families (453 people) were studied to determine the extent and severity of medical problems among the refugees. The selection process was randomized by listing all families whose ration-card numbers ended in two or seven. Educated Bengalis conducted the interviews, and the authors performed the physical examination. Anthropometric measurements included height, weight, and left-arm circumference.

From medical histories, it was clear that diarrheal diseases constituted the largest single health problem, accounting for almost half of all medical complaints. They were also the commonest cause of death. The mortality rate among the refugee population is not known. Fearing loss of rations, families often failed to report

FIGURE 11.7. At Ahespur Camp, some 70 kilometers from Calcutta, parents keep a watch over their son dying from malnutrition and diarrheal disease (courtesy of UNICEF).

household deaths to the authorities. The random survey at Barasat Camp, however, revealed 25 deaths in 94 families interviewed (Table 1). Diarrhea accounted for two-thirds of the mortalities, with trauma and measles responsible for most of the others. The young and elderly were at highest risk (12).

TABLE 1

Causes and Age of Death of Immediate Household Members among 94 Refugee Families at Barasat Camp (March 25–October 15, 1971)

| Causes of Death | Age Groups (years) | | | |
	0–15	16–49	50	All Ages
Diarrhea	11	1	5	17
Measles	2	0	0	2
Malnutrition[a]	1	0	1	2
Trauma[b]	0	3	1	4
Others	1	0	1	2
Total	15	4	8	27

a. The two victims who died of malnutrition are recorded twice. One died of malnutrition and measles and the second died of malnutrition and dysentery.
b. Traumatic deaths occurred prior to arrival in India.

Physical examination demonstrated a high prevalence of malnutrition, vitamin A deficiency, skin diseases, anemia, and positive tuberculin skin tests (Table 2). Moderate and severe malnutrition affected nearly 20 per cent of all children under 5 years of age. Approximately one-fifth of children under 10 years suffered from vitamin A deficiency. Anemia was common, being more prevalent and more severe in females than males. Nearly 25 per cent of the refugee population suffered from scabies, often complicated by pyoderma.

The data generated by this survey were extremely helpful in facilitating realistic and effective programs aimed at the most common medical problems. The finding of the high prevalence of vitamin A deficiency provided the stimulus for a program of large-dose vitamin A replacement that eventually reached 300,000

children in less than one month. Antituberculous drugs were
added to dispensary medical supplies in response to frequent diagnosis of active tuberculosis. A BCG vaccination program for children below age 16 was recommended to the authorities. Similarly,
more benzyl benzoate and long-acting penicillin were sent to the
dispensaries to combat scabies.

TABLE 2
Prevalence of Certain Physical
Findings by Age

	Proportion (Per Cent) at Following Ages (years)				
Findings	<1 (12)[a]	1–5 (50)	5–10 (92)	11–15 (72)	Adults (15) (227)
Malnutrition					
(mod. & sev. wasting)	17	20	12	3	5
Vitamin A Deficiency	8	20	23	14	0[b]
Anemia					
Moderate	50	56	42	42	52[c]
Severe	8	4	1	3	6
Skin Diseases					
(Scabies and/or					
pyoderma)	20	37	20	19	14
Tuberculin Skin Test[d]					
≥ 10 mm induration	0	2	21	31	not tested
Vaccination Scars					
(smallpox)	33	72	88	97	100

Source: From Gardner, Rohde, and Majumdar, 1972.
a. absolute number in each age group examined
b. one patient
c. In adults, anemia was more prevalent and more severe in females than
males. Prevalence: 71 per cent in females and 54 per cent in males; severe anemia 9 per cent in females and 3 per cent in males.
d. five units old tuberculin intradermally

Findings similar to those reported for Barasat Camp were published by Dr. John Seaman who conducted a house-to-house survey of Salt Lake Camp in West Bengal (13). He estimated a total
mortality of not less than 4,000—mostly infants and children—

among 170,000 refugees from March 1971 to February 1972. This represented an annual mortality rate of 23.5 per 1,000 population, which is 38 per cent higher than the death rate normally experienced by this population. From a review of records of 2,607 admissions to the camp hospital, he concluded that "most deaths were due to intestinal infections precipitating and complicating protein-calorie malnutrition."

Barasat and Salt Lake Camps had comparable facilities; their inhabitants were rural Bengalis, and the problems uncovered were similar to those reported by medical observers in other camps. Their close proximity to Calcutta, the focal point of relief operations and source of relief supplies, may have resulted in somewhat better conditions than in less accessible camps. Therefore, these surveys, if at all unrepresentative, tended to underreport the prevalence of these health problems rather than overemphasize them. Ideally, surveys with standardized criteria, should have covered several camps in each of the many border regions. In the absence of other studies, however, extrapolation of these findings provided the best approximation of the nature and magnitude of the health problems affecting the 10 million refugees.

HEALTH SURVEILLANCE

The effectiveness of surveys can be strengthened by accurate and reliable field surveillance of health conditions as they evolve with time. With continuous monitoring, health trends can be identified, facilitating any necessary adjustments of the relief effort. Moreover, ongoing surveillance can act as an evaluation mechanism to determine the effectiveness of health programs that may vary considerably in performance. In the refugee crisis, health surveillance never developed or matured due to the interruption of war and the subsequent return of the refugees to Bangladesh. However, several surveillance techniques were proposed and experimentally initiated.

Individual camps because of their disparate population, location, accessibility, administration, and supplementary inputs, presented different degrees of urgency with regard to food supplies. For the central relief administrator, the problem was to identify priority camps where nutritional state was becoming particularly precarious. One proposed nutritional surveillance technique was to monitor the nutritional status of camps by performing QUAC stick measurements on randomly selected children within each camp at regular intervals.[2] Because children are the most nutritionally vulnerable group, an increase in the number of children with a significantly low AC-height ratio would indicate inadequate food intake. Such information would alert authorities to the necessity of supplementary food supplies and a review of existing practices in the allocation of food. With many children attending some form of daily supplemental food program, random selection of children could be accomplished easily, and relocation of the same subjects at regular intervals would have also presented no problem. Comparison of QUAC stick data from individual camps would have provided a sensitive index of the nutritional trend within each camp. The technique would have provided the Nutrition Coordination Committee with valuable information in the allocation of supplemental food supplies to geographical regions of greatest need.

Although, in theory, surveillance generates accurate data; in reality, it suffers from incomplete reporting, observer variation, and poor standardization of diagnostic criteria. A physician tending to the health needs of over 200 patients daily in a rudimentary dispensary is in a poor position to diagnose accurately and to report promptly. While three clinicians may agree on a diagnosis of scabies in a given case, the same physicians may assign the diagnoses of bronchitis, pneumonia, and tuberculosis to a patient with severe cough. Similarly, a patient with diarrhea could be classified as amoebic, bacillary, or non-specific dysentery. In a three-month period, for example, the physician at Kalyani Camp-Four reported treating 641 cases of bacillary dysentery and none due to amoebae: while his colleague in Camp-Five treated no bacillary but 765 cases of amoebic dysentery over the same time period (Rohde, personal documents).

One of the authors therefore, made an effort to standardize the criteria used to arrive at a presumptive diagnosis and to facilitate

2. See Chapter 10.

regular reporting. The diseases to be reported on surveillance forms used by Oxfam, International Rescue Committee, and Caritas in more than one hundred dispensaries are listed in Table 3. The standard daily record which was submitted every two weeks provided a common format for reporting. Diagnostic criteria were standardized on an accompanying instruction sheet. While not necessarily increasing the accuracy of a diagnosis, standardization of diagnostic criteria provided a basis to measure progress or regression of disease control. It also served to focus attention on the significant, life-threatening illnesses.

TABLE 3
Diseases Under Surveillance in Over
100 Refugee Camp Dispensaries

1. amoebic dysentery	13. malaria
2. bacillary dysentery	14. undiagnosed fever
3. diarrhea	15. scabies
4. cholera	16. pyoderma, abcess
5. typhoid fever	17. measles
6. worms	18. malnutrition
7. other GI diseases	19. vitamin A deficiency
8. smallpox	20. anemia
9. influenza cold	21. eye/ear diseases
10. bronchitis	22. maternity related diseases
11. pneumonia	23. others
12. tuberculosis	

This system never fully matured because of the rapid resolution of the refugee crisis. However, it was hoped that such a system would provide continuing information with regard to the changing character of the health needs, their geographical distribution, and the impact of various health programs.

UTILIZATION OF EXISTING KNOWLEDGE
There may be circumstances under which field assessment is difficult to implement because of geographical, financial, or political

considerations. Under such conditions, the health planner need not operate in a vacuum. A vast reservoir of medical information is generally available about many regions struck by disasters. Utilization of available information can provide the planner with a framework for the direction of early health efforts. It can help with difficult decisions such as: What type of supplies and personnel are required? Should resources be directed at general public health measures or specific disease control programs? Is the preventive or curative approach more efficient?

Prevention of disease is usually more effective and cheaper than treatment; lives are saved; suffering is averted; scarce professional manpower is spared; and costly equipment, drugs, and facilities can be diverted to other priorities. Many preventable diseases are infectious in nature, and vaccines may be available. An example is smallpox vaccine, which provides nearly total protection for several years and is capable of interrupting an epidemic in progress.

Smallpox

It is known that smallpox in Bengal has appeared in approximately five-year cycles. The last major epidemic occurred in 1967 and 1968, making 1972 a likely year for resurgence. With the juxtaposition of overcrowding and favorable timing, the official Indian policy of vaccinating as many refugees as possible against smallpox at border crossings was a judicious approach. Vaccination scar surveys done in 1970 in pre-war Bangladesh showed rates of 50 to 80 per cent.[3] The 94 per cent prevalence of scars in Barasat Camp (Table 2) reflects the relative success of the vaccination program for the refugees. Despite the high over-all protection rate, the existence of certain subgroups such as children who had low prevalence of scars, allowed smallpox to break out among the refugees in four camps in December 1971. Because effective quarantine was not instituted, a significant outbreak ensued.

Cholera

Cholera control presented an entirely different problem. In West Bengal, the incidence of cholera has followed a seasonal pattern

3. See Chapter 15.

for generations, peaking in the months of April, May, and June.[4] The Indian Government program of inoculating all incoming refugees against cholera at border stations along with assignment of ration cards was a reasonable effort based on this epidemiologic pattern. In part due to the ineffectiveness of the vaccine, a cholera epidemic struck the refugee camps in late spring, leaving an estimated 10,000 deaths and three times that number with debilitating diarrhea. Many governments, international organizations, and voluntary agencies rushed cholera vaccine to India, and the immunization program was intensified. The U.S. Government, for example, flew more than 1 million doses of cholera vaccine to the refugees in June and July (14). When the epidemic subsided in mid-summer, many groups were quick to claim credit for the containment of cholera.

The decline of cholera was probably due more to its seasonal pattern than to immunization. It has been shown that the yearly incidence of cholera in Bengal, an endemic region, is approximately three cases per thousand. Thus, among 10 million refugees, one could expect approximately 30,000 cases. Furthermore, it is generally accepted that cholera vaccine provides protection to only 50 to 70 per cent of those inoculated, and then for only a few months. In addition, to be effective, the vaccine must be given weeks before the appearance of the first cases. Protection cannot be expected by massive immunization after the initial cases of an outbreak are reported. It would, therefore, appear that the second phase of intensified cholera vaccination during the outbreak had little impact on the magnitude or course of the epidemic.

It has been demonstrated that cholera treatment with oral solutions is more effective and cheaper than vaccination at preventing morbidity and mortality from cholera. Proper utilization of this knowledge would have permitted the planner to concentrate energy and resources toward curative services for cholera and other diarrheal diseases rather than toward vaccination of the entire refugee population against an epidemic that could not be eliminated.

4. See Chapter 6.

Measles

The high prevalence of malnutrition among the refugees might have prompted the institution of a massive measles-immunization program. From experience in Africa, it is known that the mortality rate of measles infection is enhanced when associated with malnutrition (15). Moreover, the catabolic state associated with measles can precipitate critical malnutrition in a marginally nourished child. In the refugee camps, the prevalence of measles was unknown. Inquiry among children hospitalized with malnutrition, however, indicated that a preceding measles infection was common. It seems likely that, as in Africa, measles was a predisposing factor in the development of severe malnutrition and high death rates among children.

The efficacy of massive community immunization against a measles epidemic was dramatically confirmed in Nigeria (16). It is probable that administration of measles vaccine to all children in refugee camps would have diminished both the incidence of measles and the alarming number of deaths due to malnutrition. These benefits, however, must be weighed against practicality and cost. Measles vaccine requires refrigeration and is expensive (approximately 25 cents per dose). Under the circumstances the Indian authorities understandably decided that a measles vaccination program was too expensive and too difficult to implement.

Other Infections

Other infectious diseases could have been more effectively contained with sound planning. The crowding and malnutrition in the camps provided optimal conditions for transmission of tubercle bacilli among the refugee population. Even during normal times, tuberculosis is a major health problem in Bangladesh; 80 per cent of adults show positive skin tests and approximately 500 per thousand have overt, active disease (17). Under field conditions, active cases even when identified could not have been isolated due to lack of facilities or properly treated due to lack of chemotherapeutic agents. Tuberculin skin tests were rarely positive among children under 5 years of age, the group at highest risk of tuberculous meningitis and osteomyelitis. While the high rate of negative tuberculin skin tests in this age group may be due in part to "false negatives" related to malnutrition (18), it seems probable that this observation is primarily related to limited previous exposure to the organism.

The juxtaposition of conditions favorable to transmission and a highly susceptible population represents a situation in which tuberculosis control through the use of BCG vaccine would have been highly desirable. The vaccine is available in large quantities for mass administration by jet injector gun and is inexpensive (less than two cents per dose). In addition, every effort should have been made to ensure that dispensaries were adequately supplied with isoniazid, streptomycin, and p-aminosalicylic acid, the mainstay of tuberculosis treatment.

Although diphtheria, pertussis, and tetanus were not highly prevalent in the refugee camps, they are known to be present year-round in Bengal, and control through immunization might have been a medium-range goal. Diphtheria/pertussis/tetanus (DPT) vaccine is durable and cheap and can be administered by jet injector gun. In addition, a tetanus immunization program for pregnant women would have been inexpensive and would have virtually eliminated neonatal tetanus.

CONCLUSION

This chapter serves to illustrate that health programs associated with medical care during disasters, such as the refugee situation, can be strengthened by survey, surveillance, and utilization of existing knowledge. Although many of the health problems in Bengal were to some degree predictable, the health crisis which mushroomed was not due to poor preparation or ineffectual relief efforts. To the contrary, the Indian authorities demonstrated a great deal of ability and expertise in recognizing and attempting to contain these problems. Where deficiencies existed, they occurred primarily because of incomplete or inadequate implementation. The vast number and rapid influx of refugees swamped the best administrative attempts to meet comprehensively the health needs of the refugees.

References

1. Ministry of Relief and Rehabilitation, Government of India.
2. Leather, A. *Oxfam Field Report on the Refugee Situation in India.* Oxfam, England. September 1971.
3. Galbraith, J. K. The Unbelievable Happens in Bengal. *The New York Times Magazine.* October 31, 1971.
4. Kennedy, E. M. *Crisis in South Asia.* A Report to the Subcommittee to Investigate Problems Connected with Refugees and Escapees of the Committee of the Judiciary, United States Senate. November 1, 1971.
5. *The New York Times,* June 13, 1971.
6. *The Washington Post,* June 11, 1971.
7. *The Boston Globe,* June 10, 1971.
8. Scrimshaw, N. S. *Nutrition and Health Problems of Pakistani Refugees in India.* Report to the Subcommittee for Refugees, Committee of the Judiciary, U.S. Senate. September 30, 1971. Appendix I.
9. Loven, F., and Foll, C. V. *World Health Organization Field Report on Refugee Health Problems.* August 4–10, 1971.
10. Ramalingaswami, V., and Tandon, B. N. *All India Institute of Medical Sciences Report on Nutrition Status of Refugee Children.* July 11–22, 1971.
11. Gardner, P., Rohde, J. E., and Majumdar, M. B. *Medical Survey at Barasat Camp.* International Rescue Committee. October 24–27, 1971.
12. Gardner, P., Rohde, J. E., and Majumdar, M. B. Health Priorities Among Bangladesh Refugees. *Lancet* 1:834 (1972).
13. Seaman, J. A. Relief Work in a Refugee Camp for Bangladesh Refugees in India. *Lancet* 2:866 (1972).
14. Kellog, F. L. *Situation Report No. 13.* Interagency Committee on South Asian Refugee Assistance. Department of State, February 10, 1972.
15. Ogbeide, M. I. Measles in Nigerian Children. *J. Pediatrics,* 71, No. 5, p. 737 (1967).
16. Smith, E. A., and Foster, S. O. Seminar on Smallpox Eradication and Measles Control in Western and Central Africa. WHO, USAID, CDC, Lagos, Nigeria (1969).
17. Hirschhorn, N. *Health in Bangladesh.* Subcommittee for Refugees, Committee of the Judiciary, U.S. Senate. February 2, 1972. Appendix II.

18. Smythe, P. M., Schonland, M., Brereton-Stiles, G. G., Goovadia, H. M., Grace, H. J., Loening, W. E. K., Mafoyane, A., Parent, M. A., and Vos, G. H. Thymolymphatic Deficiency and Depression of Cell Mediated Immunity in Protein-Calorie Malnutrition. *Lancet* 2:939 (1971).

(12) REFUGEES IN INDIA: INNOVATIVE HEALTH CARE PROGRAMS

Jon E. Rohde and Pierce Gardner

INTRODUCTION

Over the past several decades, the advances of modern medical technology have far outpaced the development of systems to deliver improved health care to a majority of mankind. Like many developing regions of the world, Bangladesh has very little organized health care infrastructure, and where present, it frequently is understaffed and poorly equipped to deal with the increasing demands of an expanding population.

When 10 million refugees poured into India, the establishment of an emergency health care delivery system was a formidable challenge indeed. Over 700 physicians and 2,000 paramedical personnel mobilized from among the refugees themselves and from all over India worked tirelessly to avert, to contain, and to treat a wide-range of nutritional and infectious diseases. Seven hundred medical dispensaries were established within the camps, and an additional fifty referral hospitals were available for the treatment of advanced or complicated illnesses. Although most of these services operated in a traditional fashion, with each patient being interviewed, examined, and treated by a physician, significant efforts were made to utilize paramedical personnel and to develop systematized approaches to handle the most common and most severe problems.

It is beyond the scope of this chapter to describe the work of hundreds of physicians and medical students who saved many lives despite the lack of medicines, diagnostic aids, and proper treatment facilities. We will instead briefly review the over-all relief operation with special emphasis on the coordination of health programs. We will discuss aspects of refugee medical care pertinent to the design of health services in a situation where physician shortage constitutes a major impediment to improved health. The chapter will focus on experimental health programs, on-the-job training of physicians, the use of paramedical personnel, public health education, and the role of foreign voluntary agencies in disaster medical care.

COORDINATION OF RELIEF OPERATIONS

The provision of relief to 10 million refugees by the Government of India represented a monumental humanitarian achievement. That mass starvation and galloping epidemics did not consume a greater portion of the refugee population is a tribute to the leadership, dedication, and energy of the Indian Government. Central control of the relief operation was assumed by the Ministry of Relief and Rehabilitation under Additional Secretary Colonel P. N. Luthra. Operating from a headquarters in Calcutta, the Ministry coordinated and supervised the procurement of resources, the logistics of transport, and the allocation of supplies. In part because of strong leadership, an unusual degree of organizational unity and efficiency was demonstrated.

In contrast to the efficient conduct of the over-all relief effort, authority over health programs was not invested in any one group or person. Certain health care decisions (such as to give cholera and smallpox inoculations) were made by the Health Ministry in New Delhi, but most medical programs were left to the control of the State Health Departments, the Relief Ministry, the Indian Red Cross, and, in many instances, to individual subdivisional health officers. Groups with a great deal of expertise and experience, such as the Hyderabad Nutrition Institute, the All India Institute of Medical Sciences, and the Calcutta School of Public Health and Hygiene were relegated to advisory roles. As a result, health policies and programs often lacked focus, direction, and coordination. Due in part to this leadership vacuum, capable and sympathetic outside expertise was not fully utilized.

OPERATION LIFELINE

Despite the lack of over-all leadership in health, many innovative programs were implemented. Unquestionably the most impressive was Operation Lifeline. Its plan to establish nutrition therapy centers (Beta) and outpatient child-feeding stations (Alpha) was an administrative model on which all health delivery could have been based. The survey conducted by the All India Institute not only quantitated the urgent need for better nutrition among the refugees but also resulted in a detailed proposal of actions to alleviate the problem (1). The Alpha and Beta plans represented a simultaneous preventive and therapeutic approach to malnutrition. Their strengths lay in pragmaticism and feasibility when confronted with scarcity of resources and personnel. Due to the short interval between the initiation of Operation Lifeline and the onset of war, this program never reached its full potential, nor could its impact on refugee health be precisely assessed. Yet much can be learned from the experience of establishing this extensive, systematic program to meet a major public health threat.

The Beta program, under the leadership of Dr. B. N. Tandon, possessed all of the essential components of a successful project: careful prospective design, strong administrative support, supervision and coordination, training of physicians and paramedical personnel, gradual expansion, and continuing surveillance and evaluation. The first Beta centers were opened in October and were staffed by nutrition experts from the All India Institute. They experimented with the acceptability of food mixtures as well as the form and frequency of feeding, and identified specific needs for equipment and supplies. Camp physicians, and often refugees themselves, were trained in the detection and treatment of malnutrition and its attendant medical problems (Figures 12.1 and 12.2). A protocol for the treatment of the most common medical problems was formulated. This protocol served as a ready reference when indigenous staff assumed more complete responsibility for the operation of the centers. Protocols were also established to give precise and detailed information covering all phases of the

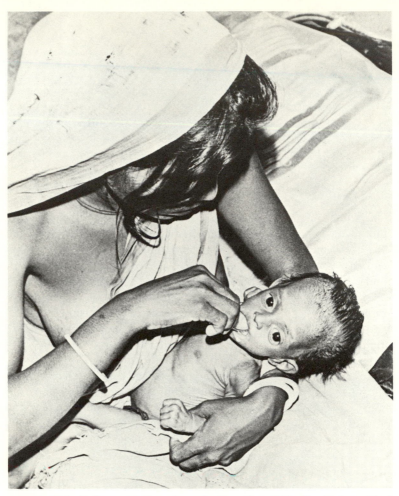

FIGURE 12.1. Refugee Mother Spoonfeeding Her Critically Malnourished Child at a Lifeline Beta Nutrition Treatment Center (courtesy of Catholic Relief Services)

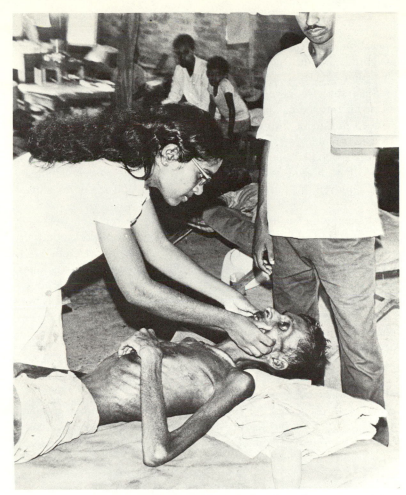

FIGURE 12.2. A Nurse Examines a Refugee Dying from Starvation and Tuberculosis (courtesy of Catholic Relief Services)

operation, including food preparation, patient registration, child weighing, and instructions to mothers on nutrition and hygiene. The plan envisaged a center staff of two cooks, six paramedics or medical students, three helpers, and two sweepers recruited from the local refugee camps. With such manpower support, one experienced physician with a jeep could oversee the operation of 15 to 25 such centers serving more than 3,000 patients. Within one month, a detailed and efficient protocol for the delivery of nutritional therapy and health care to 200 to 250 severely malnourished children in each center was field-tested and ready for expansion.

At the Beta Coordination Center, the needs for each treatment unit were estimated: special foods, medicines, transportation, personnel, shelter, and supplies. With financial support from UNICEF, a standard "kit" containing medicines, weighing machines, cots, utensils, lanterns, record cards, and other necessary equipment were prepared for each camp. Supplies of K-Mix II and CSM (high protein mixtures) designed to serve 250 children were packaged into weekly allotments to replenish the centers as needed.

During the months of October, November, and December, 88 such centers were established in the refugee camps (2). Only the interruption of war and the subsequent return of the refugees to Bangladesh prevented the Beta Program from expanding to cover all camps. The lessons learned from the Beta experience are many. Non-professional personnel can be rapidly trained to manage a large number of patients. Children with severe protein-calorie malnutrition (PCM) can be treated on an intensive out-patient feeding basis. Most important is the success that can result from integration of field survey, strong central coordination, planning, field research, utilization of local personnel, and training of physicians and paramedical personnel.

The Alpha Program, administered by the Indian Red Cross Society and assisted by foreign voluntary agencies, attempted to prevent further nutritional deterioration among refugee children. The goal was to provide a daily food supplement to an estimated 2.5 million children under 8 years of age (Figure 12.3); eventually the coverage was to extend to all lactating and pregnant women as well. The program called for the provision of 75 gms of high-protein mixtures (*balahar,* corn-soymilk or CSM, wheat-soy blend or WSB) to each child daily, a food equivalent of 15 gms of protein and 250 calories.

By the beginning of December, nearly 1,200 Alpha centers had been established. Their efficiency and extent of coverage varied tremendously. Some simply passed out dry flour into the hands of children on a first-come-first-serve basis. Others prepared a meal of high protein foods and served the ration systematically to Alpha card holders (Figure 12.4). A few required that the food be eaten under the watchful eyes of volunteers. Only in the latter instance could maximum nutritional effectiveness be assured, for often food carried home was consumed by adult family members. In one camp, the physician participated in the feeding program; as each child filed out of the food queue, he passed under the scrutiny of the doctor who was watchful for signs of malnutrition, infection, and vitamin deficiency. Although no objective data are available, it would seem reasonable to conclude that the daily food supplement provided by Alpha Lifeline spared many children from severe malnutrition and would eventually have reduced the number of new cases being seen in the Beta centers.

FISH-PROTEIN-CONCENTRATE ACCEPTABILITY TRIALS

To improve the quality of the refugee diet, Dr. Cato Aall and Dr. S. Mukherjee initiated an acceptability trial of fish-protein-concentrate (FPC) among over 10,000 refugees in November (3,4). Although FPC has been available for many years, it had never been used for large-scale protein supplement in a relief situation. The Bangladesh refugee crisis seemed an ideal opportunity to introduce FPC because Bengalis are traditionally a fish-eating people. FPC, like other animal protein mixtures, improves the protein value of vegetable diets which lack certain essential amino acids. Fifteen grams of FPC, for example, will nearly double the protein quality of a standard refugee ration of 400 gms of rice daily. If available, pulse could complement the rice diet, but it does so less efficiently and was often unavailable. FPC, on the other hand, is

FIGURE 12.3. Children Line Up for Supplementary Milk at a Lifeline Alpha Station at Changseri Refugee Camp (courtesy of UNICEF)

less expensive than pulses and is widely available from a variety of worldwide sources. FPC contains fewer calories than pulses. Although this may seem to be a disadvantage, the caloric deficit can be met by providing wheat, which is cheaper and easier to obtain than rice. In terms of supply and logistics, FPC also possesses important qualities. It is relatively resistant to environmental decay and can be transported, stored, and prepared easily.

FPC was provided as dry rations to families, as a curry sauce in Lifeline Alpha stations, and as an integral part of the food therapy to patients with severe PCM. In all instances, the results of the acceptability trials were encouraging. Enjoying the taste and smell of fish, the Bengali refugees universally accepted and indeed welcomed FPC supplements. FPC became the most popular food supplement except for infants, for whom milk was more desirable. In a population where marasmus was by far the major nutritional

FIGURE 12.4. Children Receiving High Protein Food Mixtures at Alpha Center in Salt Lake Camp (courtesy of UNICEF)

disease, high caloric intake, especially among children, was of vital importance; and FPC not only improved the protein value of the diet but also enhanced the palatability of other important nutrients. Among children who would eat only 50 gms of tasteless *balahar,* for example, the addition of FPC stimulated consumption of up to 150 gms.

The outcome of these trials has important nutritional implications for Bangladesh. Because animals compete with man for land and its resources, improved animal husbandry might be counterproductive in Bangladesh. In contrast to livestock, fish do not compete with man. Massive production and distribution of FPC could improve the quality of the diet without jeopardizing agricultural production. The possibilities of expanding offshore fisheries, of manufacturing FPC, and of promoting its use in applied nutrition programs should thus be explored in Bangladesh.

PHYSICIAN TRAINING

Physicians working in hundreds of understaffed and poorly equipped dispensaries were faced with a broad spectrum of diseases. Some camp physicians were unacquainted with the wide range of nutritional and infectious disease problems which proliferated during the crisis. Surprisingly, many physicians were unfamiliar with the treatment of PCM. All too often, vitamins were administered to patients with marasmus, and diuretics to children with edema due to kwashiorkor. Dehydration associated with diarrhea frequently was treated with gruel of barley water rather than with electrolyte enriched fluids and antibiotics.

There was clearly an urgent need for on-the-job training of physicians working in the refugee camp dispensaries. The authors therefore conducted a survey at Barasat camp (5), visited dozens of other camps, and interviewed scores of physicians. From these experiences we were able to identify the most common medical problems among the refugees and a reference pamphlet specifically oriented to the needs and resources of the refugee camp dispensaries was prepared and distributed.

Focusing on the major health problems of diarrhea, respiratory disease, skin infection, and malnutrition, *Guidelines to the Man-*

agement of Medical Problems Among Bangladesh Refugees (6) offered diagnostic "tips" and therapeutic programs designed for use by the physician caring for scores of patients without laboratory diagnostic aids. In a situation where a precise diagnosis for a symptom complex could not be accurately made, a "statistical approach" was recommended: the most prevalent disease causing a specific clinical picture was presumed to be present and treatment was offered accordingly. If improvement did not ensue, then the next most common diagnosis was adopted, and so on. Although no substitute for precise diagnosis, this method at least ensured proper treatment for the most common illnesses in a systematic fashion (Tables 1 and 2). A formulary was reduced to only 19 recommended drugs with suggested dosage by age; this reduction was aimed at focusing the attention of the physician on the most important therapeutic agents. Dietary tables offered ready reference to the caloric and protein value of foods found in the camps along with recommended daily allowances. The manual's brevity, specificity for problems faced in the camps, pragmatic emphasis, and wide distribution made it an effective tool for improving refugee health services. More than 5,000 copies were distributed and a new edition, in Bengali, has been prepared for more general use in Bangladesh.

A direct outgrowth of "Guidelines" was Oxfam's standardization of its dispensary medicinal supplies. A physician faced with a pharmacopoeia containing hundreds of drugs tended to spend too much time on minor ailments and was often tempted to use medicines unfamiliar to him. Oxfam therefore reduced its supply list to 16 classes of medicine, concentrating primarily on therapy for serious or life-threatening disease. The streamlined list of drugs is presented in Table 3. Not only were drug expenditures markedly reduced, but the efficiency of ordering, stocking, and filling of requisitions was greatly enhanced. When a new dispensary was opened, a crate containing all the items on this list, in amounts determined from previous utilization rates, was supplied and restocked as needed. Where special needs arose (for example, filariasis, congestive heart failure, seizure disorders, traumatic injuries), supplementary drugs were added. This program of selecting a limited number of first-line medicines supported the phy-

TABLE 1
Diagnosis and Treatment of Diarrheal Diseases

Complaint	Examination	Therapy
1. Acute or recurrent mild diarrhea —frequent loose motions	pulse, skin elasticity, respirations all normal	normal diet; oral glucose-saline; kaolin mixture (if available)
2. Acute severe diarrhea with dehydration	watery diarrhea, fast weak pulse, sunken eyes, dry tongue, mouth and skin, lethargic	oral glucose-saline; resume full diet; if over three days give tetracycline or sulfadiazine
3. Acute dysentery (less than one week)	bloody mucus stool, abdominal pain and tenderness, cramps and tenesmus, fever	tetracycline; opiates or lomotil for cramps; full diet
4. Chronic dysentery (10 days to several months) treat first as in (3) above; if no recovery then assume amebiasis	bloody mucus stool, flatulence and cramps, weight loss, check for enlarged tender liver	tetracycline 5 days then emetine, diiodohydroxyquinolin, if liver involved flagyl (metranidazole)
5. High fever, abdominal pain, headache, delirium, constipation or diarrhea, assume typhoid fever	abdominal tenderness enlarged spleen and liver, fever	chloramphenicol
6. Cholera and other profound diarrheas	constant watery stools, shock with absent pulse, lethargy, stupor, coma, no skin elasticity, deep rapid breathing	stuporous—give IV saline, if available in children, give push glucose IV; rehydrate with large volume and continue oral glucose-saline to equal all losses; even if vomiting occurs, fluid must

Complaint	Examination	Therapy
		be pushed; tetra-cycline, furoxone, chloraphenicol
7. Malnutrition with diarrhea	easily dehydrated and often go into shock	must be fed at least every 3 hours around the clock— if unconscious give IV glucose. Beware dehydration. Kaolin mixture

Do not use coramine, steroids, pressor agents; a patient in shock requires fluids rapidly—these drugs will only worsen the shock of dehydration.

TABLE 2
Diagnosis and Treatment of Respiratory Diseases

Symptoms	Examination	Treatment
1. Cough, runny nose, sore throat	rule out diphtheria	fluids; aspirin in children with fever; no other therapy needed
2. Recent onset cough, sputum, fever, air hunger	rib retraction, dullness to percussion, rales	penicillin force fluids
3. Persistence of (2) above after penicillin for 5 days or laryngeal block in children (croup, whooping cough)	hoarseness— severe air hunger, cyanosis, whistling obstructed breath sounds, whooping coughs	force fluids tetracycline or chloraphenicol continue feeding throughout illness
4. Persistence of (3); long history of cough, fever, sweats, weight loss-hemoptysis (coughing blood)	rales, pleural effusions with dullness, enlarged lymph nodes, meningitis in children, especially of parents with TB	fluids INH streptomycin i.m. after 21 days INH and ethambutol or PAS or Thiacetezone
5. Family of patient with TB-especially babies	may be no symptoms	INH daily along with the patient

TABLE 3
Streamlined Oxfam Drug Formulary

I. Antibiotics—Antimicrobials
   A. Penicillins (injectable, oral and pediatric suspension)
   B. Tetracyclines (injectable, capsule, pediatric suspension, ear drops)
   C. Chloramphenicol (tablets, pediatric suspension, ear drops)
   D. Sulpha Drugs (tablets, skin ointment, eye drops)
   E. Antituberculous Drugs (streptomycin, isoniazid, thiacetozone)
II. Antiparasite
   A. Amoebae (emetine, diiodochloroquin, metranidazole)
   B. Scabies (benzyl benzoate)
   C. Antihelminthics (piperazine, bipheniun)
   D. Malaria (chloroquin)
   E. Fungal (griseofulvin)
III. Antacids (tablet and liquid)
IV. Analgesics (aspirin, novocaine, ethyl chloride spray)
V. Sedatives (chlorpromazine, phenobarbital, antihistamines)
VI. Vitamins (capsule and injectable of all forms plus calcium, iron, multivits)
VII. Symptomatic (kaolin, laxatives, cough syrup, skin ointment)
VIII. Special (steroids, diuretics, intravenous fluids)

sician's attempt to focus medical attention on the most significant, treatable health problems.

TRAINING OF PARAMEDICAL PERSONNEL

In an effort to extend the reach of limited professional manpower, experimental training and on-the-job education of paramedical personnel and volunteers were undertaken. Educated nurses, midwives, and drug compounders were already serving throughout the camps. However, the health crisis necessitated a rapid expansion of the health manpower pool. The newly trained paramedical personnel proved to be most useful in sanitation control projects, in personal and community hygiene instruction, and in standardized therapy of infectious diseases and malnutrition.

The West Bengal Union for Child Welfare undertook an experimental training program for paramedical personnel (*balsevikas*). These workers were employed in Salt Lake Camp where they assisted physicians during dispensary hours and gave instructions to mothers of malnourished children in the feeding programs. They also visited huts to detect new cases, to respond to home visit requests, to offer follow-up care, and to provide intensive home education in nutrition, hygiene, and sanitary practices.

At Bandipur Camp, physicians were dismayed at the large number of cases of active tuberculosis. The prevalent attitude toward tuberculosis among refugees and health authorities alike was one of resignation because no one could offer the long-term drug therapy required. These physicians devised an effective treatment system utilizing volunteers. Each newly diagnosed case was given a card containing his name and a year's calendar. The patient was expected to appear daily before a trained volunteer who sat near the clinic, dispensing isoniazid and thiacetamide. Any patient missing two consecutive days was visited in his hut and urged to take his medication. This system reduced the physicians' work load; they made only the initial diagnosis while volunteers were responsible for the therapy and follow-up.

In Camp Bashirat, doctors became wearied by the heavy load of patients presenting with scabies. Not only did this parasite infect up to 80 per cent of the population in some camps, but also superinfection with pyogenic organisms, resulting in furunculosis, nephritis, and sepsis, caused life-threatening complications. Two physicians therefore initiated a program run by volunteers to eradicate scabies. On a set day, a drum of boiling water was positioned in front of a shelter housing five to ten families. All clothes and bedding were boiled. Each person bathed; a *purdah* or women's area was cordoned off. Before dressing in freshly boiled clothing, each refugee was painted with benzyl benzoate by a volunteer. Relief was so dramatic that additional refugees offered to expand the program or to undertake other health projects such as drainage and construction of new latrines.

When the cholera epidemic struck in West Bengal, a manpower shortage retarded the progress of inoculation, sanitation, and therapy programs. Volunteers were rapidly trained in immunization procedures and camp-wide drives to improve sanitation were led by students and village leaders. Dr. Delip Mahalanabis and Dr. A. D. Choudhuri of the Johns Hopkins Center for Medical Research and Training in Calcutta (7) organized teams to administer oral rehydration therapy in Bongoan, a refugee area 50 miles from Calcutta. Using a simplified formula containing 22 gms of glucose, 3.5 gms of sodium chloride, and 2.5 gms of sodium bicarbonate per liter of water, over 3,000 patients were orally rehydrated within a three-week period. In severe cases with shock, intravenous saline solutions were used for rehydration until strong radial pulse and good skin turgor were obtained. Then oral solution alone was given for further correction of dehydration and acidosis. Paramedical workers and relatives of patients were instructed to urge patients to drink as much as possible. Although they drank the oral solution avidly, vomiting was a major barrier to acceptance, and constant persuasion and reminders that the drink contained "medicine" was needed to ensure adequate intake. Failure of this regimen to provide adequate rehydration was generally traced to a refusal to drink.

In late June the daily admission rate of cholera patients to the Bongoan field rehydration unit reached 200 new cases, and most patients were accommodated on the floor or outside (Figure 12.5). As few as two physicians and eight paramedical personnel with recruited volunteer help handled this huge patient load. Even under these circumstances, mortality in 3,700 patients treated was 3.6 per cent, while in a group of 1,200 patients treated under the more intensive guidance of the Johns Hopkins physicians themselves it was 1 per cent.

PUBLIC HEALTH EDUCATION

Camp medical programs were hampered by the ignorance among the uneducated refugees of the basic rules of community and personal hygiene. Latrines were improperly used, and clean water supplies were neglected. Paramedical personnel were especially effective in educating the public in the practice of safe sanitation. Teams of young volunteers from groups such as the Bangladesh Volunteer Service Corps and the Bharat (Indian) Scouts tried to

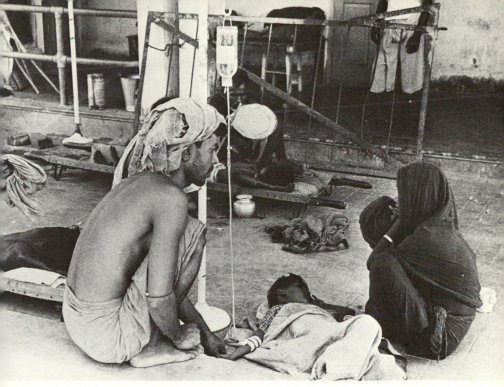

FIGURE 12.5. Parents Watch over Their Son Who Is Receiving Intravenous Saline for Cholera Outside of a Camp Dispensary Near Bongoan, West Bengal (courtesy of Catholic Relief Services)

inform their countrymen of the importance of good sanitation, personal hygiene, and sound nutritional practices. A program of displaying colorful posters and distributing handbills printed in Bengali was launched in December, but its limited scope and short duration precluded a measurable impact. The messages were simple:

"When diarrhea affects your child, barley water can kill. Continue feeding and give him water solution of glucose and salt."
"Drink only tube well water."
"Babies need extra dal to grow."

The use of radio in disseminating pragmatic medical news was initiated by Radio Bangladesh. When cholera struck Dacca and its surrounding countryside in November, daily broadcasts reiterated simple directions for the preparation and use of oral glucose-saline solutions in the treatment of severe diarrhea. The formula and constitution of the oral solution was expressed in lay terms, and the importance of drinking large volumes of the solution was emphasized. In addition, a few teams of college students who were trained in the use of this technique and were equipped with printed material and simple ingredients, infiltrated border districts to offer help within Bangladesh during the civil war. They found patients in several villages reportedly improved by following the radio instructions.

FOREIGN VOLUNTARY AGENCIES

The urgency of the refugee crisis demanded expansion of health services beyond the capacity of Indian institutions. A number of voluntary agencies with extensive experience in this area were well suited to help tackle this problem. The following section will only highlight those lessons that appear to be most important for foreign voluntary assistance.

1. Those agencies with indigenous roots seemed to be most effective. For example, Caritas, through its network of mission churches in the refugee area, was able to establish scores of medical units staffed by Bengalis. Caritas workers had intimate knowledge of local conditions and their acceptance by the people made their effort very effective. They provided 15 hospitals, 60 dispensaries, and 54 Alpha stations in 104 camps containing a population of 2.5 million refugees.

2. Those agencies with previous experience in disaster medical care function better under adverse conditions. Save the Children brought skills learned from Nigeria to bear on the problems of malnutrition in the Indian camps. Their hospitals at Salt Lake and Kalyani camps not only treated hundreds of acutely malnourished children but formed the nucleus of a training program for Bengali physicians. They also initiated camp-wide nutrition surveys, educational programs, and supplementary feeding programs.

3. Utilization of indigenous personnel greatly increased the contributions of foreign groups. The International Rescue Committee put no foreigners in the field, but instead supported a

program of the Bangladesh Medical Association of hiring refugee health professionals to work in the camps. This approach provided the means for some 300 Bengali doctors and nurses to offer needed services in over 60 camps. Other groups such as War on Want, Christian Agency for Social Action (CASA), and Cathedral Relief also staffed camp dispensaries and hospitals with refugee personnel. By drawing on the resources of indigenous personnel, a few experienced foreigners with funding were able to amplify the effect of their knowledge many times over.

Oxfam in concert with the Gandhi Peace Foundation, established several dispensaries and a central camp hospital in West Dinajpur staffed by medical students and teachers from medical colleges in Calcutta, Cuttuck, and Bombay. For concerned Indians, this provided an opportunity to volunteer a block of time for relief work within an established system. Many of the medical students were stimulated by the challenge of camp medicine and remained beyond their allotted time. Not only did they perform a humanitarian task, but they learned and devised methods of delivering health care in times of disaster. When a cyclone struck Orissa, India, in November, a cadre of young medical professionals from Cuttuck went to the newly devastated area using their experience gained in the Oxfam program only weeks earlier.

4. Independent foreign efforts often encountered insurmountable problems. A few agencies attempted to provide health facilities without any substantial indigenous participation. When entering a strange cultural, geographical, linguistic, and unique medical environment, it is difficult to introduce new technologies and concepts where traditional methods and social expectations are deeply entrenched. In most cases, the foreigners had as much or more to learn from their Indian compatriots as they had to offer. The establishment of medical units staffed largely by Western personnel too easily served as an affront to the dedicated efforts of less well-equipped Indian medical teams. Although they delivered high-quality care, these foreign model hospitals provided a double standard that could not be easily tolerated by the Indian authorities.

The exclusion of foreign medical workers from the border

camps may have been based on military or political considerations or on the expediency of avoiding criticism. The fact that officials chose "not to see" some foreign workers quietly engaged in close, effective cooperation with Indian physicians in many camps argues against a total rejection of help from the outside.

5. Effective integration of foreign voluntary agency activities requires strong central coordination by the host government. Had there been an over-all health coordinator with a comprehensive plan, foreign medical personnel might have been integrated into the system better. The conspicuous absence of such an overview created a vacuum into which many agencies poured diverse efforts. Strong leadership, comprehensive planning, and close coordination are required on the part of the host government if voluntary agency assistance is to effectively supplement indigenous medical care during disasters.

**FUTURE HEALTH CARE PROGRAMS
IN BANGLADESH**

Where few doctors are charged with the health care of millions, traditional methods of patient-physician interaction must be altered. Systems must be devised to multiply the effectiveness of the medical staff. The luxury of one-to-one consultative medicine must be replaced by a system utilizing paramedical personnel in a programmed way to diagnose and treat the most common problems. The simplest prototype of this approach is mass inoculation. Physicians are needed only to decide which vaccine should be administered; to whom; and at what interval. The population can be easily defined: for example, all refugees or a subgroup such as all below the age of 10 years. Ration cards can be utilized as immunization records. Teams of organizers, recorders, and jet-gun operators can be recruited from volunteer or civil government sources and readily trained for a single task. Thus a vast medical burden can be carried by non-medical personnel. The cholera and smallpox inoculation programs and the vitamin A supplement for children were examples of this approach. Its expansion to include

BCG vaccine against tuberculosis, and DPT and measles vaccines would be desirable in Bangladesh.

Treatment of common diseases in the camps could have followed a similar protocol. A physician acting as a triage officer would interview and briefly examine each case, assigning the patient to a treatment line according to clinical diagnosis. The volunteer staffing each line would dispense a single medicine such as sulfadiazine for dysentery, benzathine penicillin for pneumonia, benzyl benzoate for scabies, INH and PAS or ethambutal for tuberculosis. He would give directions for home treatment and follow-up therapy. A compounder would prepare standard mixtures for minor ailments and another physician would concentrate on more difficult diagnostic and therapeutic cases. Various forms of this system were used in the refugee camps and they greatly increased the number of patients that could be handled by a single physician.

Student volunteers were trained to use oral rehydration fluid for cholera in an attempt to extend medical care beyond the confines of a dispensary hospital or physician's office. Although cholera most certainly deserves the direct attention of a physician and requires around-the-clock care, early use of oral-saline in the village can alleviate the severity of the disease and allow time for travel to an established health center for comprehensive treatment. Diarrhea is the most common cause of death in Bangladesh. By simply teaching a person in each village how to mix and administer oral rehydration fluid, and providing the necessary publicity to reinforce its acceptance, health care workers could do much toward eliminating a major cause of mortality. Along with this program, an assault on the use of barley or *sago* water (which is nutritionally valueless) should be made. The vicious cycle of diarrhea leading to malnutrition leading to diarrhea can be broken only with proper rehydration and feeding.

Although a feeding supplement program such as Lifeline Alpha is not a practical suggestion for rural Bangladesh at present, two approaches to a more adequate diet for the young should be explored. A high protein supplement could be provided free in a fixed proportion to all grain purchased at government ration shops. A pilot project should be implemented as the first step.

Measures to ensure enriched food consumption by children need to be introduced and nutritional assessment of the impact of the program needs to be completed before widespread distribution could be recommended. Second, agricultural education should emphasize the nutritional value of crops like pulses, yellow and green vegetables, and ground nuts. Each family should be encouraged to cultivate such crops for home consumption, especially for children. Incentives such as the supply of free seeds and fertilizers, and broad publicity, would reinforce the educational program.

One of the few positive results of the refugee tragedy has been the general acceptance by the indigenous medical profession of the key role of nutrition in health and the diagnostic significance of wasting and edema in the young. Feeding programs similar to the Beta system should be introduced at the *thana* level in Bangladesh in conjunction with existing rural health centers. Severe cases can be referred for intensive short-term therapy with concomitant education for mothers on the use of weaning foods, grain supplements, and the preparation of vegetables. This model can be further extended as a basis for village-level health centers staffed by local persons with brief but specific training in the therapy of diarrhea, pneumonia, ear infections, vitamin A deficiency, and scabies. With a supply of only sulfadiazine, penicillin, vitamin A capsules, benzyl benzoate, and oral glucose saline rehydration solutions, a trained villager could treat the majority of significant life-threatening illnesses in rural Bangladesh.

With the institution of rural medical care, family planning should be offered and encouraged. Reduction of child mortality can remove one of the major impediments to the acceptance of family limitation in Bangladesh. Unless there is rapid acceptance and universal utilization of contraceptive measures, efforts to improve nutrition and health will be dissipated or defeated by rapid population growth.

The refugee experience, by its very urgency, facilitated experimentation and innovation in health care. If any lasting benefit is to accrue from this tragedy, those programs which met with some measure of success and which have potential application in the future must be refined, expanded, and adapted to the needs and resources of the new nation. Only through careful planning, strong central support and coordination, and extensive recruitment of new paramedical personnel will the medical profession be able to extend comprehensive health services to the 75 million citizens of Bangladesh.

References

1. Ramalingaswami, V., and Tandon, B. N. *Report on Nutritional Status of Refugee Children,* All India Institute of Medical Sciences. July 11–22, 1971.
2. Tandon, B. N. Report on the Progress of Nutrition Therapy Centers for Refugee Children from Bangladesh for the High Powered Co-ordinating and Policy Committee, memo dated January 14, 1972.
3. Aall, C., and Mukherjee, S. *Acceptability of Fish Protein Concentrate—FPC—Among Bangladesh Refugees in the Calcutta Area.* National Nutrition Council, Oslo, Norway. December 8, 1971.
4. Aall, C. *Future Potential of FPC in Fish-Eating Areas in Light of Recent Experience in India/Bangladesh.* Conference on FPC, Massachusetts Institute of Technology, June 7, 1972.
5. Gardner, P., Rohde, J. E., and Majumdar, M. B. Health Priorities Among Bangladesh Refugees. *Lancet* 1:834 (1972).
6. Rohde, J. E., Mahalanabis, D., and Gardner, P. *Guideline to the Management of Common Medical Problems Among Bangladesh Refugees.* The International Rescue Committee. Little Flower Press, Calcutta, 1971.
7. Mahalanabis, D., and Choudhuri, A. D. *Oral Fluid Therapy in Cholera Among Bangladesh Refugees.* Johns Hopkins Center for Medical Research and Training, Calcutta, India, 1972.

(13)   CIVIL WAR IN
BANGLADESH: FAMINE AVERTED?

Lincoln C. Chen and Jon E. Rohde

INTRODUCTION

The dilemma of providing adequate nutrition to a rapidly growing population afflicts much of the developing world today. This predicament is particularly intense in Bangladesh, where 75 million inhabitants carve out a subsistence living on only 55,000 square miles of land. Under such marginal conditions, even minor disruptive events can dramatically affect the precarious balance between food supply and demand, precipitating major nutritional disasters. Within the past two centuries, Bangladesh has experienced eight major famines due to intermittent drought and war (1). The famine of 1769–70, caused by drought, claimed the lives of 10 million people, one-third of the population. During World War II, a Bengal famine resulted in 3 million deaths from mass starvation and associated infectious diseases (1).

Even by conservative judgment, the bitter, nine-month civil war in Bangladesh, which erupted in March 1971, precipitated major disruptions in an already marginal economy. The fighting between an army from West Pakistan and Bengali insurgents profoundly affected every facet of life in Bengal. The economy ground to a standstill, agricultural production fell sharply, and transport and communication facilities became paralyzed. Thus, it came as no surprise that foreign journalists (2,3), voluntary relief groups (4), concerned citizens (5), and responsible international organizations such as the World Bank (6) and the United States Agency for International Development (7,8) gloomily predicted famine in 1971. The catastrophe, however, never occurred. Why? To investigate this question, we shall: (1) review the rationale for the famine forecasts, (2) analyze critically why a major famine failed to materialize, (3) examine the impact of the war on nutrition, and (4) offer some perspective on the future nutritional situation in Bangladesh.

BACKGROUND

Despite the agrarian orientation of Bangladesh's economy, East Bengal is a chronic food-deficit region (Table 1). From 1961 to

TABLE 1
Bangladesh–Foodgrain Situation

Fiscal Year[a]	Net Production	Imports (million tons)	Total Supply	Population	Per Capita Daily Grain Consumption (ounces)
1961	8.62	0.62	9.24	55.3	16.4
1962	8.58	0.32	8.90	57.2	15.3
1963	7.92	0.76	8.68	59.2	14.4
1964	9.46	0.92	10.38	61.2	16.6
1965	9.38	0.36	9.74	63.4	15.1
1966	9.38	0.88	10.26	65.6	15.4
1967	8.55	0.96	9.51	67.7	13.8
1968	9.96	1.02	10.98	69.9	15.4
1969	10.14	1.06	10.20	72.0	15.3
1970	10.76	1.48	12.24	74.1	16.2
1971	10.00[b]	1.21	11.21	76.1	14.8

Source: From Hesser, 1971.

a. The fiscal year is the one-year period from July 1 to June 30.

b. The yield of the *aman* crop of November 1970 was adversely affected by flooding and cyclone.

1970 indigenous rice production increased from 8.62 to 10.76 million tons. This increment, unfortunately, was more than outpaced by a population growing at 3 per cent per annum from 55 million in 1961 to over 70 million in 1970 (10). Thus, Bangladesh has required progressively larger quantities of imported foodgrain to feed its people. From 1966 to 1970, yearly import requirements averaged 1.08 million tons compared to an average of 0.6 for the five preceding years. These mammoth quantities of imported foodgrain have been required to maintain an average per capita daily cereal consumption of 15.4 ounces (yearly range 13.8 to 16.6 ounces), which provides approximately 1,500 calories. Supplemental foods, such as lentils, vegetables, meats, fish, oil, and fruits averaged 280 calories per capita daily (11), making 1,780 calories the total daily per capita intake.

By any objective criterion, a caloric consumption of 1,780 daily must be considered marginal (24). A detailed survey conducted between 1962 to 1964 concluded that malnutrition is endemic to Bangladesh (12).[1] Borderline malnutrition affects more than 50 per cent of preschool-age children, and approximately 3 per cent suffer from severe protein-calorie deprivation. Eighty-five per cent of Bengalis residing in the countryside have inadequate intake of essential proteins, while 0.8 per cent of the children suffer from vitamin A deficiency, which may lead to keratomalacia and blindness. In this context, even minor decreases in food availability are liable to be manifested by a marked increase in deaths due to infectious diseases and starvation. The population possesses little nutritional reserve, especially among the young.

IMPACT OF THE WAR ON
FOOD AVAILABILITY

The civil war compounded the recent disruptions caused by harsh natural disasters. Only seven months earlier, Bangladesh experienced the severest monsoon flooding in the past decade, with crop losses estimated at 500,000 tons (13). Furthermore, a cyclone and tidal bore in November 1970 devastated much of the rice surplus, southern coastal region. Approximately 650,000 acres were inundated with saline water, and crop losses totalled nearly 470,000 tons (14). The impact of the civil war on food availability was even more disastrous. An army from West Pakistan attempted to control Bangladesh in the face of a guerrilla movement. Not only did warfare envelop strategic localities such as the major cities but it also extended to thousands of villages throughout the rural

1. More precise details on the findings from this survey are presented in Chapter 4.

countryside. The army burned whole villages and destroyed rice stocks as part of an attempt to control the populace.[2] The insurgents (*Mukti Bahini*) retaliated by disruptiing transport and communication links to hinder the mobility of the army. Thus warfare affected food supply in three ways: (1) it disrupted the economy; (2) it crippled agricultural production; (3) it created logistical barriers to the movement and distribution of food.

One of the most important impediments restraining normal agricultural, economic, and commercial activity was the fear and insecurity generated by the punitive actions of the army (6).[3] Thousands of skilled, educated, and professional people were killed.[4] Those who remained behind were coerced back to their jobs, but their performance was perfunctory at best. As a result, governmental and private business activities came to a halt; industries closed down; import of essential commodities was neglected; and there was widespread unemployment. Hostile acts by the army resulted in destroyed homes, burned marketplaces, decimated towns, and loss of foodstocks. One city, Kushtia, was described by

2. Father Goedert, a priest who remained in Bangladesh during the civil war wrote in his diary: "May 14th was the day the army attacked Baira, a peaceful village of harmless farmers and fishermen who know as much about politics as they do about nuclear fission. In the afternoon we heard shooting . . . and saw the fires. Toward sundown hundreds of people came streaming into Nagari, carrying a few pitiful bundles on their heads and asking for refuge. . . . The condition in Baira is appalling. 49 people dead, and that number is still rising. 174 homes totally destroyed, and 86 more partially destroyed. About 500 tons of rice, their entire food supply for the year either burned or stolen. Most of them have only the one piece of clothing that they have lived in, bled in, and sweat in since May 14th." (From *Christian Organization for Relief and Rehabilitation Newsletter* No. 11, March 6, 1972.)

3. The World Bank Mission reported that "all-pervasive fear" and insecurity were major constraints permitting normal resumption of economic activities. People feared to venture forth, and many streets and towns appeared virtually deserted (6).

4. *The New York Times* (September 19, 1971) in its article "Dacca Still a City of Vanishing Men" reported on typical cases of deaths of civilian leaders. One example was Mr. Syedul Hassan, a prominent Bengali businessman, who disappeared after an appointment at the army cantonment in Dacca.

a foreign observer as resembling a city destroyed by aerial bombing during World War II (6).[5]

Virtually every factor relevant to rice production was adversely affected. Many laborers, especially those in the border regions, fled into neighboring India, leaving their fields unattended. The labor exodus caused food shortages because the northern border region is a traditional rice-excess area of Bangladesh (11). Rice production also fell behind normal yields owing to lack of essential agricultural inputs. Fertilizers, pesticides, irrigation equipment and fuel were not available. The aman crop (in November 1971) was severely damaged in Noakhali and Barisal by stem borer attacks (15).

The rural credit structure totally collapsed and the rural public works program stopped. With commerce halted, markets closed, and demand for labor reduced, there was widespread unemployment and shortage of cash. Even where food was available, it could not be purchased.

If decreased indigenous food production were offset by increased imports, mass starvation could in theory be averted. However, the largest ocean port, Chittagong, was working at only 40 per cent of capacity because of labor shortage (6). The smaller ports at Chalna and Narayanganj were similarly handicapped. Moreover, the capacity to transport imported grain out of the ports to the interior was sharply curtailed. In any normal year, three modes of transport are utilized for the movement of foodgrain from Chittagong: rail (37 per cent), road (24 per cent), and water (38 per cent) (8). But rail links, roadways, ferries, bridges, and trucks were selectively destroyed by the Mukti Bahini. By June, official reports indicated that rail movement from Chittagong had been reduced to 20 per cent of normal; road movement was reduced to 30 per cent; and water transport was also inhibited (8).

5. The World Bank reported that "most cities and major towns have sizable pockets of destruction where marketplaces, small shops and workers' housing once stood . . . numerous villages have suffered heavy destruction, particularly to marketplaces and bazaars. The extent of damage and destruction varies greatly both between and within districts; however, few areas have escaped altogether" (6).

The breakdown in transportation also curtailed the internal movement of foodgrains from local sources. Under normal conditions, approximately 2 million tons of food are transferred from excess to deficit regions within Bangladesh (16). In addition, the urban location of storage facilities was inappropriate to the food requirements of the overwhelming majority of the population residing in the rural regions. Most of the food was needed in the countryside. Yet, over 40 per cent of total grain storage was located in three urban centers—Dacca, Chittagong, and Chalna (6).

SPECTER OF FAMINE

Although the precise cumulative effects of reduced indigenous rice production and impeded movement of food grain are still unclear, reliable, and independent sources have estimated shortfalls of production ranging from 1 to 2 million tons from previous years (Table 2). For the following analysis, we have accepted the average figure estimated by these observers. Yields for the crop year 1971 (one-year period from November 15, 1970), therefore, approximated 10.7 million tons (*aman*, 6.1; *boro*, 2.1; and *aus*, 2.5). A 10 per cent reduction is a reasonable estimate of loss due to seed usage, animal feed, and handling (Table 3). Approximately 150,000 tons have been subtracted due to the actions of the Pakistan army. One hundred thousand tons were estimated to have been carried into India with the exodus of the refugees. Against these losses we add the amount of grain imports received, approximately 1.07 million tons (17).[6]

Thus, our calculations estimate that the total food available to Bangladesh during the crop year 1971 was approximately 10.45 million tons (Table 3). The people of Bangladesh faced an 18 per cent food deficit and a per capita daily cereal availability of 12.8 ounces. Such a level of consumption, compounded by the existing inequities of distribution, was believed to be so grossly inadequate as to provoke a famine of unprecedented proportions.

In making their prediction of famine, observers pointed to the similarities between recent events and the Bengal famine of 1943.

6. The nature and quality of the relief effort to import and distribute food under the United Nations will be covered in Chapter 14.

TABLE 2

Bangladesh–Estimates of
Domestic Rice Production
in Crop Year 1971[a]

	Crop Yield (million tons)		
	Aman	Boro	Aus
World Bank (6)	—	2.18	2.13
U.S.A.I.D. (7)	5.91	2.2	2.47
S.R. Bose (19)	6.2	2.1	2.8
Average	6.1	2.1	2.5
Previous Optimum (7)	7.26	1.9	3.07

a. The crop year 1971 is the one-year period beginning
on November 15, 1970. It is a convenient demarca-
tion because mid-November is just prior to the *aman*
harvest. Crop year 1971 includes the *aman* crop harvested in November 1970 and the *boro* and *aus* crops
of 1971.

TABLE 3

Estimation of Food Availability
in Bangladesh During
The Crop Year 1971

	Foodgrain–million tons	
	Individual	Cumulative
Indigenous production [a]	10.7	10.7
Less 10 per cent loss [b]	1.07	9.63
Less destruction due to war [c]	0.15	9.48
Less loss with refugees [d]	0.10	9.38
Plus imported food [e]	1.07	10.45

a. magnitude of indigenous rice production taken from Table 2
b. 10 per cent loss due to usage for seed, animal feed, and losses
   during the handling, processing, and shipment
c. estimation of loss due to hostilities
d. estimation of loss due to flow into India with refugee exodus
e. estimation from official import and offtake statistics of the Department of Agriculture, Government of East Pakistan

In 1943, a 6 per cent food deficit among 60 million Bengalis precipitated a famine which resulted in approximately 3 million deaths (16). Nineteen-hundred-forty-three was also a year of war, during which scarce resources and facilities were diverted from agricultural to military use. The traditional source of rice imports from Burma was cut off. The official "denial policy" of confiscating transport facilities, to hamper the enemy should they attack, reduced cultivation of fertile coastal islands, and impeded the internal movement of food. Local shortages set off a spiral of rising prices, hoarding, and profiteering. While many died from starvation, even more deaths were due to the spread of infectious diseases stimulated by the breakdown of sanitation and a more susceptible, malnourished population.[7]

During October and November annual foodstocks are at their lowest annual level,[8] and it was feared that famine would appear during these months in 1971. The number of potential victims was estimated at 21 million: 13 million in families with landholdings of less than one acre, 7 million rural laborers, and 1 million urban poor (19). Yet the expected catastrophe failed to materialize. How was a major famine averted?

FAMINE AVERTED?

The most important single factor which contributed to the attenuation of famine was the substantial reduction in the population of Bangladesh during 1971. Estimates of civilian war deaths range

---

7. The horrendous condition of those victims of the Bengal famine of 1943 was vividly described by Ghosh: "mere skeltons covered simply with skin; some gasping for their last breath; mothers hugging their dying and dead children, unable, having no strength to weep or cry; some practically in delirium precedent to death a few minutes . . . after crying for a morsel of rice. . . . Haggard, half-naked women worn out for lack of food carrying rickety babies with dried-up limbs and old wrinkled faces; small children with bloated bellies and ribs standing out . . ." (1).

8. Even during normal years, the average Bengali food consumption varies greatly from month to month. October and November are the traditional lean months before the harvest of the large aman crop. The monthly incidence of infantile malnutrition also follows this seasonal pattern (12).

from 1 to 3 million.[9] Furthermore, from late March until the cessation of hostilities in December, there was a constant and continuous stream of refugees pouring into India (20).[10] According to official Indian Government statistics, the average daily influx approximated 36,000. During the peak months of May and June, daily arrivals exceeded 100,000.

The refugee flow occurred in three waves. The first, shortly after the army crackdown, consisted primarily of people who felt politically threatened—students, intellectuals, and members or sympathizers of the outlawed Awami League. The second, during the peak flow period of May through August, consisted predominately of Hindus, the persecuted religious minority. The final wave in October and November was at least partially stimulated by fear of food shortage and starvation (21).[11] In October, a representative of the U.S. administration testified before a Senate subcommittee: "We believe people are beginning to move because of hunger" (22).

The refugee exodus afforded Bangladesh a significant food saving; the food burden was shifted to India. A calculation of the magnitude of this food saving can be made with the following conservative assumptions:

1. Civilian deaths numbered 1 million and the mean death-date was May 1.

9. There are as yet no reliable figures on the number of deaths—both civilians and military—from the civil war. Conservative observers estimate 1 million while the Government of Bangladesh, by local village and district sampling, claims 3 million lives lost.

10. Professor John P. Lewis, Dean of the Woodrow Wilson School, reported on his travels to the India-Bangladesh border at a Senate subcommittee meeting: "The scene at the border itself might have been staged by Cecil B. DeMille . . . from the other side the boats started to come—countrycraft bearing by my estimate about 25 refugees apiece—first a cluster of three, then a half dozen more. Before the nearest reached India a total of 18 approaching boats were in view." (*Hearings before the Subcommittee to Investigate Problems Connected with Refugees and Escapees of the Committee on the Judiciary,* United States Senate. U.S. Government Printing Office, September 30, 1971.)

11. Although it is well known that nearly ten million refugees poured into India, the number of refugees who migrated within Bangladesh is difficult to estimate. One U.N. survey estimated 16.6 million Bengalis left their homes for other locations within the country for at least one month (30).

2. The refugee statistics of the Indian Government are reliable.[12]
3. Each refugee or death resulted in a food saving of 14 ounces daily.

From these assumptions, one can estimate a total food saving of 681,400 tons for crop year 1971 (Table 4). The 9.5 million refugees constituted a food saving of 597,300 tons. One million deaths provided 84,100 tons of unconsumed food. If one further assumes that the 75 million people of Bangladesh cut their average con-

TABLE 4

Food Saving in Bangladesh Due to
Deaths and Refugee Outflux

Month	Monthly Arrivals of Refugees in India[a]	Cumulative Arrivals	Monthly Food Saving[b]	Cumulative Food Saving
	(thousands)		(thousand tons)	
April	1,221	1,221	110.4	110.4
May	3,158	4,379	245.6	356.0
June	2,056	6,435	133.0	489.0
July	797	7,232	41.4	530.4
August	1,055	8,287	41.0	571.4
September	804	9,091	20.7	592.1
October	400	9,491	5.2	597.3
May 1[c] (deaths)	1,000	1,000	84.1	681.4

a. figures from the Ministry of Rehabilitation, Government of India
b. Assume that monthly arrival occurred on fifteenth of each month, and food-saving for Bangladesh equals 14 ounces per capita daily. Saving calculated to November 15, end of the crop year.
c. Assume that average death occurred on May 1, and number of deaths equals 1 million.

12. The precise number of refugees has been disputed by the Government of Pakistan. However, virtually all objective observers who have visited the refugee camps agree with official Indian estimates. The refugee numbers were reliably calculated by the use of ration cards. The Pakistan Government consistently claimed the presence of only two million refugees. Some have attributed this distortion to the fact that Pakistan did not recognize the Hindu refugees (who numbered about 8 million) as legitimate citizens of the Muslim state of Pakistan.

sumption to 14 ounces per person daily, Bangladesh's total food requirement for crop year 1971 approximated 11.59 million tons. We have previously estimated the food availability to be approximately 10.45 million tons (Table 3). Thus, the major portion of the deficit could be accounted for simply by taking into consideration the refugee exodus and civilian deaths. It is an irony, indeed, that the conflict which initiated the fear of famine also stimulated the compensatory mechanisms of migrations and deaths.

Other factors tending to alleviate the food shortage may have been overlooked or miscalculated as well. The aman crop of the previous year was distributed before the onset of hostilities in March 1971. The boro crop of 1971 was fully planted and cultivated before April. This fortunately yielded a good harvest during the war. Many jute fields were converted to the cultivation of rice. The *Mukti Bahini* publicly urged this conversion to deprive Pakistan of valuable foreign exchange generated by the sale of jute abroad. To the peasants, this made good sense, for rice could be eaten while jute had to be transported and sold in uncertain markets.

The capacity of the numerous waterways to accommodate foodgrain movement by countryboats may also have been underestimated. There was a surprising lack of private hoarding, profiteering, and speculation. The insurgents publicly called for cooperation in keeping food prices down and they confiscated hoarded supplies. Farmers sold stocks earlier than usual, fearing looting and destruction.

Probably the most underestimated factor was the resiliency of the Bengali peasants. Bengalis have had to weather numerous famines and yearly fluctuations of food-intake for generations. One lesson from the Bihar famine experience of 1967 was the capacity of the peasant to adapt to food deprivation in defiance of scientific analysis (23). According to nutrition textbooks, even the normal caloric consumption pattern of Bangladesh is insufficient to reverse the effects of starvation or famine (24).

IMPACT OF CIVIL WAR ON NUTRITION

Although a catastrophic famine was averted, there is sufficient evidence to suggest that the incidence of malnutrition, starvation, and epidemics of infectious diseases markedly increased during hostilities. Thus far, we have examined the food supply and demand equilibrium with an aggregate approach; a comparison of food available to population for Bangladesh permitted us to estimate per capita food availability for the nation as a whole. There was in reality, however, wide variation between various geographic localities. Uniform distribution of food cannot be assumed in most situations. After careful analysis, members of a contingency planning force concluded that 15 subdivisions faced serious food shortage while another 17 were marginal (there are 59 subdivisions in Bangladesh averaging 1.2 million people and 1,000 square miles each) (15). Although reliable morbidity and mortality statistics are not available from these critical subdivisions, there are numerous reports indicating widespread hunger, starvation, and deaths.[13]

The most striking results come from QUAC stick measurements performed on children in Matlab, Comilla District, before and after the hostilities (25–27). Using the same anthropometric criteria for the same population, these studies conclusively demonstrated a twofold increase in the prevalence of severe malnutrition among children after the war. Only 27 per cent of the children were found to be normally nourished after independence as compared to 50 per cent before the war. Similar findings were reported from Faridpur District where the severe malnutrition rate was also increased twofold from pre-war levels.

Previous studies in regions of mass starvation have shown that many, if not most, deaths are due to infectious diseases breaking out among a more susceptible, more malnourished population (23). In November 1971, Dacca and the surrounding countryside experienced the worst cholera outbreak in recent years. By Janu-

13. Father Goedert's diary graphically describes the situation in Nagari, a town within walking distance of Dacca: "Each day is worse than the previous one. Because of the intense army activity, the food situation now is difficult. With almost 5,000 people to feed, we are not even one day ahead on supplies. For two days we had to turn hungry people away. When we finally got in a boat-load of flour (from private relief) and began the distribution, one old woman couldn't wait until she got home. As she was walking away with her flour, she stuffed a handful of the stuff in her mouth. Try it sometime. You've got to be hungry." (*Christian Organization for Relief and Rehabilitation Newsletter* No. 11, March 6, 1972.)

ary 1972, the epidemic had spread to Comilla District (26). One need only consider the normal annual death rate due to diarrheal diseases and to cholera (estimated at 250,000) to appreciate the proportions of this epidemic. Other infectious diseases also broke out in epidemic proportions. Dysentery was common, and during early 1972 Bangladesh experienced a resurgence of smallpox.[14]

In a recent symposium sponsored by the Swedish Nutrition Foundation, famine was defined as, "a severe food shortage accompanied by a significant increase in local or regional death rates. Among the signs of a famine are rapid increase in the prevalence of persons who are markedly underweight and/or have hunger edema" (23). The nutritional catastrophe in Bangladesh during the civil war fulfilled all of these criteria of famine. Not only did Bangladesh experience the severest food shortage since the famine of 1943, but according to a reliable post-war health survey sponsored by the United Nations, the crude mortality rate (number of deaths per 1,000 population) due to natural causes increased by approximately 31 per cent during the conflict (30). Although a famine failed to approach levels predicted, that a famine occurred seems likely.

PROSPECTS

With the achievement of independence, Bangladesh faces the monumental task of rehabilitation and reconstruction, while inheriting a bankrupt economy, crippled industries, disrupted transport and communication links, and burned homes, market places, and towns. Faced with this destruction, the refugees from India poured back. By the end of March 1972, nearly all of the refugees had returned to their homes. These refugees joined another 17 million displaced and destitute persons within Bangladesh.

There is thus little room for complacency in the immediate future. Rice production in the future remains an uncertainty. Virtually no imported foodgrain was delivered from November 1971, until the end of February 1972, and the capacity of the inland transportation system is still severely restricted. Due to drought,

14. The large smallpox epidemic which struck Bangladesh in early 1972 is covered in Chapter 15.

yields from the *aman* crop of 1972 failed to reach normal levels. It has been estimated that at least 2 million tons of imported food grain will be needed during 1973.

With independence, Bangladesh should be able to devote its energy to its food and population problems. The beneficial impact of any advance will depend greatly upon the ability of Bangladesh to limit its population size. But it need not remain a chronic food-deficit nation. At present, Bangladesh possesses one of the lowest rice yields per acre in the world; only 3 per cent of the arable land is chemically fertilized; 15 per cent is sprayed with pesticides; and irrigation is underutilized. Formation of farming cooperatives, introduction of high-yielding rice strains (the Green Revolution), better water control with joint implementation with India and basic social and economic reforms could help provide adequate food for the people of Bangladesh.

References

1. Ghosh, K. C. *Famines in Bengal, 1770–1943.* Calcutta, 1944.
2. *The New York Times,* September 23, 1971.
3. *The Washington Post,* June 25, 1971.
4. Press Release from Oxfam and War on Want, April 1971.
5. Chen, L. C., and Rohde, J. E. Famine and Civil War in East Pakistan. *Lancet* 2:557 (1971).
6. *Report of the World Bank Mission to East Pakistan.* The International Bank for Reconstruction and Development. July 8, 1971.
7. Hesser, L. F. *Rice Production in East Pakistan: Prospects for the Year 1971–1972.* United States Agency for International Development. July 1971.
8. Ryan, J. A., and Weiss, E. J. *A Report on the Food and Transportation Situation in East Pakistan.* United States Department of Agriculture and Agency for International Development. June 3–21, 1971.
9. Revelle, R., and Thomas, H. A. Population and Food in East Pakistan. *Industry and Tropical Health* VII:27–43 (1970).
10. Mosley, W. H., and Hossain, M. Population: Background and Prospects. Part One, Chapter 2.

11. Rashid, H. E. *East Pakistan: A Systematic Regional Geography and Its Development Planning Aspects.* Second edition. Ghulam Ali and Sons, Lahore, 1967.
12. *Pakistan: Nutrition Survey of East Pakistan: March 1962–January 1964.* United States Department of Health, Education and Welfare. May, 1966.
13. *Food Plan for East Pakistan,* Department of Agriculture, Government of East Pakistan. August–December 1971.
14. Department of Agriculture, Government of East Pakistan, 1971.
15. Schwarzwalder, A. M., Unti, J., and Myers, D. *Contingency Planning for East Pakistan Food Shortages.* United States Agency for International Development. November 1971.
16. Muhith, A. M. A. *Report on Famine and Starvation in Bangladesh.* Embassy of Bangladesh to the United States. October 1971.
17. Department of Agriculture, Government of East Pakistan.
18. Muhith, A. M. A. *The Economy of Bangladesh: Is It Really an International Basket-Case?* Embassy of Bangladesh to the United States. October 1971.
19. Bose, S. R. *Foodgrain Availability and Possibilities of Famine in Bangladesh.* A Report Financed by the Ford Foundation. January 1972.
20. Kennedy, E. M. *Crisis in South Asia: A Report to the Subcommittee to Investigate Problems Connected with Refugees and Escapees of the Committee on the Judiciary, United States Senate.* U.S. Government Printing Office, Washington, D.C., 1971.
21. Galbraith, J. K. The Unbelievable Happens in Bengal. *The New York Times Magazine.* October 31, 1971.
22. Williams, M. J. *Hearings Before the Subcommittee to Investigate Problems Connected with Refugees and Escapees of the Committee of the Judiciary,* United States Senate. U.S. Government Printing Office, October 4, 1971.
23. Blix, G., Hofvander, Y., and Vahlquist, B. editors: *Symposium on Famine: Nutrition and Relief Operation in Times of Disaster.* Almqvist and Wiksell, Stockholm, 1971.
24. Passmore, R., and Davidson, S. *Human Nutrition and Dietetics.* Williams and Wilkins Company, Baltimore, 1963.
25. Loewenstein, M. S. The Cyclone: Nutritional Assessment with the QUAC Stick. Part Two, Chapter 10.
26. Zerfas, A. J. Correlation of Clinical Measurement Findings in Pre-school Age Children with Known Ages. February 1972. International Union for Child Welfare (unpublished).

27. Clark, A. Report on Nutritional Survey, Madaripur Subdivision, Faridpur District, March 28–30, 1972. Quaker Field Service (unpublished).

28. Chen, L. C. *Hearings Before the Subcommittee to Investigate Problems Connected with Refugees and Escapees of the Committee of the Judiciary, United States Senate.* U.S. Government Printing Office. February 2, 1972.

29. Hesser, L. F., and Suttor, R. E. *A New Look at the Food Situation in East Pakistan.* United States Agency for International Development. December 1971.

30. *Bangladesh Health Nutrition Survey.* Information paper No. 13. United Nations Relief Operation Dacca, June 23, 1972.

(14) CIVIL WAR IN BANGLADESH: RELIEF PLANNING AND ADMINISTRATION IN AN INSURGENCY SITUATION

Desaix Myers III

INTRODUCTION

Because the vast majority of the 75 million people of Bangladesh live at subsistence or near subsistence level, any breakdown in the food supply line places critical stress on survival (1). The outbreak of civil war in March 1971 posed a serious threat to health by simultaneously disrupting the three major sources of foodgrain: agricultural production, local marketing, and foodgrain import. Production was hurt by migration of cultivators and dislocation of critical production supplies and services: seeds, fertilizers, pesticides, credit, and pump fuel. Local markets were burned, traders were forced to flee, and transport routes were disrupted. Food imports, representing about 15 per cent of total consumption, clogged the ports and could not be transported or distributed in the countryside (Figures 14.1 and 14.2).

Fear of impending famine led the United Nations to make offers of assistance to the Government of Pakistan, and from June 18 to December 16, 1971, the UN operated an international relief program in Bangladesh. Given Bangladesh's logistical constraints, the problems of donor-recipient relations, and conflicts in distribution during an insurgency, the task of providing relief to a population the size of Bangladesh's was to prove extremely difficult. This chapter discusses some of the difficulties encountered in trying to plan and administer relief during the civil war in Bangladesh.

DESAIX MYERS III, staff member of the United States Agency for International Development, remained in Bangladesh during the civil war and participated in the international relief effort.

BACKGROUND: EARLY DISASTER PLANNING

Bangladesh is an area with a long history of disasters. One of the earliest references to Bengal, which dates from the third century B.C., cites an imperial order to a local ruler to distribute food-grains and money from the government storehouse to the famine

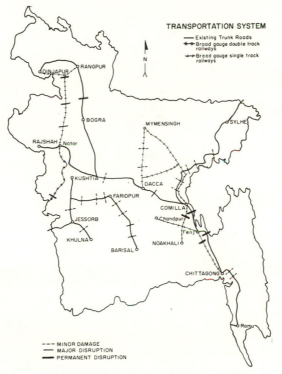

FIGURE 14.1. Rail and Road Routes in Bangladesh and Disruptions During the Civil War. Damage was extensive. The disruption to the rail network at Feni prevented upcountry movement of foodgrain from the port at Chittagong to Dacca. Food delivery to all rural regions was hampered by the damage to the transport infrastructure.

affected people in the area (2). Cyclones, droughts, and floods have been common, and repeated emergencies have forced governments in Bengal to develop an administrative approach to disaster relief.

Approaches and administrative tools were codified in the 1913 Famine Code and the 1941 Famine Manual. Strict guidelines concerning classification of relief recipients (according to tax rolls, marital status, and estimated need), methods of distribution, types

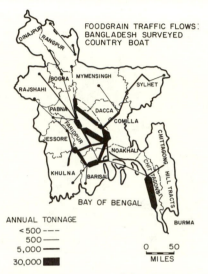

FIGURE 14.2. Countryboat Transport of Foodgrain in Bangladesh. This mode of transport is the most important for the inaccessible rural regions. In Faridpur District, hostilities impeded water movement and resulted in significant food shortage. Due to UN efforts, foodgrain from Chittagong to Chandpur was increased by importation of barges and coasters, but movement into some rural regions was hampered by hostilities and shallow waterways.

of loans and gratuitous relief, and organization of relief-work programs are set forth in these two documents.[1] Special instructions

1. Rationing was divided into two types: statutory and modified. Statutory assures distribution to government-affiliated employees and to residents of large cities. Modified rationing attempts distribution to rural population centers and nongovernment employees. Rationing, a continuous process in effect during normal time as well as crisis, aims to force free market rice prices to reasonable levels. Two additional distributions systems can be effected: open market distribution and gratuitous feeding. The latter proceeds according to classifications (tax assessment, personal and family status) as determined by the local council.

are given on taking readings of rainfall, crop estimates, flood level, and prices. Regular reporting on general economic conditions of the area under the District Officer's purview is required. District Officers are permitted to institute rationing, open market distribution, and gratuitous feeding. To meet fund shortages, Officers are permitted to initiate work programs, to give cash grants, and to make agriculture loans (3).

Although methods of dealing with disaster are well understood, relief implementation often breaks down. Inadequate supplies, lack of available personnel and transport, biased distribution at lower levels, and overburdened bureaucracy at higher levels, all serve to hamper effective distribution. Some of these problems (transport, planning, and supply of funds and materials) can be affected by international donors. One of the least likely to be changed by external assistance, however, is the administration of relief.

RELIEF ADMINISTRATION

Relief program administration in Bangladesh primarily involved four departments: Relief, Food, Transport, and Local Government (Figure 14.3).[2] Funds for relief were allocated by the Relief Department. A two-man department, Relief was not responsible for implementation;[3] distribution was handled by the Food Department working with the Transport Department, and final distribution fell to the jurisdiction of Local Government (BDLG). At the local level, relief committees were formed, based on established local councils (*thana*, union, and ward committees).[4] These com-

2. The Local Government Department was the Department of Basic Democracies and Local Government (BDLG) established by President Ayub Khan in the early sixties. It replaced the traditional Local Government instituted by the British. Although there was much talk of abolishing the Basic Democracies aspect of the Department after Ayub's fall in 1969, the Department was still referred to as a BDLG in 1971.

3. The Relief Department was staffed by a Secretary and a Deputy Secretary. Additional officers were deputed from other departments during a crisis. The Department allocated funds and food supplies for delivery and distribution by other departments.

4. The *thana* or county consisted of an area approximately 100 square miles with a population of 150,000 to 200,000. There are 356 *thanas* in

mittees were responsible for drawing up lists of those in need, classifying needs into categories, and deciding on distribution of food, cash grants, and work-relief funds. A *thana* Food Inspector was to check lists periodically for accuracy, and the distribution operation was supervised by the *thana* Circle Officer, a non-gazetted officer in the civil service. Government officers from other departments (Health, Family Planning, Agriculture) might be deputed to assist in relief distribution, but the ultimate responsibility fell upon the Deputy Commissioner (DC), the chief District

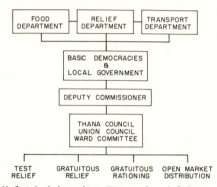

FIGURE 14.3. Relief Administration. The major deficiency of this organizational structure is lack of built-in leadership. Effective relief requires optimal coordination among four departments which may be difficult to attain during a crisis.

Officer. Weighing the severity of the crisis and his availability of funds and stocks, the DC would allocate relief supplies to the *thana* Circle Officer; the Circle Officer would in turn allocate to the unions; and the unions to the wards. If the situation was critical and stocks were available, gratuitous distribution could be instituted; if less severe, the DC might order open market distribution. To raise purchasing power the DC could distribute test relief funds to pay wages at less than market rate for work done on embankments, clearing of ponds, and building of roads. By paying

Bangladesh. The Union Council succeeded the old British Union Board and served a population of approximately 10,000. The Ward Committee served a population of approximately 1,000.

less than the market rate, the DC would "test" the need for work-relief. If the severity warranted and he had funds available, he could also allocate cash grants to be distributed through the local councils.

RELIEF DURING INSURGENCY

East Bengal did have, therefore, both disaster experience and a traditional system for coping with disaster. Against this framework four major forces would become involved in affecting relief operations during the civil war: the UN, the Pakistan Army and the Government of Pakistan, the Mukti Bahini (guerrilla insurgents), and the Bengali civil servants in the administration. Objectives for the four groups differed. Where they overlapped, the relief program enjoyed some success; where they conflicted, it became frustrated.

The United Nations

With the Secretary General's appeal for assistance to the people of East Pakistan on June 16, 1971, the United Nations became the prime international organization involved in relief assistance. The objective was stated as "an attempt to forestall a situation in which a very large number of human beings may perish from famine and other causes associated with the dislocation of life in their country" (4). It was designed to be a neutral effort to move foodgrain to areas in need, and by October over $143 million worth of food, cash, and transport supplies had been pledged to that effort (5).

Fear of famine was based upon projections from current stock levels, production estimates, and assessment of disruption to the transportation infrastructure (1). Reports called for imports of up to 200,000 tons per month in order to maintain stock capacity required for minimum consumption requirements. The transport system, badly disrupted by army and insurgent activities was hardly capable of sustaining the load. Railroads supplying 60 per cent of the transportation north from Chittagong (the main port) under normal conditions had been cut off (Figure 14.1), and the line north from Khulna which had played an even more important role in transporting foodgrain to the northwest was badly damaged. Ports became clogged, and office buildings in Chittagong were being used to store the overflow (Table 1).

TABLE 1
Movement of Imported Foodgrain into and out of
Major Ports During the Civil War

	June	*July*	*August*	*September*
		(metric tons)		
Arrival at Ports	—	84,000	181,000	211,000
Movement from Ports	50,000	54,000	88,000	150,000

The UN attempted to circumvent the impeded up-country movement of food by chartering low-draft vessels to move foodgrain by the numerous waterways in Bangladesh. Even with the supplementary transport, however, movement up-country was not fast enough to unclog the ports. By fall, stocks in storage depots around the country had fallen from 687,000 tons in June to 350,000 tons in October (4).

While the chief UN objective was the supply of food relief, the principal operating concern was to establish the UN operation as neutral, independent, humanitarian, and "above the battle" (6). Unless such neutrality could be established, there was little hope that implementation could be effected. Coasters, minibulkers, and trucks carried large UN markings identifying the vehicles as part of the UN program for humanitarian relief; coasters and minibulkers were operated by foreign crews. Orders were issued by the UN and assurances given by the Government of Pakistan that both trucks and UN boats would carry nothing other than foodgrain. Jute transport was not permitted, despite pressure from the Government of Pakistan. Even jute gunny bags were prohibited. Plans called for the import of 26 vessels and 1,000 trucks (4). By November, 100 trucks had arrived, and 17 vessels (8 minibulkers and 9 coasters) were in place (4).

To monitor distribution the UN had hoped to place observers in field stations. In November, reports were filed that UN person-

nel had indeed been posted in field positions. In fact, fears of insecurity had kept the UN from posting field personnel except in a
very few cities (Khulna, Chittagong, Rajshahi). The areas of greatest need, (parts of Faridpur, Noakhali, and Rangpur Districts) were
also areas of greatest insecurity (Figure 14.4). Although these
areas were touched on field visits, no field stations were established. It is doubtful, given the inadequacy of local transport and

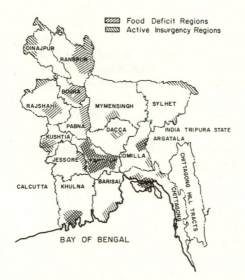

FIGURE 14.4. Areas of Insurgent Control and Food Shortage. The most impressive fact is that areas of greatest need were controlled by the *Mukti
Bahini*. Yet UN food was not channeled through the insurgents. By delivering food solely through the army controlled civil administration, food
rarely reached the regions of greatest need.

the lack of government stocks, that field stations could have been
successful in ensuring adequate distribution, although regular field
reports would have helped determine priorities and allow focus of
scarce resources. In the end the UN decided that implementation
of the program was to be done primarily through the existing administrative structure, and the UN operation was limited to supply
and transportation to terminal points from where local administrators would handle distribution.

The Government of Pakistan and the Role of the Army

Relief assistance would have been impossible without some degree of cooperation from the Government of Pakistan. The UN could not initiate efforts until invited. Although Secretary General U Thant offered assistance to Pakistan on April 1, it was not until late May that President Yahya Khan accepted his offer. It was not until mid-June that the UN was able to establish offices in Dacca. There had been considerable reluctance on the part of the Pakistan Government to recognize the possibility of famine until international pressure made it impossible to ignore (7). The Government stressed the availability of adequate stocks in the country and minimized transportation disruption. Only in August did they officially recognize the acute problems facing Bangladesh (8).

It is impossible to document the rationale either for the Government of Pakistan's delay or for its acceptance of international assistance. During the early months, the Government wanted to suppress all news coming out of Bangladesh, to hide what it considered a domestic problem. When it became clear that the situation would not return to "normalcy" through military suppression and that the threat of guerrilla activity could continue indefinitely, the Government might have seen advantages to an international relief operation: to supply food and other needed inputs, to assist in repair of the transport system, and to replace such things as coasters and trucks which had been requisitioned for military use. United Nations participation in food distribution within Bangladesh, working with the Government of Pakistan, gave the Government a certain legitimacy in world opinion that it may have felt it had lost through the suppression.

In any event, relief itself was not the principal objective of the Government's permitting UN operations to proceed. Unwillingness to return requisitioned vehicles or boats to relief organizations, reticence to allow field stations, reluctance to appoint full-time personnel to relief operations (7), preoccupation with military operations, and attacks against the Hindus and other "anti-social elements" demonstrated the Government's lesser interest in relief activity.

At the field level, control was delegated to the army Majors in individual sectors. The field personnel operated independently of Government statements of amnesty, and on several occasions, Deputy Commissioners reported quietly to foreigners that the local Majors had refused them the right to distribute foodgrain to areas of suspected guerrilla activity.

The Insurgents

In late November, the *Mukti Bahini* succeeded in mining three UN minibulkers. Almost simultaneously an effort was made to fire-bomb UNICEF trucks in Chittagong. The trucks and the mini-bulkers had been well marked; there was no doubt that the *Mukti Bahini* had been aiming specifically at the UN operation. It was the first direct action against the UN operation.

Although some international relief representatives had been taken aside during the summer months and told by the insurgents that their efforts were being viewed as contributions to a return to normalcy and therefore collaborationist, no serious attempt had been made to stop the operation until November. Indirect messages from the *Mukti Bahini* had given the impression that the relief effort was recognized as humanitarian assistance and the *Mukti Bahini* did not "wish to stand in the way of people being fed as long as the effort is truly under the United Nations' auspices and is truly a neutral effort" (6).

There was great fear among Bengalis, however, that UN vehicles would be misappropriated, that foodgrains would be diverted, that the army and their sympathizers would benefit, and that relief distribution at the local level would be handled by the Peace Committees [5] to exclude all Bengali sympathizers. In order to reassure the *Mukti Bahini* of the neutrality of its operation, the UN needed to deliver to areas of insurgency as well as to pacified areas. It had become evident by November that delivery to these pocket areas of greatest need and also greatest guerrilla insurgency

5. The army attempted to control the countryside by forming "Peace Committees" in rural villages. Those appointed to the Committees consisted primarily of pro-army segments of the population. By in large, the Committees were composed of ultra-conservative Muslims, opportunists, or "Biharis" (non-Bengali Muslim immigrants to Bengal).

would be impossible, and this realization may have influenced the *Mukti Bahini* move to interdict the UN operation.[6]

Civil Administration

During the critical months of the civil war, the district and local administrators found themselves in extremely ambiguous and precarious positions. To cooperate with the Martial Law Administration would be to collaborate; not to cooperate would be to deny that the people for whom they were responsible needed food, rehabilitation, and funds. The functional administration, the Bengali members of the elite Civil Service of Pakistan, were generally sympathetic to the *Mukti Bahini;* yet they were accountable to the army. They sought to establish a degree of apparent neutrality (neutrality at least to the Martial Law Administration, with perhaps loyalty visible to the insurgents). Most succeeded and were able to operate limited cash and food relief programs under duress.

At the lower levels the *thana* and union officials were in an even more difficult position. By August the *Mukti Bahini* controlled close to 25 per cent of the territory. In these areas the *Mukti Bahini* aimed their attacks at *thana* headquarters and these raids jeopardized *thana* personnel. Although *Mukti Bahini* recognized the necessity for an ongoing civil administration and allowed officials to remain at their jobs, the army, upon recapturing a liberated *thana,* was likely to view the officials as *Mukti Bahini* sympathizers. The union officials were in the least desirable position. As local leaders they were forced into collaborationist peace committees; as rich men who had profited from the Pakistani rule, they were targets of guerrilla assassination. Many union council chairmen fled their homes to find shelter in the more secure subdi-

6. Although informal talks were held between UN representatives and representatives of the Bangladesh Government (Bengali insurgents), open contact could not be made. Nor could the UN consider channelling relief supplies through the *Mukti Bahini* into insurgent-controlled territory. Some attribute this lack of formal contact as a sign of UN insensitivity and as a cause for *Mukti Bahini* disaffection. In reality, it was due primarily to the UN's feeling that its legitimacy in Bangladesh at the reticent behest of the Pakistan Government without the support of a UN General Assembly resolution was extremely tenuous.

visional headquarters; many others were attacked. The system of local council distribution was severely disrupted, and although new leadership was emerging, it was with much conflict.

RELIEF ASSISTANCE

International relief assistance can have only marginal impact on such a situation as existed in Bangladesh during the civil war. It cannot rectify the imbalance, supply all needs, or ensure equitable distribution. It can be effective only in particular areas: planning, supply, and certain levels of transportation. The final step, distribution, must depend primarily on the local and traditional administration.

Planning

The most important task facing international donors in Bangladesh was to establish priorities and to focus Government will and resources on needs in defined areas. At first the Government showed little interest. Two assessment reports finally moved the Government to become involved (1,7), but the potential problem was so vast and the resources so limited, that it was critical that an early defining of geographic priorities be made.

Under normal conditions it would have been possible to work directly with the Food and Local Government Departments, assessing needs, outlining priorities, using bi-weekly field reports from officers (both Local Government and Food Departments) deputed to Relief. Such information had become classified by the Martial Law Administration, however, and although occasional reports were passed to international relief organizations, to do so involved great risk for the government officer. Relief donors were forced to do planning in a relative vacuum. Despite the hazards of such planning from limited data, it was important that donors make some effort to establish geographic priorities. In September, the United States Agency for International Development (USAID) prepared a contingency plan for food shortages in Bangladesh (9). This plan combined a simple survey of existing information with projections and encouraged the UN and the Government of Pakistan to look at the alternatives available, to set up an information system that could signal population areas of greatest need, and to conduct field operations to check on data projections. It provided a geographical delineation of requirements. Focusing on a few critical areas as examples, it offered case studies of logistical alternatives.

Information was available or could be approximated for a country breakdown analysis at the subdivision level. The subdivision level was selected as the lowest level of accurate Food Department accounting. There were 59 subdivisions in Bangladesh, averaging fewer than 1.2 million people and 1,000 square miles. Data was collected on population, agriculture production by season, daily consumption requirements, public stocks available, and monthly offtake rate. From these data "Profiles" were made for each subdivision.

A ratio of food availability to monthly consumption requirement was made, and subdivisions were divided into three categories: (a) those with negative availability; (b) those with less than one month's consumption requirement; (c) those with availability equal to one month or more. A ranking was made, putting 15 subdivisions in the most likely to experience food shortage category and 17 in the category requiring close monitoring. The effort was to gather and set forth available statistics to identify geographical priorities.

The Profiles did offer relief donors some framework for program development. USAID field trips concentrated in areas of greatest need, and although some discrepancies became evident, the Profiles generally proved reliable in assessing relative need. Madaripur, in Faridpur District, for example, did suffer acute shortage, prices rose as high as 80 *rupees* from 40 *rupees* per *maund* (82 pounds). Insurgency action had prevented food delivery, and subdivision officers reported rumors of famine from the interior.

The Profiles, while encouraging some concentration of resources and energy, did not solve the problems of delivery to the interior. The Government of Pakistan was preoccupied with military priorities. The local administration was upset by insurgent action and at the *thana* level by lack of supply and personnel. Test Relief programs were estimated at affecting less than 2 per cent of the population.[7] Food delivery was hurt by absence of ration shop dealers, local traders, ox carts, and countryboats.

Transport

The Profiles demonstrated the tremendous difficulties in trying to meet food shortages in a country as rural, as riverine, and as populated as Bangladesh. The permanent disabling of the main rail and road routes by the incision at Comilla, and the repeated guerrilla attacks on the road and rail system from Khulna, severely limited transportation in these areas (Figure 14.1). Countryboat operators, frightened by army operations (many boatmen were Hindu, or taken for Hindus, and were fired upon or killed) or guerrilla attacks, refused to ply in certain areas. Even with offers of incentive payments some boatmen would refuse to travel in the interior areas of Faridpur for fear of violence.

With the destruction of the traditional supply routes, the USAID report (9) discussed the possibility of air transport of food under contingency planning. A closer look at the potential size of the population, the consumption requirements to be met, and the logistical constraints involved, however, discouraged the use of helicopters, short-take-off-and-landing craft (STOL), or even large transport planes (C-130) in any but the most dire of circumstances. In a country as populated as Bangladesh, famine in one isolated area can affect as many people as famine across all of Scandinavia. A small village of 25,000 could require a fleet of four helicopters operating daily. Some of the potential "pockets" of food shortage had populations in the millions, and air delivery would have required fleets of helicopters and armies of support personnel. During the cyclone relief effort, for example, 8 helicopters flew a total of 1,250 sorties over a period of 25 days to deliver 500 tons of relief supplies. Sixty-three men were required to keep 8 helicopters flying; 8 hours of service were estimated as required for each flight hour. Because range is limited, helicopter services require numerous support centers supplying petroleum, oil, lubrication (POL), and giving transport problems that could be as serious as that for food itself.

7. Estimated from data gathered by the author on a field tour in October 1971.

STOL service also has severe limitations, both because of small cargo capacity (two tons) and required landing strips. Perhaps, the best air transport alternative is the C-130 with a twenty-ton carrying capacity. Consideration still must be given to logistical constraints: in this case location of adequate landing sites. Since food dropped from C-130's needs to be double bagged to prevent loss at dropping, sufficient manpower and an efficient bagging operation are necessities (9).

Distribution

Planning and transport represent only two of three major difficulties in large relief operations. The third is distribution. In the relief effort to Bangladesh, the UN had hoped to have complete control over relief operations from the import of the foodgrains to the final distribution. The World Food Program temporarily debated food for work programs and massive free-food programs, but analysis of the tremendous numbers and the areas to be covered underscored the impossibility of foreign organizations handling food distribution alone. Also to be considered was the Government of Pakistan's desire to have the ultimate responsibility for all relief operations. The UN at one time contemplated the free distribution of 280,000 tons of wheat and rice (10). It was decided that the only feasible way to deliver amounts of this magnitude was through the established administrative structure, through the Deputy Commissioners, to the *thana* Circle Officer, through the Union Councils and Ward Committees to the people (Figure 14.3).

Difficulties in using the traditional systems were rife. The local storage depots lacked supplies; ration shop dealers had fled; *thana* headquarters were not in operation; and Union chairmen had been killed or were collaborationist. There was no choice. Indigenous administrators had to take charge of local level distribution. A large-scale relief effort cannot operate if it is dependent on distribution by foreign groups. There are not enough donor staff members to go around; they lack experience with local customs and institutions; they are unable to judge need accurately. Local level politics have usually already decided which power group will play the major role in distribution. During the civil war this was difficult for relief organizations to accept since often it meant that Peace Committees would be able to use relief supplies for their own political ends. Only rigid central and district supervision could have prevented this, and both District and Central Government personnel found this extremely difficult to do both for political and logistical reasons.

There were certain exceptions to this generality of ultimate local dominance in distribution. The Catholic Organization for Relief and Rehabilitation with an established hierarchy of local personnel, substantial field experience, and local language on its side was able to effect an efficient relief operation. Other voluntary agencies, already in the field, notably British Consortium and CARE, were able to function with some effectiveness, but their projects were limited and were aimed more at rehabilitation than immediate relief.

The lack of committed Government of Pakistan supervision, the difficult position of government administrators, and the frequent lack of field officers, gave negative demonstration of the importance of in-country local administration assuming relief responsibility. In those areas where relief operations were effective, in areas of Comilla and Faridpur, it was because of competent and hard-working local administration. In large-scale relief operations, donor countries and voluntary agencies can supply only resources; the fulfilling of the ultimate objective, distribution, will depend on the will and the effectiveness of the Government and the local administration.

DISCUSSION

Of the three areas outlined, planning, transport, and distribution, the latter two proved to present insurmountable problems. The UN operation was not able, given time constraints and security problems, to place permanent teams in the field to monitor or effect distribution. Although UNICEF made considerable efforts toward and eventually succeeded in establishing a feeding program to some 160 schools, its impact on the total food situation was marginal at best. Trucks, minibulkers, and coasters donated by the UN were able to make only a small dent in the transport crisis; by November, only 100 UN trucks had arrived in country and minibulkers and coasters had provided transport for 78,000 tons in four months, the equivalent of slightly more than 2 per cent of the total consumption requirement during that period. Transport upcountry to the areas of greatest need could not be effected. Areas of greatest need had proved, in many cases, to be areas of greatest insurgency: areas which could not be reached by international transport both because of logistic and security difficulties and because the army (at least local level Majors) viewed food as a resource to be withheld from insurgents. Because the UN was unable to reach these areas in time (the food crisis was to come in late October and November and by the end of November most of the pledged grain lay in the ports, Central Supply Depots, or in transit), the *Mukti Bahini* withdrew endorsement of the UN operation. Food was not being transported to areas the *Mukti Bahini* considered of primary importance.

Although it is improbable that the UN operation could have enjoyed more than minimal success under the circumstances, certain things might have been done to enhance the likelihood. The delay in delivery of food and transport vehicles meant that most of the resources were unavailable until after the crisis had passed. Preplanning and pre-pledging of foodstuffs, relief supplies, transport equipment, logistics staff, to a United Nations Organization could have resulted in quicker arrival and a greater chance for timely distribution.

In relief assistance the donor can offer three things: relief supplies, transport, and planning. Of these three, planning is the easiest and the most likely to have some success in an insurgency situation. It can be done, at least superficially, in isolation from the Government without encountering the logistical constraints of transport and distribution. Planning is empty, however, without implementation. Implementation can be encouraged by planning, by the timely supply of relief goods and by transport and logistic support; but in the end, the success of a larger relief operation, particularly one the size of that attempted in Bangladesh, is dependent of the will and administrative capacity of the Government and its local administration.

The planning effort succeeded to a certain extent in alerting the Government of Pakistan and international donors to problems and dangers ahead. To the extent possible, the Profiles made some contribution to geographical focus. Planning for disaster relief, however, cannot ensure that relief requirements are met, but can only encourage the use of common sense in a situation in which emergency conditions urge decision makers and citizens to act irrationally. The planning reports provided through the UN operation offered some encouragement to common sense and responsible action, but emergency conditions and political irrationality prevented the implementation of planning recommendations.

References

1. Hesser, L. F. *Rice Production in East Pakistan: Prospects for the Year 1971–1972*. United States Agency for International Development. July 1971.
2. Ahmed, Nazerhuiddin. *Mahastan*. Department of Archeology and Museums in Pakistan. Karachi, 1964.
3. *Famine Manual,* Government of Bengal, Revenue Department. Reprint Series No. 6, June 1967.
4. Henry, Paul-Marc, United Nations Press Release GA/SHC/1717/IHA/94, November 19, 1971.
5. Fong, Hiram L. *Hearings Before the Subcommittee to Investigate Problems Connected with Refugees and Escapees,* U.S. Government Printing Office, October 4, 1971.
6. Williams, M. J. *Hearings Before the Subcommittee to Investigate Problems Connected with Refugees and Escapees,* U.S. Government Printing Office, October 4, 1971.
7. Ryan, J. A., and Weiss, E. J. *A Report on the Food and Transportation Situation in East Pakistan.* United States Department of Agriculture and Agency for International Development. June 3–21, 1971.
8. *Food Plan for East Pakistan,* Department of Agriculture, Government of East Pakistan. August 1971.
9. Schwarzwalder, A. M., Unti, J., and Myers, D. *Contingency Plan-*

ning for East Pakistan Food Shortages. United States Agency for International Development. November 1971.

10. *Plan for Free Distribution of Food in East Pakistan.* United Nations East Pakistan Relief Organization, Dacca. November 1–December 31, 1971.

(15) POST-CIVIL WAR IN BANGLADESH: THE SMALLPOX EPIDEMIC

Alfred Sommer, Nilton Arnt, and Stanley O. Foster

INTRODUCTION

In 1966 the World Health Organization's General Assembly voted to launch a worldwide program to eradicate smallpox. By December 1971, the number of endemic countries had been reduced from 28 to 8, and 4 countries, Ethiopia, Sudan, India, and Pakistan, accounted for over 95 per cent of the reported cases (Figure 15.1) (1). These persistent pockets of endemicity continue to pose a significant health threat to these countries and to the international community at large.

Smallpox eradication requires not only programs in individual countries, but also regional and international coordination and cooperation. In West Africa, 20 countries with a total population of 110 million people successfully eradicated smallpox through a four-year program from 1966 to 1970 (2,3). In other areas, countries that had successfully eradicated smallpox were reinfected by importations from neighboring nations (4).

In 1968 Bangladesh, then East Pakistan, with technical assistance from the World Health Organization, launched a nationwide program to eradicate smallpox. By 1970 the reported incidence of smallpox had fallen to undetectable levels, and transmission may well have been terminated. But in January, February, and March 1972, the return of infected refugees re-established endemic smallpox in the country. This chapter documents the reintroduction of smallpox into Bangladesh and delineates the problems that migrations between countries pose for worldwide smallpox eradication.

The authors were members of a WHO Smallpox Eradication Team which assisted the Ministry of Health, Government of Bangladesh, in 1972.

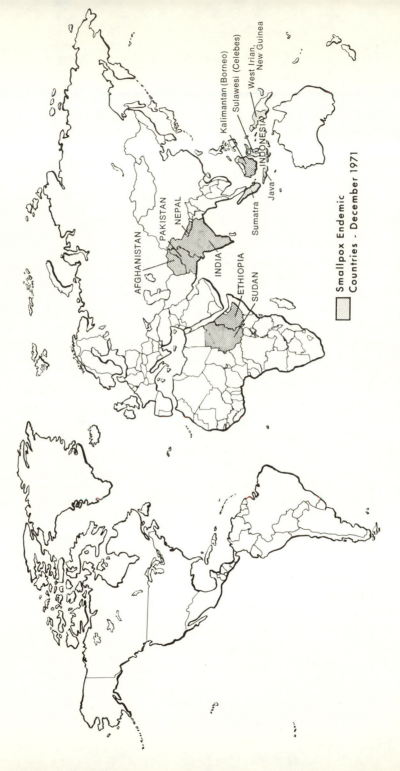

FIGURE 15.1. Smallpox Endemic Countries—December 1971

SMALLPOX IN BANGLADESH

Smallpox in Bangladesh follows a cyclical pattern with a peak incidence every five to seven years (Figure 15.2). Of the years from 1951 to 1970, the most cases occurred in 1958 (79,060 cases) and the fewest in 1964 (45 cases). The last peak year was 1968, when 3,735 cases were reported. The disease also follows a seasonal pattern, with the majority of cases occurring during the first five months of the year.

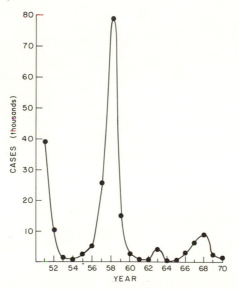

FIGURE 15.2. Annual Reports of Smallpox Cases in Bangladesh (1951–1970)

In 1968 the Provincial Government of East Pakistan launched a province-wide program to eradicate smallpox. Mass vaccination programs with concurrent assessment were begun in 10 of the 19 districts, but progress was slower than anticipated (5). At the end of the first year only 26 per cent of the target population had been vaccinated (Table 1). A scar-survey sample assessment of vaccinated areas in 1970 showed vaccination scars in 65 to 86 per cent of the population (Table 2).

In addition to the mass vaccination campaign, four special containment teams were established to investigate and control all reported outbreaks, and efforts were directed at improving surveillance. This latter program resulted in a twofold improvement in

TABLE 1
Progress of Mass Vaccination Program, Bangladesh
January–November 1970

Age Group (Years)	Target Population	Number Vaccinated	Percentage Vaccinated
0–4	3,367,280	907,866	26.9
5–14	4,810,400	1,588,761	33.0
15+	9,011,120	2,022,790	22.4
Total	17,188,800	4,519,417	26.2

TABLE 2
Percentage of Population with
Vaccination Scar by District
(1970 Survey)

District	Per Cent with Vaccination Scar
Bogra	64.9
Dacca	72.1
Dinajpur	71.5
Faridpur	69.0
Jessore	77.5
Kushtia	75.6
Pabna	86.2

reporting from recognized outbreaks from 1969 to 1970 (Table 3). Although the eradication program was interrupted by the civil war that began in March 1971, significant success in interrupting transmission of the disease appears to have been achieved before that time. No smallpox cases were reported between September 1970 (six months before the disturbances began) and January

1972. Although the absence of reported cases during the latter part of this period could represent a breakdown of the surveillance system, an active search for cases was carried out by the containment teams without success, and physicians interviewed in April 1972 were unable to recall any cases between August 1970 and January 1972. In all probability, smallpox transmission had been interrupted by the fall of 1970.

TABLE 3
Percentage of Smallpox Cases
Reported from Known Outbreaks,
Bangladesh, 1969–1970

Year	Number of Smallpox Outbreaks Investigated	Reported Cases	Total Cases	Percentage Reported
1969	11	105	1139	9.1
1970	11	150	715	21.0

THE 1972 EPIDEMIC

Early in 1972, soon after the cessation of hostilities, WHO received reports of smallpox in the Salt Lake Refugee Camp, outside Calcutta. Although a mass vaccination program was initiated, the camp eventually recorded a total of 784 cases with 369 deaths. Three additional camps, two in 24-Parganas and one in Cooch Behar, all in the state of West Bengal, were also reported to be infected. By February 1972, the first cases of smallpox in Bangladesh in 18 months were being reported from Rangpur District in the extreme northwest (Figures 15.3 and 15.4). Two months later a total of 2,055 cases with 734 deaths had been officially reported to the Smallpox Eradication Program in Dacca (Figure 15.5). These reported cases probably represent only a small fraction of the total cases. Intensive investigation of one large outbreak in Barisal revealed that the official figure of 241 cases represented only 12 per cent of all the cases. Although a majority of the 19 districts have reported at least an occasional case, major outbreaks have occurred in only two widely separated areas (Figure 15.6),

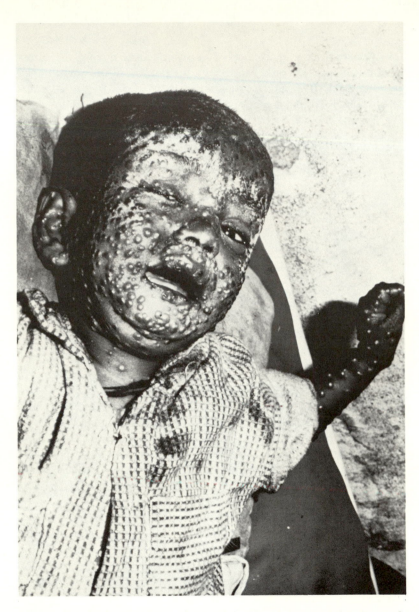

FIGURE 15.3. Bengali Refugee Child During the Acute Eruptive Stage of Smallpox

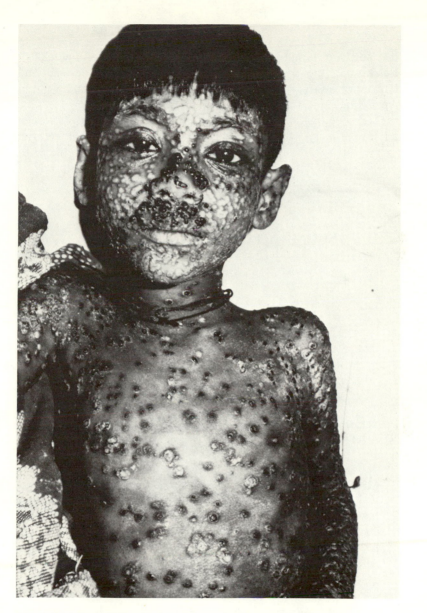

FIGURE 15.4. Bengali Boy in the Recuperative Stage of Smallpox

the northern promontory of Rangpur District adjoining Cooch Behar, and the southwestern districts of Khulna, Barisal, and Faridpur. Attack rates are provided for the period January 1 to April 8 in Table 4.

Case investigations revealed the following epidemiologic points:

1. The primary source of almost every outbreak was a refugee returning from one of the smallpox endemic states of India. In the majority of cases, the source's exposure occurred in one of

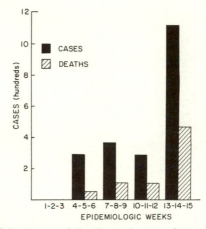

FIGURE 15.5. Officially Reported Smallpox Cases and Deaths in Bangladesh (1972) by Three-Week Intervals Ending April 8

the four infected camps, although some reported having been exposed en route to their homes, either in the vehicle bringing them back to Bangladesh or in one of the reception camps on the Bangladesh side of the border.

2. The epidemic is confined almost entirely to the returnee population. Very little spread to nonrefugees has occurred, even within the same village. This is probably related to the social, religious, and familial insularity of the individual *bari,* a cluster of patrilineally related families living around a common courtyard. This system breaks down in the densely populated urban areas, and there the disease has spread to the nonrefugee community.

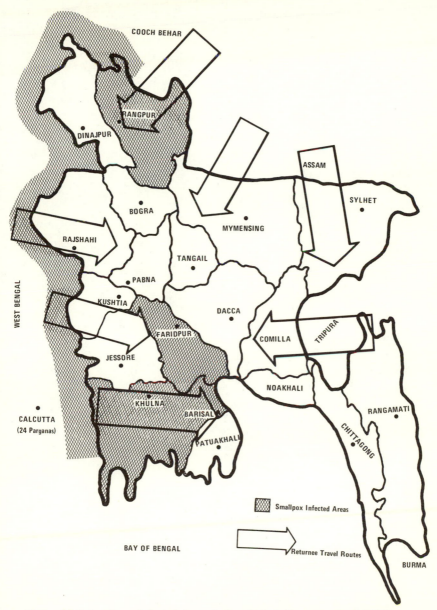

FIGURE 15.6. Smallpox Infected Areas in Bangladesh (January–April 1972)

TABLE 4
Reported Smallpox Incidence in Bangladesh
January 1–April 8, 1972

District	Cases	Sub-division	Cases	Rate Per 100,000	Per Cent Population with Vaccination Scar[a]
Barisal	745			16.9	
Bogra	0			—	64.9
Chittagong	7[b]			0.2	
Chittagong Hill Tracks	0			—	
Comilla	1			0.0	
Dacca	8			0.1	72.1
Dinajpur	0			—	71.5
Faridpur	778[c]			17.0	
		Goalonda	0	—	74.3
		Gopalganj	601	61.0	57.8
		Madaripur	142	8.1	49.9
		Sadar	0	—	81.4
Jessore	20			0.6	77.5
Khulna	189			5.4	
Kushtia	0			—	75.6
Mymensingh	0			—	
Noakhali	0			—	
Pabna				—	86.2
Patuakhali	7			0.4	
Rajshahi	0			—	
Rangpur	307			5.6	
Sylhet	1[b]			0.0	
Tangail	0			—	

Total Officially Reported – 2,063

a. 1970 assessment data
b. identified by WHO Advisor—not officially reported
c. In 35 cases the sub-division was not identified.

3. More than 80 per cent of all the patients lack evidence of prior vaccination. This appears to have had important geographic implications. Those areas of Bangladesh found to be well vaccinated in a 1970 scar survey have remained relatively free of disease. For example, Kushtia (zero cases) and Jessore (20 cases) both had large influxes of refugees from the smallpox endemic state of West Bengal, and also served as transit stations to the more heavily infected neighboring districts of Khulna, Barisal, and Faridpur. Table 4 indicates that the vaccination status of their populations is better than that of the infected subdivisions of Faridpur, the only one of the three neighboring districts for which data are available. The majority of cases are confined to Gopalganj and Madaripur subdivisions, both of which are poorly vaccinated (57.8 and 49.9 per cent respectively). The vaccination status of the two remaining subdivisions is considerably better (74.3 per cent and 81.4 per cent).

4. The distribution of cases by patient's age (Table 5) approxi-

TABLE 5

Age Distribution of 209 Smallpox Patients
in Barisal District

Age Group (years)	No. of Cases	Per Cent Distribution of Cases	Per Cent Distribution of Population[a]
0–4	43	20.5	21.3
5–9	62	29.7	13.3
10–14	35	16.8	14.7
15+	69	33.0	50.7
Total	209	100.0	100.0

a. represent 116,909 individuals under study by the Cholera Research Laboratory in Matlab Bazaar, a rural area 40 miles south of Dacca

mates that of the general population at large (6), except for the 5 to 9 years age group. The disproportionate representation of this age group probably reflects a combination of two factors: relatively low levels of immunity and high mobility. The latter probably accounts for the greater prominence of this age group over those 0 to 4 years of age, who according to previous vaccine scar surveys are the least protected.

5. Although the nutritional status of the returnees is significantly poorer than pre-war baseline standards (7), the case fatality rate of 34 per 100 (for variola major) is similar to that reported elsewhere in Asia.

CONTROL MEASURES

Although faced with an overwhelming number of nonmedical problems, the Bangladesh Government, with the help of WHO, has launched an aggressive smallpox control program combining the technique of mass vaccination with surveillance and containment. While the former has gone a long way toward satisfying public demand and is the initial step in reinstituting a systematic eradication program, it cannot by itself materially affect the present epidemic. If the present outbreak follows the usual seasonal pattern in Bangladesh, it will abate before the coming of the monsoons, a total duration of three to five months. Given the experience of the well-organized and financed campaign of 1970–71, no more than 5 to 10 per cent of the population can be reached within that time period.

The major emphasis has therefore been placed on case-finding and containment. The entire rural health structure was employed in making a village-by-village search for new cases. Specially trained containment teams were being established to respond to each reported case with a house-by-house search for additional cases and contacts. The primary focus of these activities was the patrilineally related *bari,* containing between 15 and 50 individuals. Each house within the affected bari was revisited on three successive days, at least once at night, and at one, three, and six weeks. This resulted in the vaccination of over 95 per cent of reported contacts, effectively blocking further transmission and eliminating the outbreak as a source of further infections.

DISCUSSION

Epidemic diseases such as cholera and smallpox have often accompanied disasters in Bengal. Although there has been much conjecture as to the factors which could be responsible for the epidemic spread of infection during both manmade and natural catastrophes, there have been few facts with which to judge the relative importance of the many variables which are always involved. The migration of vast numbers of people from refugee areas in India back to their homes within Bangladesh has been clearly shown to be closely related to the epidemic spread of smallpox in Bangladesh during the spring of 1972.

While in India the refugees were housed in crowded camps in smallpox endemic districts, such as Cooch Behar and 24-Parganas (Calcutta) in West Bengal. Returning home to Bangladesh, they brought the disease with them. Of the many reasons why this relatively captive population went unprotected, the most important was undoubtedly the sheer magnitude of their number which overwhelmed the capacity of refugee health services. Efforts at smallpox vaccination competed with other, more pressing needs, such as food, shelter, and clothing. Even in the purely medical sphere, smallpox loomed as a future threat, while cholera was an immediate one in the refugee camps. By the time cholera was under control and the nutritionally important feeding programs were under way, it was already too late. Under these circumstances, the hurried attempt to vaccinate the refugees against smallpox was only partially successful. Lack of trained personnel, insufficient resources, use of antiquated equipment—all contributed to incomplete implementation. In addition, many of the refugees resisted vaccination when offered to them. Their reasons were manifold: the vaccination scar was seen as a physical blemish (many parents therefore allowed themselves, but not their children, to be vaccinated); many feared contracting smallpox from the vaccination process itself; and perhaps most important, the Hindus, who made up the bulk of the refugee population, believe that smallpox is the curse of the Goddess *Shitala* for past sins, and vaccination was therefore viewed not only as useless but, even worse, as a further provocation of the Goddess.

Two major factors seem to have determined the geographic distribution of the 1972 epidemic: the pattern of migration of individuals from the four infected refugee camps in India and the prewar vaccination status of the different areas within Bangladesh. Refugees from the better vaccinated areas were more likely to be protected, and therefore less liable to infection while in India, and any infections they might have brought home would have had less opportunity to spread.

The course of the outbreak during the second half of 1972 seems to support this hypothesis. The major outbreaks remained confined, for the most part, to the same two geographic areas noted above, although as time progressed increasing numbers of cases were being reported from outside these regions. This spilling over of infection into the initially smallpox free segments of the population was even more rapid within the affected areas themselves. While the vast majority of cases were initially Hindu refugees (who make up less than 10 per cent of the population of Bangladesh), the bulk of the subsequent cases were in nonrefugee Muslims.

Previous studies (8) have implicated cities as the major foci of maintenance and subsequent dissemination of smallpox to the countryside. This seems to have been the pattern of the large southern epidemic (Khulna, Barisal, and Faridpur). Khulna town, the commercial and transportation hub of the region, experienced a mammoth outbreak (9). Numerous introductions into the town were traced first to returning refugees, and later to families and factory workers arriving from infected areas in the countryside. Crowded into squalid slums or *bustees,* they exposed other workers and families who introduced the disease in turn into their own previously unaffected villages. Thus a vicious cycle was established between the town and countryside which, because of the large proportion of transients, has been very difficult to interrupt.

Attempts to control the epidemic have centered on mass vaccination and case-finding and containment. While we have already pointed out that mass vaccination is a relatively inefficient method of influencing the course of the 1972 epidemic, it forms an integral part of the smallpox eradication program and has gone a long way toward reassuring the public. The real danger inherent in any mass vaccination campaign is the false sense of security provided by the feeling that "something is being done," further obscuring the need for intensive surveillance and containment of active cases. In 15 "contained" outbreaks we investigated, approximately 50 per cent of the close contacts of the index case lacked recent vaccination, and over a third of the children lacked primaries. In the quest for vaccinating the greatest number of people, the immediate contacts of the index case, who were at the greatest risk of becoming infected and perpetuating the chain of transmission, remained unprotected. By concentrating instead on case detection and containment, there is the hope of limiting the number of endemic foci that will persist into the inter-epidemic period, when transmission is naturally decreased and total eradication might be more easily accomplished (10).

Unlike many of the other health problems of the underdeveloped world, such as amebiasis, tuberculosis, cholera, malnutrition, and overpopulation, smallpox is eradicable with present technology. There are no inapparent infections or chronic carriers capable of silently spreading the disease, and there is no known reservoir of infection besides man. Vaccination with lyophilized vaccine by means of bifurcated needles is simple, inexpensive, benign, and highly effective. By combining the techniques of routine vaccination, to raise and maintain the general levels of immunity, with surveillance and containment of all cases (especially during the inter-epidemic period), smallpox can be eradicated. But as long as a single country remains infected, it poses a serious threat to the rest of the world.

References

1. *Wld. Hlth. Org. Weekly Epidemiol. Rec.* 47:17–26, 1972.
2. Millar, J. D., and Foege, W. H. Status of Eradication of Smallpox (and Control of Measles) in West and Central Africa. *J. Infect. Dis.* 120:725–732, 1969.

3. *Wld. Hlth. Org. Weekly Epidemiol. Rec.* 46:17–18, 1971.
4. *Wld. Hlth. Org. Weekly Epidemiol. Rec.* 47:161–162, 1972.
5. Markvart, K. *Report of World Health Organization Smallpox Advisor,* Dacca, Bangladesh, 1971.
6. Chowdhury, A. K. M. A., Aziz, K. M. A., and Mosley, W. H. *Demographic Studies in Rural East Pakistan—Third Year, May 1968–April 1969.* Cholera Research Laboratory, Dacca, Bangladesh.
7. Clark, A. *Report of Nutritional Survey, Madaripur Subdivision, Faridpur District,* Quaker Service, Bangladesh, March 1972.
8. Thomas, D. B., McCormack, W. M., Arita, I., Khan, M. M., Islam, S. M., Mack, T. M.; Endemic Smallpox in Rural East Pakistan. I. Methodology, Clinical, and Epidemiologic Characteristics of Cases, and Inter-village Transmission. *American Journal of Epidemiology* 93:361–372, 1971.
9. Sommer, A., Foster, S., Arnt, N.; A Massive Outbreak of Smallpox in Khulna Municipality, Bangladesh. I. Methodology and Basic Epidemiologic Characteristics. Manuscript in preparation.
10. Foege, W. H., Millar, J. D., and Lane, J. M. Selective Epidemiologic Control in Smallpox Eradication. *Am. J. Epid.* 94:311–315, 1971.

(16) POST-CIVIL WAR IN BANGLADESH: HEALTH PROBLEMS AND PROGRAMS

William B. Greenough III and Richard A. Cash

INTRODUCTION

It is perhaps presumptuous for individuals who are not citizens of a country and have surveyed only briefly the end result of events which witnessed immense dislocation of people and services to comment on the results. However, an external point of view may lend some objectivity to observations on the general subject of health in Bangladesh. At the outset one must realize that it is unlikely there will ever be data that could stand the test of scientific critique with regard to even such gross events as loss of life. The more subtle idea embodied in the concept of "health" clearly must be commented on from a vantage point which cannot be statistically enumerated with any accuracy: for health is not just the absence of disease but rather a state of physical, mental, and social well-being.

In Bangladesh, as in other parts of the world, good health is a blessing and those who possess it are thankful, while those who do not aspire to achieve it. Although ill health is more common and disease a greater risk in Bangladesh, people are neither less anxious to achieve a healthy state nor less grieved by loss of health than in areas which are better insulated from the ravages of social dislocation, malnutrition, and epidemic diseases. The idea that because death is so common, there is lesser grief or sense of loss of loved ones is erroneous. An ingrained acquaintance with catastro-

DR. GREENOUGH and DR. CASH worked under the auspices of the International Rescue Committee during the early months of 1972 in Bangladesh. Both worked at the Cholera Research Laboratory before the war: Dr. Greenough from 1962 to 1965 and Dr. Cash from 1967 to 1970.

phe perhaps makes one savor health and life even more intensely.

In this chapter we shall comment upon the effects of the civil war on health, the problems generated during the period from March 1971 to December 1971, and the programs for health care in the post-war period. The prospects for improved health in Bangladesh depend on this matrix as well as upon an awakened awareness by the population in general of the opportunities for improved organization of health services by better control of their fate through their own intervention in the political, social, and economic arenas.

IMPACT OF WAR ON HEALTH

During the civil war which erupted in March 1971 and extended through the succeeding nine months, concern about health was reduced for the majority of people to a fight for survival. The most immediate problem was to avoid being shot or burned as the army of Pakistan swept out from the cities into the rural areas burning a vast number of villages. The scope of this manmade tragedy cannot be tallied accurately or adequately but millions of people were forced to flee from their homes. The migration did not only pour into India where an estimated 10 million refugees sought refuge, but according to a post-war health and nutrition survey conducted under the sponsorship of the UN, an estimated 16.6 million persons were displaced from their homes within Bangladesh for at least one month (Table 1) (1). Those persons who lived in close proximity to the border were more likely to flee into India while those from more central regions preferentially migrated within Bangladesh.

Mortality rates during the conflict are not known precisely. Impartial foreign observers and the Government of Bangladesh have estimated 1 to 3 million civilian deaths. The UN estimated that the crude mortality rate due to natural causes increased from a normal level of 1.6 per cent to 2.1 per cent during the war (1). This represented an increase of 31 per cent from normal years and indicated that a minimum of 1.6 million deaths occurred. The actual mortality figure is much higher since those deaths that resulted directly from military hostilities are not included in this estimate.

Many deaths during the civil war were due to disruption of the basic needs of food and shelter as well as the inevitable attrition of the very old and very young or those too frail or sick to survive the stresses of walking many miles to remote areas or to India.

TABLE 1

Per Cent of Population Migrating by District (1)

District	Remained at Home	Fled Within Bangladesh for One Month or More	Fled to India	Total Displaced
Barisal	84.9	12.8	3.2	15.1
Chittagong	59.1	28.7	12.1	40.9
Comilla	78.9	13.2	8.0	21.1
Dacca	66.5	32.3	1.2	33.5
Dinajpur	26.2	30.7	43.1	73.8
Faridpur	81.2	10.8	8.0	18.8
Khulna	38.7	14.9	46.4	61.3
Kushtia/Jessore	65.6	13.7	20.7	34.4
Mymensingh	76.1	15.9	8.0	23.9
Noakhali	59.9	31.0	9.1	40.1
Pabna/Bogra	57.9	37.2	5.0	42.1
Rajshahi	42.1	32.4	25.6	57.9
Rangpur	56.3	25.2	18.5	43.7
Sylhet	58.9	22.9	18.2	41.1
Rural Bangladesh	64.2	22.1	13.7	35.8

Source: From Bangladesh Health Nutrition Survey, United Nations, 1972.

The severity of the food shortage has been documented in previous chapters. The UN has estimated that 2.1 million persons were living without any home of their own in June 1972 and that 1.5 million houses had been completely destroyed (Table 2) (1,2).

Although health services were rudimentary at best before the war, they became non-existent in the disrupted areas during the war. The loss of such services, in reality, has greater impact on the sense of security than on actual reduction of morbidity or mortality. The inability to provide antibiotics or other potentially life-saving medicines cannot be estimated as their efficacy as used before the war is unknown.

Epidemics did occur during the war and it is likely that their spread was enhanced by the increased movement of people as is

TABLE 2
Per Cent of Families by Housing Status and District
in Bangladesh (June 1972)

District	Puka^a	Kutcha Adequate^b	Damaged	Inadequate	No House
Barisal	1.3	32.0	9.5	54.7	2.7
Chittagong	2.5	37.5	22.2	32.2	5.5
Comilla	1.3	43.9	6.5	46.5	1.9
Dacca	0.6	52.5	3.5	40.6	2.7
Dinajpur	0.0	48.3	18.0	33.7	0.0
Faridpur	0.6	45.9	13.5	37.9	2.1
Khulna	5.6	30.3	25.0	31.3	7.8
Kushtia/ Jessore	5.0	35.8	16.0	40.3	3.0
Mymensingh	0.1	37.9	3.9	57.6	0.6
Noakhali	0.9	35.0	6.6	51.9	2.8
Pabna/Bogra	0.2	37.6	7.5	51.9	2.8
Rajshahi	3.8	32.6	12.1	46.8	4.7
Rangpur	0.0	35.0	8.3	55.6	1.0
Sylhet	3.3	52.4	4.9	35.7	3.6
Rural Bangladesh	1.6	39.8	9.8	46.0	2.8

Source: From Bangladesh Health Nutrition Survey, United Nations, 1972.
a. Houses which were classified as *puka* were made of substantial building materials such as brick or concrete.
b. Houses made of less durable materials such as mud or woven mats but still able to withstand the monsoon were classified as *kutcha* adequate.

shown in Chapter 15. During November 1971, more than 2,000 severe cases of cholera were admitted to the hospital of the Cholera Research Laboratory in Dacca which was the largest monthly number of patients cared for by this unit in its ten-year history.

At the Matlab Bazaar rural treatment center a similarly large number of cases was seen. In the past the number of cases seen at these hospitals have roughly reflected the numbers in the community. It is likely with this large number arriving at a hospital when transportation was disrupted and a war was in progress that cholera took an enormous toll during the epidemic in November and December 1971. It is of interest that the upsurge of cholera took place at the time of the anticipated seasonal increase in this disease, so it could have been expected and, in fact, was by the Cholera Research Laboratory. Hence, the mortality rate at this institution was under 1 per cent. In the community, the death rate is usually between 30 and 50 per cent.

Accurate appraisal of deaths due to the cholera epidemic will never be known except anecdotally. It is clear, however, that many thousands of people both within Bangladesh and in refugee areas in India died of cholera. Since all deaths due to this disease are preventable, this epidemic should be of particular concern.

POST-WAR HEALTH PROBLEMS

Between the end of the war in December 1971 and March 1972, the 10 million people who fled into India returned to their homes (Figure 16.1). In addition, 16.6 million displaced persons also returned to their villages. Simply stated, this represents the largest dislocation of any population in recorded human history. When they began to return, they not only lacked basic needs of food, shelter, and the minimum tools to begin rebuilding their shattered existence, but they also carried with them diseases such as smallpox and malaria (3) which further harassed them during resettlement.

The number-one priority in the post-war period was the rapid and effective distribution of food. Indigenous rice production had been crippled. Imported food could not be distributed because of a devastated transport infrastructure. Furthermore, means to plant and harvest the coming crops had to be provided to the farmers. The threat of famine, which peaked in November 1971, was far from over.

Expressed in a different way, the lack of food was objectively

manifested and could be documented in the population which was at greatest risk, i.e., the 1- to 10-year-old children. Although in normal times there is considerable malnutrition in Bengal, the war markedly increased the proportion of malnourished children (Table 3). Using the QUAC stick measurement on the same pediatric population in Matlab, studies performed prior to and after the war showed a twofold increase in the percentage of severely malnourished children. Normally nourished children fell from 50 per cent to 29 per cent (4,5).

The various population groups seemed to possess varying degrees of nutritional deterioration. By far, the hardest hit group was the refugees. Over half of the children in Salt Lake Refugee Camp were classified as severely malnourished as compared with 9 per cent in Matlab prior to the war (5). There appears to be two explanations for this disparity. First, the refugees were predominately Hindus who constitute the poorer segment of Bangladesh's population during normal times. Second, the refugees obviously suffered enormous hardships: the actions which forced them to flee and a long trek without food and shelter to India.

A QUAC stick survey in Faridpur District in March 1972 provided further evidence of the poor nutritional status of the population as well as the disparities between various population groups (6). The returned refugee population possessed the largest percentage of severely malnourished children. Displaced persons, although healthier than refugees, fared worse than the stable population. These disparities were due in part to the degree of losses the groups suffered during the war. Although the stable population was the healthiest group, it compared unfavorably to the prewar Matlab standards. Confirmation of the significant deterioration of nutritional status is also provided by the results of QUAC stick measurements made on carefully selected sampling sites nationwide. The 14 per cent severely malnourished children nationwide indicate significant deterioration from the 9 per cent encountered prior to the war.

FIGURE 16.1. Refugees Returning to Bangladesh from Refugee Camps in India on a Road near Bagdha (courtesy of UNICEF)

As during the war, destruction of transportation facilities was the largest single obstacle to the distribution of food (3,7). Fortunately, the Bangladesh Government was able to employ the indigenous transport system comprised of countryboats, ox carts, and people to meet immediate and urgent food needs. By April a great

TABLE 3

Impact of the War on Nutritional Status of Children
as Determined by QUAC Stick Measurements

Percent of Children[a]

Reference	Location	Date	Normal	Moderately Mal-nourished	Severely Mal-nourished
(3)	Matlab, East Bengal	November, 1970	50	41	9
(4)	Matlab, Bangladesh	February, 1972	29	54	17
(4)	Salt Lake Refugee Camp	January, 1972	9	38	53
(5)	Faridpur District	March, 1972			
	Average Stable		—	—	17
	Population		—	—	15
	Displaced Persons		—	—	18
	Returned Refugees		—	—	31
(1)	Nationwide, Bangladesh	May, 1972	44	42	14

a. The same QUAC stick criteria were employed for the data presented in this table.

deal of road rebuilding had been completed under the test works program of the Government and Christian Organization for Relief and Rehabilitation (CORR) (8). Ferries, trucks, and railroads were beginning to carry a larger proportion of the needed goods and the ports of Chittagong and Chalna were functioning better.

In addition to immediate needs the urgent requirement to plant and harvest the best possible crop by the fall of 1972 was obvious. During the war much of the seed stock was destroyed and many improved strains of rice, vegetables, and particularly of jute, the major cash crop, were lost. Agriculture was second only to the needs for food and shelter in terms of urgency. It is likely that food production will be lower in quality as well as quantity over an indeterminate period due to insufficient agricultural credit and lack of fertilizer, proper tillage, and good seeds. Planning will have to take this into account in the near future and the international community will need to assist in fulfilling the deficit.

POST-WAR HEALTH PROGRAM

It is of utmost importance to realize that the most effective projects which improved the health of people after the war were not those labeled as health projects. In order of efficacy, feeding, housing, providing income through the test works program, and repair of water supplies rank well above any program of medication or clinics in their over-all impact. The best way to prevent disease is to provide conditions of optimum housing, sanitation, and nutrition. Health workers, when confronted with a situation such as the one that took place in Bangladesh, must bear this in mind when considering priorities in the expenditure of money and effort.

If one looks at what are considered "health programs" in Bangladesh after the war, one can easily be critical because there were many deficiencies. This is particularly true if one was an observer unacquainted with the state of health prior to March 1971. There were major lacks in the distribution of medicines and skilled medical personnel. However, it is equally important to bear in mind that adequate health care was sorely lacking in prewar Bangladesh and that sensible health priorities properly focused on the supply of food and provision of shelter. We believe that the successful moves on the part of the Bangladesh Government which averted famine and provided shelter with a maximum of speed indicated a good grasp of health priorities. The fact that by the summer the price of coarse rice was going down or remaining stable is indicative of initial efficacy in programs of distribution and prevention of hoarding (9). Improvement of nutritional status was confirmed by a second UN nutrition survey conducted in September and October of 1972.

The test works program of employing jobless men to construct homes, roads, bridges, and embankments not only provided labor to rebuild the society but also supplied many people with the money they desperately needed to buy food. The increased purchasing power also stimulated the small shops and bazaars to spring back rapidly into commercial activity. It was striking to us to see in early April such a rapid return to flourishing activity of so many of the market places in both rural and urban areas of the country. This rapid return of internal commerce was the correlate of the vast amount of earth moving by the people to repair damage and construct new roads and dikes in the works program (Figure 16.2).

The areas that are classically assigned as the domain of health were not ignored in that a large portion of the effort and the resources of the private voluntary agencies were directed toward health services. As of the end of March 1972, $7.8 million out of $68.9 million spent by private groups were for health-related activities (9). The performance of the various 48 agencies varied considerably. Where the effort was directed at supporting and making use of the existing medical facilities and personnel the results were often striking. Examples are the supply of medicines and of salaries for the staffs at existing hospitals or rural health centers, the financial support for the treatment of cholera and diarrheal diseases, and the training programs to extend the reach of effective treatment methods. Least successful in our opinion was the importation of teams of foreign medical specialists to give primary medical care, since they often had little knowledge of the indigenous problems or priorities and were not able to communicate well with their patients. Much money was wasted on elaborate surgical supplies and facilities and on medicines which were not essential and often outdated.

In disasters relief teams often seem lured by glamourous activities and overlook what may be cheaper, more effective, yet not nearly so newsworthy. Field hospitals, operating rooms, specialists in plastic surgery, etc., are given support before vaccinating teams

FIGURE 16.2. Workers Under the Test Relief Program Moving Earth to Reconstruct a Road (courtesy of Dr. R. A. Cash)

or paramedical persons. It is very costly to fly hospital beds half way around the world and to bring in complete field hospitals geared to caring for battle casualties. The foreign staff members of such hospitals often find their skills inappropriate to the major needs. In addition, the availability of sophisticated care to a limited few, tends to raise the expectations of the people. This creates unnecessary difficulties for future health-related activities. Most important, these programs are inefficient in terms of cost-effectiveness.

In contrast to such expensive efforts, several model projects were initiated by agencies working to support local efforts. One such project was initiated by a group of Bengali physicians who had established an excellent field hospital in the Agartala region during the fighting and subsequently sought funds for implementing a long-term plan to care for the health needs of the rural population. The goal of their effort is worth quoting in their own words (11):

The purpose of our project is to evolve some system by which the medical care of the whole population of a particular area can be undertaken efficiently and effectively with the minimum expenditure and maximum benefit with the employment of limited medical manpower. To make this project viable we have to find (and train) a large number of paramedical workers, family planning personnel, social and health education workers. . . .

From this statement it seems evident that the time and money devoted to transporting large amounts of outdated medicines or elaborate equipment is better devoted to establishing facilities and recruiting people to train paramedical personnel. Efforts should be directed at training indigenous personnel to treat the common diseases which are susceptible to simple health measures. Clearly, immunization against the very prevalent diseases, such as tetanus, diphtheria, smallpox, and measles, would at far less cost save many more lives than the building of modern hospitals and certainly more than the services for a few weeks of a surgical team.

A specific example in pre-war Bangladesh of the effectiveness of paramedics was documented in a rural area in Comilla District in 1963. Briefly trained, uneducated health workers, previously local health practitioners, were taught to treat cholera with intravenous rehydration and antibiotics. They were able to reduce mortality from 40 per cent to less than 10 per cent. This occurred at a time when the death rate in the city hospitals in Dacca was about 30 per cent. Now field hospitals established by the Cholera Research Laboratory are able to treat thousands of cases cheaply with a loss of life that is less than 1 per cent. Care in such rural treatment centers is provided mainly by paramedical personnel.

PROSPECTS

With the urgent needs of food and shelter being met, the Government was by early summer 1972 moving to develop and implement plans for effective health care for the entire population. There seems to be a genuine commitment to seek a more equitable and effective distribution of services. This is an enormous task and it is one that the people of Bangladesh should develop to fit indigenous needs.

Regardless of the system employed, Bangladesh will have to address itself with considerable urgency to the three major health problems it now faces—overpopulation, malnutrition, and infectious diseases. Effective approaches on the basis of current knowledge are available but will require unprecedented social and organizational changes. In our opinion, it is crucial to move on all three fronts simultaneously, for these problems are intimately interrelated and interdependent. Better nutrition cannot result from sheer increase in food production alone without a concomitant decline in the spiraling population growth rate. Control of infectious diseases will be greatly hampered by malnutrition, overcrowding, and poor sanitation, conditions exacerbated by rapid population growth. Yet, most important, efforts to reduce the population growth rate may not realize maximal impact unless they are coupled with programs aimed at reducing morbidity and mortality from malnutrition and infectious diseases. The people of Bangladesh now demand better health as a human right, and unless there is some reasonable assurance of survival of their offsprings, voluntary limitation of family size will be extremely difficult to induce.

The state of health in Bangladesh cannot be regarded as an isolated problem. In our modern world, the health of one area impinges directly on the well-being of people in distant areas. The transmission patterns of the smallpox outbreak in Bangladesh and the recent worldwide spread of cholera are examples of the dangers of disease in distant corners of the world. Hence, in addition to urgent humanitarian needs, even enlightened self-interest urges that all nations concern themselves with better health for the people of Bangladesh.

References

1. *Bangladesh Health Nutrition Survey,* Information Paper No. 13, United Nations Relief Operation Dacca. June 23, 1972.
2. *Informal Report of the Secretariat,* United Nations Relief Operation, Dacca. February 29, 1972.
3. *Report of the Mission of High Level United Nations Consultants to Bangladesh.* Vol. II. March–April 1972.

4. Loewenstein, M. S. The Cyclone: Field Assessment of Nutritional Status with the QUAC Stick. Chapter 10.
5. Zerfas, A. J. *Correlation of Clinical Measurement Findings in Pre-school Age Children with Known Ages.* International Union for Child Welfare, Dacca. February 1972.
6. Clark, A. *Report on Nutritional Survey of Madaripur Subdivision Faridpur District, Bangladesh.* Quaker Service, March 28–30, 1972.
7. *Report of the Mission of High Level United Nations Consultants to Bangladesh.* Vol. I. March–April 1972.
8. *Christian Organization for Relief and Rehabilitation, Bangladesh.* Vol. 1, No. 3, p. 3. April 1972.
9. *United Nations Relief Operation Dacca Weekly Summary Report.* March–June 1972.
10. *Report to the Office of the Coordinator of External Relief "List of Foreign Voluntary Agencies in Bangladesh" and Summary Statement of Their Plans and Activities at End of March, 1972.* United Nations Relief Operation Dacca. March 1972.
11. *Proposal by the Bangladesh Hospital and Rehabilitation Center,* Dacca, Bangladesh. February 1972.

Part Three
RECOMMENDATIONS

(17) FRAMEWORK FOR DISASTER RELIEF

Lincoln C. Chen and Robert S. Northrup

INTRODUCTION

Disasters by their very nature seem to defy efficient relief planning and administration. Governments, international organizations, and private agencies are called upon to act immediately to restore some degree of equilibrium. Because of this urgency, there is often little time taken for planning, assessment, coordination, and implementation. As a result, personnel may be inefficiently utilized, and scarce resources may be misdirected or wasted. Such *ad hoc* actions are not only less than optimal but may be counterproductive as well.

Yet this need not be the case. Disasters can be anticipated and contingency plans can be formulated before they are needed. During the crisis, field assessment can identify the approriate relief requirements. Leadership and coordination of the over-all relief effort can be improved. National and international operational structures can be strengthened.

The disasters and relief operations described in this book serve as important models for a discussion of what might be done to establish a framework for relief efforts at times of disaster. The cyclone that struck Bangladesh in November 1970 came during peacetime and within the geographical boundaries of one nation. Responsibility for the relief operation rested solely with the Pakistan Government. The problems produced by the civil war of the following year, occurring at a time of major political and military

The editor is grateful to the following contributors for their suggestions: R. A. Cash, S. O. Foster, W. B. Greenough, M. S. Loewenstein, W. H. Mosley, D. B. Myers, J. E. Rohde, and A. Sommer. The helpful comments of E. Griffel, R. Timm, and N. Borton are also gratefully acknowledged.

differences, demanded other approaches. Refugee relief was carried out in India and was supervised by the Indian Government. Relief in Bangladesh was carried out by the United Nations in a rather uneasy partnership with the Government of Pakistan. These three different events (cyclone in Bangladesh, refugees in India, and famine in Bangladesh) necessitated varying approaches and solutions to the wide range of problems they encountered. The lessons learned from these diverse experiences can provide valuable information for the future.

The intent of this chapter is not to provide a "how to" or step-by-step manual for disaster relief operations; such information is available from other sources (1–10). Rather our purpose is to offer a constructive approach to effective relief planning and administration for future disasters in developing regions of the world. The chapter is divided into the following sections: Pre-disaster Planning, Field Assessment, Relief Operations Under Peaceful Conditions, Relief During Military Conflict, Rehabilitation and Development.

PRE-DISASTER PLANNING

Pre-disaster planning is essential to anticipate disasters before they occur and to provide a prearranged framework, at both national and international levels, for rapid, coordinated, and effective response. Planning can identify disaster-prone regions, coordinate warning systems against natural disasters, provide background information on local conditions, and offer contingency plans. With such preparation, flexibility and optimal effectiveness in the response to a disaster can be achieved more easily.

International and National Organizations for Disasters

Despite the frequency and regularity of disasters throughout the world, there is as yet no international organization capable of assuming full responsibility for pre-disaster planning. There is no single office to give guidance, no focal point of decision-making, no evaluation or assessment machinery, and no one to discriminate in the efficient allocation of worldwide resources. An effective international disaster planning and coordination body is urgently needed. The United Nations recently established a Disaster Office, but its experience and resources are limited. It should be strengthened and needs more support.

An effective international disaster body should coordinate two phases of disaster relief: pre-disaster planning and international assistance. It should encourage the formation of national units to plan and prepare for disasters within their territories, providing technical assistance if requested. National plans should be centrally collected and used to promote mechanisms for regional coopertion. Moreover, other international agencies (within and outside the United Nations) should be asked to participate. Planning of certain areas of disaster assistance may be delegated to other organizations along traditional lines of strength. Food procurement and delivery might be delegated to the World Food Program and Food and Agriculture Organization (FAO). Similarly the World Health Organization (WHO) might be assigned health; the UN High Commissioner for Refugees, refugee care; and the International Committee of the Red Cross, protection of minorities and prisoners.

When a disaster strikes, the international disaster body should act as the focal point for international assistance. Prospective donations to the disaster-affected region should be cleared and channeled, not through multiple bilateral assistance programs, but through the international organization. This will produce a more integrated response. The organization also would provide the affected government with technical assistance in carrying out the relief operation.

Pre-disaster planning should include the following components: 1. identification of disaster-prone regions, 2. coordination of warning systems, 3. provision of information on local conditions, 4. pre-arranged contingency plans.

Identification of Disaster Areas

Most natural disasters, i.e., cyclones, earthquakes, floods, and drought, occur in predictable geographical regions. Recognition of such disaster-prone areas should permit the disaster planner to focus his attention on specific localities. In Bangladesh, for example, the vulnerable southern coast is swept by an average of forty cyclones from the Bay of Bengal per decade. Other regions which have experienced repeated natural disasters include: the St. Andreas fault in the Americas (site of the Peruvian and San Franciscan earthquakes), the territory in the path of the yearly Caribbean hurricanes, and various regions along major rivers subject to flooding, such as the Ganges and Yangtze.

Manmade disasters, usually war and civil disturbances, evolve more slowly with time, thereby providing an opportunity for specific pre-disaster planning. The civil war in Bangladesh erupted in March, some months before the peak refugee exodus to India in early summer and before famine threatened Bangladesh in November. Time was therefore available for planning and coordination. Other recent manmade disasters have also exhibited an evolution with time, including the Palestinian refugee problem, the Indochina refugees, and the Biafran famine.

Coordination of Warning Systems

Pre-disaster planning can also minimize the impact of natural disasters by coordinating the various types of detection instruments to warn potential victims before disasters. Seismological equipment, weather satellites, and hurricane warning stations require international coordination. In technologically advanced nations, communication systems are sufficiently sophisticated and widespread to provide this service. The communication networks of the developing countries, however, where many natural disasters occur, are inadequate. Although the Bangladesh cyclone was clearly visualized by weather satellites two days in advance, farmers along the southern coast received insufficient warning. Little or no information reached the rural regions, where even radios are in short supply. Disaster-prone regions must devise comprehensive warning systems. This might include the placement of radios in each village and education on the significance of various warning classifications. Each village might institute a house-to-house notification procedure. Nations with technological expertise can participate by strengthening international cooperation and by providing funds and technical assistance to national programs in developing countries.

Information on Local Conditions

Accurate and up-to-date information on existing local conditions should be centrally collected from all nations of the world, especially disaster-prone regions. Readily available information facilitates the donation of appropriate supplies and expedites the relief operation. The Bangladesh experience has demonstrated that the complexion of a tragedy and the requirements for relief are determined to a large extent by pre-existing conditions. Such a "data bank" should include the following types of information: food availability and consumption pattern, clothing worn during different seasons, type of shelter and construction materials, medical facilities and nature of indigenous health problems, transportation and communication facilities, and social and cultural traditions relevant to assistance needs and operations.

The availability of such information would greatly assist relief operations. In Bangladesh, knowledge that the harvest of the *aman* crop coincided with the November cyclone permitted anticipation that food would be a major relief requirement. The two cholera epidemics (in the refugee camps during the spring and in Bangladesh during the fall) were simply accentuations of the seasonal incidence of cholera in an endemic region. An appreciation of the marginal nutritional status of Bengali children during normal times would have provided clues to the magnitude of the malnutrition crisis which affected the refugee population.

Such information also permits formulation of realistic relief goals. An average rural Bengali lives in a thatch-roofed house, wears a T-shirt and *lungi,* and consumes mainly rice and pulses. For him, sophisticated shelter, Western clothing, and fortified or enriched foods may be inappropriate during the early stages of a crisis. It would be far more useful, and economically beneficial, to supply resources appropriate to local conditions.

Contingency Plans

From such an information system, contingency plans to deal with possible disasters can be formulated. Contingency plans would facilitate rapid, decisive, and effective relief operations. Such planning might consider the following:

1. *Cataloguing of potential needs.* For specific regions, as for specific disasters, certain supplies are more likely to be needed than others. These items should be identified, assigned a priority, and evaluated on a cost-effectiveness basis.

2. *Stockpiling of essential supplies.* Readily available resources would permit a more rapid response to disaster needs. Physical possession of supplies prior to disasters may not be necessary; but negotiations with prospective donor groups by the international disaster body could be carried out in advance of disasters. Prepledged items could then be mobilized rapidly when needed. Some have proposed, for example, a "food bank" where pledged food can be called for at a moment's notice for relief assistance.

3. *Listing of potential procurement sources.* After requirements and available resources have been identified, a list of potential sources should be drawn up. Maximum utilization of domestic or nearby sources should be made, while foreign or distant supplies should be kept at a minimum. For example, sending rice from Burma to Bangladesh (if available) is more appropriate than shipping wheat from the United States.

4. *Acquiring sufficient foreign exchange.* The international disaster body should be funded with sufficient unrestricted foreign exchange. Since most donations are made in kind (commodity) rather than in cash, international assistance organizations are unable to make sustained plans or commitments. Sufficient uncommitted funds are essential to permit a rapid, flexible, and sustained response.

5. *Planning of logistical alternatives.* Perhaps the most difficult aspect of disaster relief is the logistics of movement of large quantities of supplies within short periods of time. Thus, contingency plans dealing with alternate modes and routes of transport are mandatory.

6. *Publishing disaster manuals.* Prior publication and distribution of "how to" handbooks for disaster procedures are extremely useful during crisis. India, for example, has published an excellent "Famine Code" since 1913.

FIELD ASSESSMENT

The impact of disasters creates great confusion, making planned and coordinated assistance extremely difficult. For this reason, accurate field assessment is desirable. The effects of disasters of short duration, often dramatic in character, usually subside rapidly, but field assessment is necessary to allay fears, to clarify needs, and to project long-term effects. With disasters of moderate or longer duration, however, there is a need not only for rapid initial surveys, but also for continuous field surveillance. Data generated from the field assessments should be incorporated into an integrated information system to monitor the disaster as it evolves.

An international disaster office can direct national attention toward the desirability of field assessment. The office should be prepared to offer resources and personnel to assist with or to participate in such assessments. It should maintain a list of field epidemiologists, water specialists, public health workers, agriculturalists, nutritionists, etc., who can be rapidly mobilized in the event of a disaster. Because the data generated from surveys may be politically sensitive, all information should be considered the property of the indigenous government. In particular, release of field information to the public should be decided upon solely by the host government.

It is urged that initial surveys be conducted after all major disasters. Although delay is attendant upon field assessment, it does permit more time for planning and coordination thereby resulting in more effective relief assistance and more efficient utilization of scarce resources. Initial surveys should focus on issues of immediate concern to the survivors: housing, food, and health hazards. The surveys conducted after the cyclone and in the refugee camps demonstrate that they can be performed rapidly, efficiently, and at low cost. Such information helps to identify relief needs and geographical disparities and provide a framework for early relief efforts.

After the initial survey, a more detailed assessment should be conducted with the aim of establishing a continuous surveillance system to keep abreast of changes in the field situation. Surveillance should first statistically establish a baseline to judge future trends. For comparative purposes, surveillance information must be standardized (standard forms, questions, diagnostic criteria, etc.) and reported at regular intervals to the disaster coordinating office. Having pre-disaster information regarding local conditions available would strengthen the reliability of such a baseline and document the degree of difference from normal conditions. But pre-disaster information is not crucial since one is primarily interested in changes in the field situation as the disaster relief operation evolves with time.

The type of data collected will depend upon the nature of the disaster, local conditions, and the most urgent problems. Information on the number of lives lost, morbidity, number of homes destroyed, crop losses, foodstock, etc., will be of value to the overall relief effort. In the health field, one would focus on the progress in the control of existing health hazards, the emergence of new diseases, and the trends of nutritional status of the population.

If the participants of surveillance are not directly involved in the relief effort, the information generated can be used to evaluate the effectiveness of various relief measures. When the surveillance team members are directly involved in relief activities, it would be important to establish an independent evaluation mechanism to gauge the success or failure of various programs. Such impartial information permits the relief coordinator to strengthen weak programs and to expand successful programs.

An integrated information system is vital to the support of relief operations. A national disaster coordinating body can coordinate this function. It would utilize field information to plan, procure supplies, assign priorities, and supervise the logistics of supply movement. Such information would be used to inform the press, donor groups, and interested governments. Moreover, informing the *affected* public of current developments is of particular importance, as it will alleviate fears, curb panic, and foster the psychological feeling that "something is being done." After assimilation, information would pass back to the field workers, keeping them informed of new developments so that they may better coordinate their individual efforts. Such feed-back to the field staff also acts as an incentive for continued field-reporting.

An integral part of the relief program should be the ability to respond rapidly and appropriately to needs detected by the surveillance team. Thus, supplies, equipment, and personnel must be able to respond and contain a nutrition crisis as it is identified. Similarly, smallpox vaccination teams must be readily available to vaccinate potential victims during an epidemic.

The coordinating body will be required to process large volumes of survey and assessment data rapidly. The use of management experts, data processing equipment, and even computers to store, digest, and retrieve information will facilitate this task. The physical presence of a computer may not be necessary since a teletype connected to a computer terminal may be sufficient and can be installed in many areas of the world at short notice. Disaster data should be broken down into geographical units each of which might include the following: (a) food—production, size and location of stocks, consumption patterns, storage facilities; (b) health—nutritional status, deaths and their causes, incidence of infectious and other diseases, medical facilities, drug supplies; (c) transport—number and type of vehicles, capacity of various modes and routes, fuel availability, spare parts, maintenance units; (d) supplies—projected requirements, allocations, delivery, location, distribution; (e) communication—messages, data, information, orders, requests; (f) water—rainfall, sanitation, tubewells, contamination; (g) relief programs—number of workers, progress of projects, success, failure, problems, needs; (h) social parameters —civil unrest, sale of land or livestock, disruption of family nit, migration patterns.

RELIEF OPERATION DURING PEACETIME

The host government is ultimately responsible for the conduct of relief operations. This point cannot be overemphasized. Since the host government is responsible for the welfare and safety of its people, it must be permitted to exercise final control of all phases of the relief operation. We thus accept the fact that the success or failure of assistance efforts is to a large extent determined by the commitment, dedication, and determination of that government.

The host government should immediately establish a central co-ordinating body to assume full leadership and responsibility for relief operations. Its members might consist of full-time disaster planners supplemented by skilled administrators from other governmental agencies. Although a committee arrangement is feasible, the decision-making should be concentrated as much as possible to a small nucleus. Management specialists should be consulted to streamline the organizational structure.

A smoothly functioning and well-coordinated relief operation depends on integration of many factors. Inefficiency or delay in any one phase may result in a poor over-all performance. This perhaps is the most difficult aspect of relief. It is very much like a large military operation in which supply, transport, distribution, and personnel all must be integrated into one smooth running operation to achieve success.

International donor groups should view themselves primarily as donors and technical advisers. Through pre-arranged joint agreement, international donor groups should operate within established parameters of responsibility. Actions undertaken by foreign groups should support, not threaten, indigenous efforts. All voluntary agencies should be assigned specific projects by the national coordinating body. The more successful foreign private agencies in fact usually attempt to confine their activities to specific geographical regions or to specific activities, such as child-feeding, health care, or housing programs. Frequently, merger with indigenous counterparts facilitates success.

Voluntary agencies can make a significant contribution to the over-all relief effort. Although their resources are limited, they frequently possess dedicated, experienced, and skilled personnel. Because of their size, they maintain flexibility; they can demonstrate how and what type of programs can succeed. The quality of their performance, however, varies widely; the best are well-established charities or those with indigenous roots such as religious or missionary societies; the worst serve primarily as channels by which well-meaning but ineffectual personnel are brought to the scene of the disaster, where they do little, function primarily as tourists, and in the process take up much of the time and energy of harried field workers and supervisors.

Relief Supplies

Disaster after disaster, inappropriate goods are sent to the stricken area. Not only are these items wasted, like ineffectual personnel, but they also hamper the delivery and distribution of badly needed supplies. Expensive hospital beds, whole field hospitals, long underwear, miniskirts, high-heel shoes, woolen gloves, and many other superfluous items were sent to Bangladesh during the recent disasters. One group imported eight-ton electric water distillation units after the cyclone when water contamination was not a problem and no electricity was available to power the units in the devastated region. The cause of this wasteful practice is probably inaccurate or incomplete information. Some donations, however, are made for tax purposes. Certain drug firms, for example, donated outdated unmarketable drugs, apparently in order to benefit from the resulting tax deductions.

Every effort should be made to identify and to standardize appropriate supplies. Local and domestic sources should be utilized as much as possible in as much as purchase of local goods helps to stimulate the local economy. One must avoid large-scale purchases which may cause inflation, however, and as a result, decrease the purchasing power of others.

The inappropriateness of many foreign commodity donations presents a dilemma to the recipient nations. For the sake of greater efficiency, they may wish to refuse to accept inappropriate gifts. Yet a refusal may well discourage the donor from offering more essential items. Obviously, a balance must be maintained. Accurate information would help considerably to inform donor groups of the most urgent needs.

Transportation

This is usually the most difficult aspect of major relief operations. Movement of supplies should be planned and directed by the national coordinating body. Alternative modes and routes of transport should be carefully weighed and selected. Although airpower (helicopters, STOL aircrafts, and transport planes) has enormous speed and psychological advantages, its limited capacity often precludes its use. For large-scale movements during the disasters of moderate or long duration, surface transport must be established.

Under these circumstances, an understanding of the local transport infrastructure is vital. Imported vehicles and boats may be necessary to supplement local vehicles. Consideration should be given to necessary supportive supplies and personnel. Fuel is a necessity for mechanized transport. Spare parts and maintenance of vehicles are very important. In this regard, an effort should be made to coordinate vehicular donations and to provide for maintenance teams and spare parts. If a wide variety of vehicles are donated, servicing and spare parts become difficult and these vehicles might fall into disrepair.

Distribution

When requirements are massive, distribution ideally is channeled through existing institutions. The local administrative structure of the disaster region can most effectively provide the backbone for the distribution system. Success depends on local initiative and impartiality. Outside or foreign observers may be desirable under circumstances where impartiality requires reinforcement, but should be careful to avoid local sensitivities. Aggressive although well-intentioned actions may result in antagonism, misunderstanding, and counterproductive activities. Foreign groups may feel that local institutions are inefficient. Even under these circumstances, foreigners would better function as advisers and impartial observers rather than take a direct role in the distribution process.

Distribution must reach those in greatest need. A reliable survey can define geographical regions of need. But even within these regions, disease, illness, and social customs should be taken into account in the formulation of a distribution system. For example, in Bangladesh, women rarely leave their homes because of *purdah* and the sick and malnourished may be unable to reach the distribution areas. It is important to devise a distribution arrangement that will include, and in some instances be weighed toward, those who urgently need attention but may be inaccessible by routine distribution procedures.

Food

An understanding of the dietary and nutritional background of a disaster region is crucial to any food program. Food supplied to a disaster region should possess the following qualities: acceptability, easy preparation, requiring little fuel and utensils, resistance to environmental decay, packed in easily stacked containers, and easy transportation and distribution. In disasters of short duration, something to eat is often more important than a balanced diet. After the cyclone, a diet of rice and pulses would have been sufficient to avert malnutrition. If the crisis is of moderate or longer duration, a carefully formulated food program based on accurate field assessment of nutritional status and specific deficiencies (protein, caloric, or vitamin) is essential. Caloric insufficiency on a wide scale is more difficult to treat than specific deficiencies because it involves large volumes and weights of food, taxing transportation facilities, while protein deficiency can be contained by using high-protein food mixtures. There is generally an overemphasis on multivitamin preparations as vitamin deficiency is not an acute problem during food deprivation since requirements for vitamins diminish with malnutrition and slower metabolism. An exception to this may occur, however, when specific vitamin or mineral deficiencies become identified in the affected population.

In Bangladesh during the civil war, there was a lack of both calories and proteins. Yet the famine relief effort focused nearly totally on the provision of sufficient rice and wheat (good sources of calories and poor sources of proteins) to avert starvation. This was wise because by providing sufficient calories for short-term needs, protein breakdown by the body for caloric demands was avoided. During starvation, proteins are preferentially metabolized for caloric purposes. Thus protein deficiency cannot be fully corrected unless caloric demands are also satisfied.

In the refugee camps, the situation was somewhat different. Those children who consumed their ration of rice or wheat received nearly adequate caloric intake. In many camps, however, pulses, fish, meats, and other food sources of protein were often not available. Thus, some striking successes (such as the Lifeline Programs) were obtained by supplementary feeding with high-protein food mixtures. Specific vitamin deficiencies, in particular vitamin A deficiency, were also found among the refugee population. Large doses of vitamin A replacement were therefore indicated. Ideally, if circumstances permit, sufficient calories, proteins, and multivitamins should all be provided, but this is rarely possible with major disasters.

Special feeding programs aimed at the most severely malnourished and most vulnerable age groups are a good way to combat malnutrition. Infants, children, and lactating and pregnant women deserve special nutritional consideration. As these groups may constitute close to 50 per cent of a population, this may become a massive distribution and supply problem. To be more discriminating, a screening procedure might be instituted to identify those who require special nutrition attention. Objective and clinical criteria can be established and malnourished individuals can be assigned into different categories: such as those requiring weekly supplements, those requiring daily rations, and those to be hospitalized.

Schools, community centers, and other public buildings can be used as feeding stations. But it should be confirmed that distribution can reach children who are not attending school as well. Schools have been the traditional food outlet, but do not reach those who are at greater nutritional risk (the preschool-age child or the poorer child who cannot afford to attend school).

Disease Control

Disease control should receive the same priority as food distribution during disasters. Diseases which are amenable to control, such as smallpox, measles, worms, scabies, and amebiasis, should receive the most attention. During starvation, infectious diseases may cause more morbidity and mortality than starvation alone. Therefore, it is important to treat a victim against both his disease and his malnutrition. Survey and surveillance provide a framework for the application of health programs.

Sophisticated field hospitals and roving foreign medical teams have a limited place within an effective health care program during disasters. Health care should be provided by local physicians, nurses, nutritionists, administrators, and auxiliaries. In situations where local manpower is numerically inadequate, as in the refugee camps, success can be achieved by training local paramedics (medical students, pharmacists, midwives, and volunteers) on the spot. Foreigners can more effectively assist by training indigenous personnel and by assisting with health planning.

RELIEF OPERATIONS DURING MILITARY CONFLICT

Implementation of relief operations during conflict may not differ significantly from that during peacetime. During hostilities, however, an impartial international organization should provide assistance to all parties regardless of politcal loyalties. It is urged that the international disaster planning and coordination body act as that neutral body. Such an organization should be free of national influences and should establish its credibility as a truly unbiased humanitarian agency. It should be permitted to gain immediate entrance into disaster regions to assess the relief needs and to operate a neutral relief effort.

World opinion can play an important role in strengthening such an organization. Bacteriologic and biologic warfare have been renounced through international convention because they affect the innocent. World opinion should similarly renounce the use of starvation or lack of medical care as an instrument of suppression because, worse than indiscriminate, they affect the young, the aged, women, and the infirm. The civil war in Bangladesh demonstrates that world opinion can influence the action of parties at war. It was in large part because of its public image that the Pakistan Government publicly recognized the threat of famine in Bangladesh and invited the United Nations to operate an unbiased relief effort.

In order for such an organization to operate effectively, it must negotiate with all combatants regardless of their state of legitimacy in the eyes of the world. If impartiality cannot be maintained, the relief effort may well be doomed to failure, for armed resistance against any operation would place insurmountable barriers to effective implementation. In this regard, circumstances may well lead one to consider the possibility that no relief may be preferable to relief distributed in a biased manner. In Bangladesh, for example, the United Nations maintained and operated independent facilities for the transport of food to local storage depots.

Subsequent distribution was not handled, or supervised, by the UN, but by civilian administrators who were under the control of the Pakistan army. As a result, many felt the distribution to be biased and not impartial. This incurred the opposition of the insurgents, who in fact controlled many of the food shortage areas, and doubtless was a major factor in the decision of the *Mukti Bahini* in November to oppose the UN operation openly. In this situation, a lack of impartiality jeopardized the entire operation. It is unfair to criticize the UN operation harshly, as it is virtually impossible for a foreign group to import, transport, and distribute food to a population as large as that of Bangladesh. In retrospect, however, no relief at all might have been better.

This view is in direct contrast to those who contend that getting any food into a shortage region (regardless of the channel) is better than no food at all. This dilemma is a difficult one to resolve. It is, however, important to recognize that post-conflict requirements often exceed those during hostilities. Operations during hostilities must maintain the credibility of the international organization in order to ensure effective post-conflict operations.

REHABILITATION AND DEVELOPMENT

Relief has been traditionally viewed as an emergency, temporizing measure aimed at preventing further deterioration of a disaster situation. Properly planned and conducted, however, it need not be merely a give-away with lines of victims waiting for their share of free goods. While under some circumstances, such as the refugees in India, alternative other than a gratuitous ration system are not realistic, in most cases relief can play an important role in the rehabilitation process. Examples are the provision of tools to the carpenter, boats and nets to the fisherman, and livestock and plows to the farmer. These items can be given free, provided on a loan-basis for future repayment, or sold at reduced rates. Another example is food-for-work programs. If the population is fit, food in exchange for public works (reconstruction of homes, bridges, roads, etc.) can provide an effective incentive for community action. These activities, rather than fostering a passive attitude, encourage indigenous initiative, self-help, and pride.

The relief administrators, both national and international, need to recognize the long-range implications of immediate actions. They should seek advice from existing governmental institutions with the aim of coordinating a concerted approach to rehabilitation. Moreover, as relief activities evolve with time, a gradual transfer of authority and responsibility should be made from *ad hoc* relief groups to existing governmental institutions. Part of the rehabilitation process should include concrete plans to avert future catastrophies. For the cyclone-prone region of Bangladesh, for example, construction of embankments, planting of trees, and building of cyclone shelters, which can double as schools and community centers would ideally be integrated into the rehabilitation process.

Relief is not a static process. On the contrary, many new techniques, innovations, and institutions may be introduced during relief operations and old ones strengthened. The bureaucracy may become less rigid; tradition may be shaken; people may be more willing to accept innovation; and local motivation and initiative may be raised. Thus, disaster relief may provide an ideal vehicle to accelerate socio-economic development. After the 1970 cyclone, the formation of farming and fishing cooperatives took place in the affected area. Such cooperatives, in which individual families pool their resources to optimize production, holds enormous promise for rural development in Bangladesh. The use of paramedical personnel in the refugee camps is another striking example. This approach to medical manpower has profound implications for the later establishment of a comprehensive health care system. Such new programs have a better chance of acceptance during disaster times. The confidence and rapport which develops between relief workers and local inhabitants may also facilitate acceptance.

One benefit of disasters is that they expose neglected conditions which prevail even during normal times. Disasters draw the attention and purse strings of the world to the plight of the victims. During such times, funds can be generated to support development processes. After the cyclone, for example, the World Bank committed over $30 million to the rehabilitation and development of the devastated region. After the civil war, the United Nations was able to attract nearly $500 million to be used for the reconstruction of Bangladesh. Properly directed, such funds can provide the necessary resources for an acceleration of the development process.

References

1. All, C. Relief, Nutrition and Health Problems in the Nigerian/Biafran War. *J. Trop. Pediat.* 16, No. 2, June 1970.
2. Blix, G., Hofvander, Y., and Vahlquist, B. eds. *Famine: A Symposium Dealing with Nutrition and Relief Operations in Times of Disasters.* Almquist & Wikselle, Uppsala, Sweden. 1971.
3. *Famine Code (1913) and Famine Manual (1941).* Ministry of Relief and Rehabilitation, Government of India.
4. Jelliffe, D. B. Emergency Feeding of Young Children. *J. Pediat.* 75:153 (1969).
5. Masefield, G. B. *Famine: Its Prevention and Relief.* Oxford University Press, London, 1963.
6. Masefield, G. B. *Food and Nutrition Procedures in Times of Disaster.* FAO, Rome. Nutrition Studies No. 21, 1967.
7. Miller, J. P. Medical Relief in the Nigerian Civil War. *Lancet* 1:1330 (1970).
8. Saylor, L. F., and Gordon, J. E. The Medical Components of Natural Disasters. *Am. J. Med. Scs.* 234:342 (1957).
9. Sommer, A., and Mosley, W. H. The East Bengal Cyclone of November, 1970: Epidemiologic Approach to Disaster Assessment. *Lancet* 1:1029 (1972).
10. World Health Organization. Prevention and Treatment of Severe Malnutrition in Times of Disaster. *Wld. Hlth. Org. Techn. Rep. Ser.,* 45, 1951.

GLOSSARY

absorption, intestinal: the taking up of a substance from the lumen of the bowel into the body.

acetate: a salt of acetic acid; a weak base; used in the treatment of acidosis.

acidosis: a condition of excess acid or reduced alkali (bicarbonate) in the body.

adipose: fatty; relating to fat.

age-specific: according to age.

albumen: a protein distributed throughout the tissues of animals.

Alpha Lifeline: the preventive part of Operation Lifeline; its goal was to provide daily food supplements to refugee children in India.

AMAN: a rice cultivation season from July to December; the main rice crop harvested in early winter.

amebiasis: infestation with *ameba histolytica* or other pathogenic ameba; usually causes a colitis.

amino acid: a compound containing the radical groups NH_2 and COOH; the primary constituent of protein.

anthropometric: dealing with measurements of the human body.

antibody: a body protein formed in response to foreign antigens; it may neutralize the effects of various toxins.

anuria: total suppression of urine.

ASCARIS LUMBRICOIDES: round worm; intestinal parasite found especially in children.

attack rate: the number of people affected by a disease divided by the total number in the community.

AUS: a rice cultivation season from April to July; the rice crop harvested in early summer.

auxiliary: non-professional health worker; paramedical worker.

AWAMI LEAGUE: the dominant political party of Bangladesh which won the Pakistan national election prior to the civil war.

AYURVEDIC relating to ancient Hindu system of medicine still in practice in many rural areas of Bangladesh and the Indian subcontinent.

Bacille Calmette Guerin (BCG): a vaccine for the prophylaxis of young infants against tuberculosis.

BALAHAR: high protein mixture of peanuts, lentils, and wheat.

BALSEVIKAS: briefly trained paramedics who worked in the refugee camps.

BARI: a house or a household of patrilineally related members.

barley water: solution made from boiling seeds from a cereal plant, often used in the treatment of diarrheal diseases.

Bengal: a province of an ethnically, linguistically, and culturally homogeneous people in pre-partition India; divided into East and West Bengal in 1947. East Bengal, formerly the province of East Pakistan, is now the nation of Bangladesh.

Bengali: the people of Bengal; the language of Bengal; an adjective of the word Bengal.

benzyl benzoate: a chemical compound used to treat scabies.

beriberi: a disease resulting mainly from deficient thiamine intake; it may affect peripheral nerves.

Beta Lifeline: the curative part of Operation Lifeline; its goal was to treat severely malnourished refugee children and adults in treatment centers.

BHAT: cooked rice.

bicarbonate: a compound containing the radical group HCO_3; alkali; used for correction of acidosis.

biopsy: removal of tissue from a living patient.

birth rate: number of livebirths per year divided by midyear population; usually expressed as per 1,000 population.

    age or sex specific: according to age or sex.

    crude: birth rate of the entire population including all ages and both sexes.

BORO: a rice cultivation season from December to April; rice crop harvested in the spring.

bronchitis: inflammation of the mucous membrane of bronchial tubes of lungs, frequently causing symptomatic cough and sputum.

brucellosis: infectious disease due to brucella characterized by fever, sweating, weakness, pains, and aches.

C-130: large capacity cargo plane made in the United States; frequently used for movement of large quantities of supplies.

CSM: a high protein vegetable mixture containing corn, soy bean, and milk.

calorie: value of foods standardized by the quantity of heat (energy) it produces; one calorie is defined as the quantity of heat required to raise the temperature of 1 kg of water 1 degree centigrade.

capillaria: a genus of worms.

case-fatality ratio: the ratio of the number of fatal cases to the total number of cases of any disease.

Chalna: the second largest seaport of Bangladesh; situated approximately 50 miles south of Dacca.

CHAPATTI: flat, round, unlevened bread made from whole wheat flour.

chemotherapeutic agent: antibiotic or chemical used in the treatment of infectious or other diseases.

chloramphenicol: an antibiotic.

cholera: acute infectious diarrheal illness due to intestinal infection with Vibrio cholerae marked clinically by profuse watery diarrhea.

cholera cot: hospital bed used in the treatment of cholera and other diarrheal illnesses; hole under the buttocks facilitates collection of stool to provide a guideline to replacement of fluid losses.

CIRRA: beaten and husked rice cooked by boiling.

coccidia: protozoan parasite which may infest the human intestinal tract.

colitis: inflammation of the large bowel or colon.

congestive heart failure: inability of the heart to pump and circulate the blood.

containment: control of infectious diseases by interrupting transmission from an infected person.

contusion: a bruise.

crypt, intestinal: narrow space between intestinal villi.

countryboat: indigenous wooden boats powered by oar or sail.

curry: a highly spiced dish cooked with vegetables, fish, or meat eaten in the Indian subcontinent.

cyclone syndrome: term coined to describe medial arm and thigh lacerations from holding on to sharp objects during the cyclone.

DAI: midwife.

DAL: pasty soup made from pulses.

DATTA: green stem of a vegetable plant.

death rate: number of deaths per year divided by midyear population; usually expressed as per 1,000 population.

demography: scientific study of human populations.

dependency ratio: number of persons under 15 years and over 65 years divided by number of persons between these two ages in a population.

deputy commissioner: the chief civil service administrator of a district.

diphtheria: infectious disease due to *Kleb-Loeffler* bacillus marked by fibrinous exudates of mucus membrane of respiratory tract and systemic symptoms.

diuretic: an agent that promotes the excretion of urine to relieve the body of excess fluid.

duodenum: the upper-most segment of the small intestine; segment from the pylorus of the stomach to the jejunum.

dysentery: a disease marked by fever and diarrhea with stools often containing blood and mucus; usually due to shigella, ameba, or other infectious agents.

edema: accumulation of excess fluid in the body and tissues.

electrolyte: any compound which in solution conducts an electrical current; usually refers to sodium, potassium, chloride, and bicarbonate found in body fluids.

endemic: present continually in a community.

enrollment ratio: number of children in school divided by total number of children eligible to attend.

ENTAMEBA HISTOLYTICUM: species of ameba which causes amebic or tropical dysentery.

enteric: relating to the intestine.

enteritides: infectious or other diseases involving the intestine.

enteropathogenic: capable of producing disease of the intestine.

enterotoxin: a protein elaborated by certain bacteria capable of producing disease of the intestine.

eosinophilia: increase of the number of eosinophils (a white blood cell) in the blood.

epidemiology: the field of science dealing with the relationship of the various factors which determine the frequency and distribution of an infectious process, a disease, or a physiological state in a human community.

epithelium, intestinal: the cellular layer of tissue lining the luminal side of the intestinal tract.

ESCHERICHIA COLI (E. COLI): a gram negative bacillus commonly found in the feces; most types of this organism are benign but recent studies have demonstrated that certain strains may be enteropathogenic.

ethambutal: a compound used to treat tuberculosis.

etiology: the study or theory of the causation of any disease process.

exanthematous: pertaining to an eruptive disease.

exotoxin: enterotoxin.

Faridpur: a district in Bangladesh.

fertility rate: number of livebirths per year divided by a defined female population of specific age groups.

filariasis: a tropical disease caused by the presence of filariae in the tissues of the body.

Five-Year Plan: economic development plan covering five year periods; the first five-year plan in Pakistan covered 1955–60.

flora, intestinal: various bacteria in the intestinal contents.

folate: a salt of folic acid; an essential ingredient for the production of red blood cells.

furizolidone: an antibiotic.

furunculosis: condition marked by presence of boils or furuncles; a pyogenic infection of the hair follicle.

gastrointestinal: relating to stomach or intestine.

GHEE: clarified butter.

giardia: a genus of flagellates which may be parasitic in the human intestine.

glucose: sugar.

glycine: an amino acid.

goiter: enlarged thyroid gland.

goitrogenic: causing goiter.

gourd: vegetable such as cucumber, pumpkin, mellon, or squash.

gram negative bacillus: a class of microorganisms.

gratuitous distribution: free distribution of relief goods.

hemoglobin: a protein in red blood cells.

hepatitis: inflammation of the liver.

histology: branch of anatomy that deals with the cells and the minute structure of the tissues and organs.

hookworm: a worm which may infest the intestine causing loss of blood and anemia.

hyperlipemia: high fat levels in the blood.

hypoalbumenemia: low albumen protein levels in the blood.

hypoglycemia: low sugar levels in the blood.

hyponatremia: low sodium levels in the blood.

hypotension: low blood pressure.

hypovolemia: low blood or body fluid volume.

iatrogenic: relating to difficulties resulting from activity during treatment.

ileum: third portion of the small intestine in between the jejunum and the colon.

incidence: an expression of the rate at which a certain event occurs, as the number of new cases of a specific disease occuring during a certain period.

incubation period: time interval from the contraction of an infectious disease and the onset of symptoms or signs.

infant mortality rate: the death rate expressed as number per 1,000 livebirths per year of children under one year of age.

inflammation: a body response to injury.

International Rescue Committee: an international voluntary relief agency.

isoniazid: a compound used to treat tuberculosis.

jejunitis: inflammation of the jejunum.

jejunum: the portion of the small intestine between the duodenum and ileum.

jute: a glossy fibre from a plant used to make burlap and twine.

K-II mix: high protein mixture of casein hydralysate, sucrose, and milk.

kala azar: a parasitic disease caused by *Leishmania donovani* which infests the body; transmitted to man by the bite of the sandfly.

kaolin: aluminum silicate powder used to treat diarrhea; used to absorb bacteria and toxins in the intestine; not an antibiotic.

keratomalacia: debilitating eye disease with dryness, ulceration, and/or perforation of the cornea due to severe vitamin A deficiency.

KITCHURI: mixture of rice and pulses cooked together.

KOI: small freshwater fish.

kwashiorkor: a severe disease of children due to deficiency of protein with anemia, edema, depigmentation of the skin, loss or change of hair color.

lactation: the secretion of milk.

lamina propria: a connective tissue coat of a mucus membrane just deep to intestinal epithelium.

lentil: pulses.

leprosy: chronic infectious disease caused by *Mycobacterium leprae;* may affect skin and peripheral nerves.

licentiate: a physician in Bangladesh with ten years of primary school and high school training and four years of medical training; this educational program has been phased out.

LUNGI: a large piece of cloth wrapped around the waist; worn by Muslim men in Bangladesh.

lymphocyte: a white blood cell formed in lymphoid tissue.

lyophilize: to separate a solid from solution by freeze drying.

MAGUR: small freshwater fish.

maintenance: replacement of diarrheal stool loss with fluid and electrolytes.

malabsorption: failure or inability to absorb nutrients from the intestine.

malaria: disease caused by presence of a protozoan parasite in the red blood cell.

marasmus: extreme emaciation or wasting especially in children due to inadequate caloric and other food intake.

Matlab: a bazaar or thana in Comilla District of Bangladesh; site of the cholera vaccine field trials by the Cholera Research Laboratory.

measles: rubeola; an acute exanthematous viral disease marked by systemic symptoms and a generalized body rash.

metabolic ward conditions: carefully supervised hospital conditions to facilitate accurate data collection for research.

millet: any of various small seeded annual cereal grasses; a grain; often made into a flour.

monsoon: a period wind from the Indian ocean with heavy rains; occurs from June to September in Bangladesh.

morbidity: a diseased state; the ratio of sick to total population in a community.

mortality rate: death rate; the ratio of number of deaths to the total population.

mucosa, intestinal: mucous membrane of intestinal tract.

MUKTI BAHINI: Bengali guerrilla army which fought against the Pakistan army during the civil war.

MURI: puffed rice.

mustard oil: oil formed from compressing the seeds of the mustard plant.

MYCOBACTERIUM TUBERCULOSIS: the causative agent of tuberculosis in man.

Narayanganj: the third largest port city in Bangladesh; about 10 miles from Dacca.

nasogastric tube: a hollow tube inserted through the nostrils into the stomach for the purpose of delivering or withdrawing solutions.

neonatal: relating to the period immediately succeeding birth and continuing through the first month of life.

nephritis: inflammation of the kidney.

oliguria: scanty urination.

Operation Lifeline: nutrition program in the refugee camps.

oral therapy: replacement of diarrheal stool losses by ingestion of salt-

glucose containing solutions orally; in contrast to replacement intra-
venously.

osteomalacia: a disease characterized by softening and bending of
bones; may be due to deficient vitamin D, calcium, or phosphorus.

outpatient: a patient who is treated but who is not hospitalized.

Oxfam: a charitable voluntary agency.

paddy: wet land on which rice is grown; threshed unmilled rice.

para-amino salicylic acid (PAS): an agent used in the treatment of
tuberculosis.

PARATHAS: round bread made from wheat flour fried in rich oils.

peace committee: civil administrators established by the Pakistan army
during the civil war in an attempt to control the rural regions.

pellagra: disease characterized by gastrointestinal disturbances, skin involvement, and nervous and mental disorders; mainly caused by deficiency of niacin in the diet.

peristalsis: circular contraction and relaxation of the intestine leading
to movement of luminal contents.

pertussis: whooping cough.

phagocyte: a cell possessing the property of ingesting bacteria, foreign
particles, and other cells.

poliomyelitis: a viral disease due to poliovirus which may result in
paralytic disease.

post-neonatal: relating to the period one month to one year of life.

potassium: an element; essential electrolyte in the human body.

pressor agent: drug which affects the blood vessels or heart and used
to maintain adequate blood pressure.

prevalence: the number of cases of a disease in existence at a certain
time in a designated area.

prodrome: a premonitory symptom or precursor; a symptom indicating the onset of a disease.

pronatalist: relating to favoring increased number of births.

protein: an important component of animal tissue; formed by combination of amino acids; essential for tissue growth.

protein-calorie malnutrition: a syndrome of faulty nutrition with inadequate calories, proteins, and commonly other nutrients as well;
may be precipitated by infection or other disease states.

protein synthesis: production of protein by the body.

prothrombin: a protein factor necessary for coagulation; low levels may be encountered if the intestine fails to absorb certain nutrients.

pulse: a widely cultivated Eurasian annual leguminous plant with edible seeds.

PURDAH: a practice of secluding women from public observation among Muslims and some Hindus, especially in the subcontinent.

pyogenic: pus forming.

QUAC (QUaker Arm Circumference) stick: anthropometric measurement expressed as the ratio of left bicep circumference divided by linear height; a field measure of nutritional status.

rapeseed oil: oil from rapeseeds.

rehydration: replacement of body fluids and electrolytes.

riboflavin: vitamin B_{12}; essential nutrient abundant in liver, eggs, milk; also synthesized.

rickets: a disease of infants and children with disturbance of bone formation caused by deficiency of vitamin D.

RUPEE: Pakistan monetary currency note; one U.S. dollar officially equals 11 rupees.

STOL (short-take-off-and-landing): aircraft.

sago water: barley water.

saline: salty; solution containing sodium and chloride, and often other electrolytes, used to replace diarrheal stool losses.

salmonella: bacterium which may be pathogenic in human intestine.

scabies: a disease with intense itching caused by the burrowing into the skin of a mite.

scar survey: examination of the prevalence of either scars from smallpox vaccination or scars from the disease process.

Schilling Test: a test of intestinal absorption of vitamin B_{12}.

scurvy: a disease marked by inanition, debility, anemia, edema, ulceration of gums, hemorrhage into the skin due to lack of vitamin C.

sepsis: the presence of pathogenic organisms, or their toxins, in the blood.

sex-specific: according to sex.

shigella: bacterium capable of causing dysentery.

skin test: test performed on skin to determine previous exposure to tuberculous organisms.

skin turgor: elasticity and texture of skin which is a clinical sign of hydration status.

SHING: a freshwater fish.

SHITALA: Hindu Goddess of smallpox.

sign: any objective evidence of disease in the body.

smallpox: variola; acute eruptive contagious disease marked by systemic symptoms and skin reddening, pustules, and scabs; leaves permanent pox marks.

small intestine: segment of the intestine from stomach to colon; consists of duodenum, jejunum, and ileum.

sodium: an element; essential electrolyte in human body.

stem borer: a pest which may attack crops.

strongyloides: a class of nematodes which may infest human intestine.

subclinical: denoting a state of disease where symptoms and signs are not yet detectable.

subdivision: administrative unit of Bangladesh; average size—1.2 million people and 1,000 square miles.

submucosa: below the mucosa.

sulfadiazine: a sulphur antibiotic.

symptom: subjective evidence of disease.

syndrome: an aggregate or concurrence of symptoms associated with any disease state.

TAKA: Bangladesh monetary currency note; one U.S. dollar officially equals 7.2 takas.

TAKURIA: an evil spirit believed to be the cause of neonatal tetanus.

tetanus: an infectious disease marked by painful tonic muscular contractions; caused by toxin of Clostridium tetani.

tetracycline: an antibiotic.

THANA: administrative unit in Bangladesh; smaller than a subdivision and larger than a union; approximately 100,000 to 200,000 people.

thatch: plant material such as straw used for roofing.

thiacetamide: a drug used in the treatment of tuberculosis.

triglyceride: a fat.

tropical sprue: tropical diarrhea with chronic inflammation of the intestinal tract and associated with malabsorption.

tube well: a well driven into the earth often lined for the purpose of obtaining water for drinking or irrigation.

tuberculosis: an infectious disease caused by *Mycobacterium tuberculosis* and characterized by the formation of tubercles in tissues.

undernutrition: a form of malnutrition resulting from reduced supply of food or from inability to digest, assimilate, or utilize nutrients.

United Nations Relief Organization Dacca (UNROD): specially established UN organization for relief in Bangladesh.

union: a civil administrative unit in Bangladesh; average size 10,000 to 20,000 people.

union council: the civil governing body of a union.

United States Agency for International Development (USAID):

branch of the U.S. federal government concerned with international assistance.

vaccination: inoculation of a killed culture or of a specific bacterium as a means of prophylaxis.

vaccine: the modified or attenuated virus or cells product of any organism which confers immunity if inoculated prior to exposure of the virulent organism.

VIBRIO CHOLERAE: organism responsible for cholera.

vibriocidal antibody: protein which neutralizes infections due to Vibrio cholerae.

villus: minute projection from the surface of mucous membranes.

vitamin A: fat soluble compound necessary for vision; found in spinach, carrots, egg yolk, milk, and other green or yellow vegetables and fruits.

vitamin A deficiency: interferes with the production and resynthesis of rhodopsin (visual purple) thereby causing night blindness and/or keratomalacia.

vitamin C: ascorbic acid; contained in fresh vegetables, citrus and tomato juices, and other fresh fruits; deficiency leads to scurvy.

vitamin B_{12}: compound absorbed in the ileum essential for the formation of red blood cells.

WSB (wheat-soy-blend): high protein vegetable mixture made from wheat and soy bean.

ward: administrative unit in Bangladesh; approximately 1,000 to 2,000 people.

ward committee: civil governing body of a ward.

West Bengal: western portion of Bengal; a state of India.

World Health Organization (WHO): international agency concerned with health problems worldwide; arm of the United Nations.

xylose: a five-carbon sugar.

Index